👁 INSIGHT **CITY GUIDE**

NEW YORK

Discovery
CHANNEL

APA PUBLICATIONS **L**
Part of the Langenscheidt Publishing Group

✳ INSIGHT GUIDE
NEW YORK

Project Editor
Martha Ellen Zenfell
Editorial Director
Brian Bell

Distribution

UK & Ireland
GeoCenter International Ltd
The Viables Centre, Harrow Way
Basingstoke, Hants RG22 4BJ
Fax: (44) 1256-817988

United States
Langenscheidt Publishers, Inc.
36–36 33rd Street 4th Floor
Long Island City, NY 11106
Fax: (1) 718 784-0640

Canada
Thomas Allen & Son Ltd
390 Steelcase Road East
Markham, Ontario L3R 1G2
Fax: (1) 905 475 6747

Australia
Universal Publishers
1 Waterloo Road
Macquarie Park, NSW 2113
Fax: (61) 2 9888 9074

New Zealand
Hema Maps New Zealand Ltd (HNZ)
Unit D, 24 Ra ORA Drive
East Tamaki, Auckland
Fax: (64) 9 273 6479

Worldwide
Apa Publications GmbH & Co.
Verlag KG (Singapore branch)
38 Joo Koon Road, Singapore 628990
Tel: (65) 6865-1600. Fax: (65) 6861-6438

Printing

Insight Print Services (Pte) Ltd
38 Joo Koon Road, Singapore 628990
Tel: (65) 6865-1600. Fax: (65) 6861-6438

©2005 Apa Publications GmbH & Co.
Verlag KG (Singapore branch)
All Rights Reserved

First Edition 1991
Fifth Edition 2005

ABOUT THIS BOOK

This guidebook combines the interests and enthusiasms of two of the world's best-known information providers: Insight Guides, whose titles have set the standard for visual travel guides since 1970, and Discovery Channel, the world's premier source of nonfiction television programming.

The editors of Insight Guides provide both practical advice and general understanding about a destination. Discovery Channel and its Web site, www.discovery.com, help millions of viewers explore their world from the comfort of their own home.

How to use this book

The book is carefully structured both to convey an understanding of the city and its culture and to guide readers through its sights and activities:

◆ The Best of New York at the front of the book helps you to prioritize what you want to see. Unique experiences, the best buys, best walks and top family attractions are listed, together with money-saving tips.

◆ To understand New York, you need to know something of its past. The city's history and culture are described in authoritative essays written by specialists who have lived in the city for many years.

◆ The main Places section details all the attractions worth seeing. The main places of interest are coordinated by number with the maps.

◆ A list of recommended restaurants, bars and cafés is printed at the end of each chapter. Some of these are also described and plotted on the pull-out restaurant map that accompanies the guide.

Zenfell, rated by *New York* magazine as one of the best contemporary guide books to New York City. Zenfell wanted to convey the fresh optimism sweeping the city after the mourning for the World Trade Center victims ended, and made a point to include coverage of the new Museum of Modern Art, and formerly down-beat, now hot-spot areas like the Meatpacking District and Alphabet City.

The main updater of this edition, **Kathy Novak**, has lived in New York for three decades. A writer, TV producer, radio presenter and university professor, she is Insight's chief correspondent in the Big Apple and writes a weekly column there called *Inside New York*.

David Whelan, writer, designer and musician, went through the updated text and gave it new energy and a bright new outlook in keeping with this edition. From the previous book, we would like to thank **Divya Symmers**, who wrote the original Downtown chapters and the Green Spaces essay, **John Gattuso**, who wrote the history section, **A. Peter Bailey**, **Michele Abruzzi**, **John Wilcock** and **John Strausbaugh**.

This edition uses many new images contributed by **Britta Jaschinski**, **Anna Mockford** and **Nick Bonnetti**, in addition to **Catherine Karnow** and **Tony Perrottet**. **Hilary Genin** and **Jenny Kraus** were visually invaluable. The book was proofread and indexed by **Penny Phenix**.

◆ Photographs throughout the book are chosen not only to illustrate geography and buildings, but also to convey the moods of the city and the life of its people.

◆ The Travel Tips section includes all the practical information you will need for your stay, divided into four key sections: transportation, accommodations, activities (including nightlife, shopping and sports), and an A–Z of practical tips. Information may be located quickly by using the index printed on the back cover flap.

◆ A detailed street atlas is included at the back of the book, complete with a full index.

The contributors

This new edition was edited by **Martha Ellen Zenfell**, and builds on another earlier edition, also edited by

CONTACTING THE EDITORS

We would appreciate it if readers would alert us to errors or outdated information by writing to:

Insight Guides, P.O. Box 7910, London SE1 1WE, England. Fax: (44) 20 7403-0290. insight@apaguide.co.uk

NO part of this book may be reproduced, stored in a retrieval system or transmitted in any form or means electronic, mechanical, photocopying, recording or otherwise, without prior written permission of *Apa Publications*. Brief text quotations with use of photographs are exempted for book review purposes only. Information has been obtained from sources believed to be reliable, but its accuracy and completeness, and the opinions based thereon, are not guaranteed.

www.insightguides.com

Contents

Maps

Travel Tips

THE BEST OF NEW YORK

Riverside walks by movie-classic views, dining where Sinatra's Little Town Blues just melted away. With tips for the budget, be a part of it in old and new New York

BEST SHOPPING IN NEW YORK

- **Bloomingdale's**
  If you have time for only one store, this is it. *See page 109.*
- **Barneys New York**
  A store for fashionistas of both sexes. *See page 109.*
- **Macy's**
  More than 100 years of retailing in a store the size of a city block. *See page 93.*
- **FAO Schwarz**
  Fifth Avenue toy store that attracts generation after generation. *See page 230.*
- **Tiffany's**
  Who will ever forget the store, the song, the breakfast? *See page 77.*
- **Strand Bookstore**
  America's largest secondhand bookstore. *See page 144.*

- **Zabar's**
  Zillions of people call in at Zabar's for high-quality deli fare. Famous for smoked fish. *See page 120.*
- **Myers of Keswick**
  British specialty shop where Elton John and Keith Richards stock up on homemade pork pies. *See page 148.*
- **Kiehl's**
  Old-fashioned looking beauty and toiletry range. There's also a branch in the East Village. *See page 120.*
- **Dean & Deluca**
  Gourmet heaven with a great coffee bar. *See page 172.*
- **Century 21**
  Designer discounts for high style with low outlay. *See page 229.*
- **Chelsea Market**
  Indoor market selling specialty foods and home-design items; part of an ambitious renovation scheme. *See page 139.*

CLASSIC NEW YORK

Where to follow in the footsteps of Sinatra, Bacall, Dylan Thomas and Dorothy Parker.

- **21**
  This former speakeasy is still a haunt of the beautiful and the powerful. *See page 78.*
- **Algonquin**
  Dorothy Parker may have departed, but the Round Table is back. *See page 97.*

- **P.J. Clarke's**
  Sinatra preferred the back room, along with Louis Armstrong. Johnny Depp comes now. *See page 91.*
- **White Horse Tavern**
  Dylan Thomas drank here. And then he died. *See page 148.*

BEST BOOKS TO READ

If you read nothing else before or while you are in New York City, choose one of the titles from this list of five classic works of fiction:
The Age of Innocence by Edith Wharton. Modern Library Classics, 1999.
Another Country by James Baldwin. Vintage, 1993.
A Tree Grows in Brooklyn by Betty Smith. First Perennial Classics, 1998.
The Bonfire of the Vanities by Tom Wolfe. Bantam Books, 1990.
Washington Square by Henry James. Modern Library Classics, 2002.

ONLY IN NEW YORK

Culture Vulture
Choose from up to 200 events each month at Lincoln Center, and see everything from the New York Philharmonic to the final operatic performance of a star like Luciano Pavarotti. *See page 119.*

Moon over Manhattan
Take a late elevator to the top of the Empire State Building, and watch the moon light up Gotham. *See page 73.*

Gaze on Greatness at the Chrysler Building, arguably the most beautiful skyscraper in the world *See page 86.*

Sail the Statue of Liberty
Climb aboard a Circle Line tour or have brunch on a sleek 1929 sailboat. *See pages 190 and 192.*

Eat and Drink
Partake of the most expensive hamburger imaginable at DB Bistro Moderne, or sip a $10,000 martini at the Algonquin. *See pages 78 and 97.*

Be Merry
Join sports stars, superstars and jovial shoppers for the annual lighting of the Christmas tree in Rockefeller Center. *See page 75.*

Shop and Skate
Take in the galleries and small treasures of Chelsea, then don ice skates for a midnight spin around the Sky Rink at Chelsea Piers. *See page 139.*

Dine with Diplomats in the dining room of the United Nations building. *See page 86.*

Muse over Music
Visit the home of a jazz legend, and find out why some called him "Dippermouth." *See page 202.*

Get Sporty
Cheer on the New York Knicks or the Harlem Globetrotters at Madison Square Garden. *See page 94.*

Cultivate Irony
Mingle with models and banter with butchers in the trend-setting Meatpacking District. *See page 147.*

Be Bemused and Confused by History
Study a lock of George Washington's hair; also his tooth. *See page 185.*

RIGHT AND BELOW: The Chrysler Building was erected in 1930. Its distinctive spire was designed in secret and lifted into place as one solid piece. The Statue of Liberty was shipped from France in 350 pieces, and reassembled in New York harbor.

NEW YORK FOR FAMILIES

These attractions are popular with children, though not all will suit every age group.

- **Carousels**
The entire family can ride on New York's carousels. The one in Central Park *(see page 80)* operates all year round, while the carousels in Bryant and Prospect parks are seasonal.
- **Children's Museum of Manhattan**
A kiddy kingdom with inventive interactive exhibits; let them touch everything. *See page 120.*
- **Central Park**
From rowing in the lake to a specially designed children's area, the park is fun any time of the year. *See page 80.*

- **Sony Wonderlab**
Wondering how to entertain the bored and grumpy pre-teens? Look no more. *See page 89.*
- **South Street Seaport**
Sailing ships and all things nautical, in an outdoor atmosphere where kids can let off steam without embarrasing their parents. *See page 189.*
- **Fabulous Food**
Inexpensive snacks

don't come any easier. Try two NY specialties: Nathan's Famous hot dogs on Coney Island *(see page 202)* and bagels, bagels, bagels.
- **Bronx Zoo**
The largest urban zoo in America. What's stopping you? *See page 208.*
- **Circle Line Tour**
View the Statue of Liberty, watch all of Manhattan cruise by, and let the kids go wild. *See page 231.*
- **American Museum of Natural History**
Four city blocks to keep the kiddies informed, including a planetarium, an Imax theater and dinosaurs. *See page 118.*
- **Brooklyn Children's Museum.** Founded in 1899, the oldest kids' museum in America. *See page 200.*

CLOCKWISE: Hans Christian Andersen and a young fan, Central Park; food fit for New Yorkers; the fabulous Guggenheim Museum.

NEW YORK FOR FREE (OR ALMOST FREE)

- **Major Museums**
Some of the city's museums have "pay what you wish" evenings on Fridays. These include the Guggenheim *(see page 107)*; the Whitney *(see page 108);* and MoMa *(see page 100).* Thursday is the Jewish Musem *(see page 108).*
- **Native American Art**
is free to see at the George Gustav Heye Center of the National Museum of the American Indian in the US Custom House. *See page 185.*
- **Culture in the Park**
The New York Philharmonic, the Metropolitan Opera and the Public Theater offer free performances in Central Park during the summer months.
- **Jazz, tapas and drinks** are offered the first Friday of every month under the Hayden Sphere at the American Museum of National History. Suggested donations to the museum, but the fun is free.
- **Free Flowers**
The Brooklyn Botanic Garden *(see page 200)* is free Monday through Friday

and until noon on Saturday; while the Queens *(see page 203)* and the Staten Island *(see page 206)* botanical gardens are free all the time.
- **Free Food**
Some vendors offer tasty samples at the Union Square Greenmarket. *See page 137.*
- **Free Tours**
Times Square offers free tours with guides. *See page 102.*
- **Free Travel**
Statue of Liberty views are still absolutely free on the Staten Island Ferry *(see page 192),* while Lower Manhattan has a free bus service *(see page 189).*
- **Free Fashion**
The Fashion Institute of Technology (Seventh Avenue at 27th St) shows off thousands of designer costumes and the work of famous photographers in its museum.
- **Surf for Free**
Most libraries have email facilities, as does the Times Square Visitor Center. Free WiFi access in Union Square; also at several locations in Lower Manhattan.
See page 186.

ABOVE:
Chinese New Year has great dragons and food, but the traditional fireworks may be in trouble *(see page 164)*.

BEST TOURS

The best tours of New York's buildings are:

- **Radio City Music Hall**. *See page 97.*
- **Grand Central Terminal**. *See page 85.*
- **Rockefeller Center** *See page 75.*
- **Lincoln Center** *See page 119.*
- **Carnegie Hall** *See page 98.*
- **NBC Studios** *See page 76.*
- **Gracie Mansion** *See page 111.*
- **Madison Square Garden** *See page 94.*

BEST WALKS

- **Fifth Avenue**. *See pages 73 and 105.*
- **Madison Avenue**, from 42nd to 96th streets. *See pages 85 and 108.*
- **Central Park** *See page 80.*
- **Times Square** *See page 102.*
- **Battery Park Esplanade**. *See page 184.*
- **Brooklyn Heights Promenade**. *See page 198.*

BELOW: The Christmas Spectacular at Radio City Music Hall, starring the Rockettes, is corny but cozy *(see page 97)*.

BEST FESTIVALS AND EVENTS

For a more complete list of festivals, see page 226.

- **New Wave Festival** From October through December, some of the most innovative sounds around at the Brooklyn Academy of Music (BAM). Guaranteed hot tickets. *See page 199.*
- **Harlem Week** Streets are jumping in the daytime and clubs are jiving at night. Every August. *See page 130.*
- **Museum Mile** A street festival in June when all nine of the grand museums on "Museum Mile" are free. *See page 114.*

- **St Patrick's Day** Watch the wearing o' the green and the rousing parade on Fifth Avenue every March. *See page 76.*
- **Thanksgiving Day Parade**. Started in the 1920s, this is the longest-running show on Broadway, brought to you by Macy's. *See page 95.*
- **Feast of San Gennaro** A 10-day festival in September where Little Italy shows off, and the air is heavy with the scent of garlic. *See page 161.*

MONEY-SAVING TIPS

Theater Tickets The **TKTS booth**, at Broadway and 47th Street, by Times Square, has discounted seats (25–50 percent off) for that night's performances. It's open Monday through Saturday 3pm to 8pm for evening performances, Saturday and Wednesday 10am to 2pm for matinees, and Sunday 11am to 7.30 pm for both shows. Near South Street Seaport in Lower Manhattan, a booth at 186 Front Street sells tickets for the following night's shows. S*ee page 52.*

Special Passes A way to save on New York's buses and subways is to buy a **MetroCard** (for instance, you get 11 rides for the price of 10). Available for 30 days, 7 days or one day. Go to www.mta.nyc.ny.us
CityPass saves if you plan to visit attractions. Buy the pass at the first destination; then you have nine days in which to visit six others. You also avoid most ticket lines. Savings of almost 50 percent; plus discounts on meals. Go to www.citypass.com. The **New York Pass** is a similar scheme. Go to www.newyorkpass.com

Shopping International visitors can take advantage of the free **Macy's Savings Card**, which offers 11 percent off most purchases. Multiple visits are allowed, within a certain time frame. Tel: 212-494-2118.

All visitors can find great bargains at New York's **sample sales**, where designers sell off end-of-season clothes, or smaller sizes. Check the listings pages of *Time Out New York* for dates. **Woodbury Common**, an outlet mall about an hour from the city by bus, offers big discounts on many items. *See page 228.*

BIG LIGHTS, BRIGHT CITY

**New York's glittering charms
are gleaming more brightly than ever.
Parks and open spaces are blooming
and business is booming**

New York changes. Almost as often as the Empire State Building's light show shifts from one celebration to another, the Big Apple's identity evolves. Ever since a land deal between a few Algonquin Indians and a Dutchman in 1626, the city has been in continuous, rapid transformation.

Manhattan's famous charms – the Empire State Building, the Chrysler Building, Central Park and Lady Liberty herself – are preened and gleam like never before. Classic attractions, like the Algonquin and the Chelsea Hotel, have had make-overs, while MoMA and Columbus Circle have been completely reborn.

Alphabet City, formerly a perilous demi-monde, has sparkled into a club- and bar-land. The old Meatpacking District parts red-velvet ropes for designers like Stella McCartney, and über-hip haunts like Soho House and Meet. From the ashen wake of 9/11, Lower Manhattan rebounded with free buses, waves of free WiFi internet access, and a calendar bursting with free festivals.

Parks and open spaces have bloomed, and the city has gained a fresh, open outdoors to complement the metropolitan Gotham glamour. The Hudson River Park has opened the riverside from Battery Park at the southern tip of the island to 59th Street on the West Side, and on along Riverside Park up to 145th Street. The dream of an "emerald necklace" around the island for walkers, cyclists and skaters, is coming true.

Tourists throng in record numbers, from home and abroad. Mayor Michael Bloomberg said that in 2004, the airports of New York welcomed 11.3 million international guests. Foreign travelers may not have felt the welcome at immigration, but still, they come. Nearly 40 million people arrived in Manhattan in 2004, bringing around $23 billion in business for the town. And that's definitely something to shout about.

Always one of the world's great cities, New York's present incarnation is more optimistic, more exciting and more dazzling than ever. Come and experience it for yourself. ❏

PRECEDING PAGES: runners cross the Verrazano-Narrows Bridge at the start of the New York City Marathon, in which more than 30,000 people compete; Zabar's on the Upper West Side is a deli with a difference.
LEFT: Downtown view near the Flatiron District.

BRAVE NEW WORLD

Discovered by accident during the hunt for the Northwest Passage, and bought for a box of trinkets from an unwary Indian tribe, Manhattan was poised to become a crossroads for the world

Anthropologists say that mythology is a way to explain and explore our origins. Fitting then that, according to local myth, New York began with a real-estate deal – and a swindle at that. In 1626 Peter Minuit, an official working for the Dutch, bought Manhattan island from the Indians for a box of trinkets worth 60 guilders, about $24. Today in Manhattan, $24 won't buy one square inch of office space.

The Algonquin

The Indians Minuit did business with were of Algonquin stock, a loosely associated family of tribes ranged along the northeast coast. They led fairly settled lives, moved seasonally within tribal territory, and lived by hunting, fishing and farming. Despite occasional skirmishes, their relations with Europeans began as cordial, if not exactly friendly, but when the Dutch settled for good, the peace deteriorated.

Theft, murder and squabbles over land escalated into a cycle of revenge that kept both Indians and colonists in constant fear. In 1643, Dutch soldiers fell on two Indian camps, savagely murdering about 120 men, women and children, and two years later massacred 1,000 more in villages north of Manhattan.

In 1655 the Indians launched the so-called Peach War, to avenge the murder of an Indian woman caught stealing from an orchard. Two thousand warriors responded by terrorizing the town for three days, killing 100 colonists, burn-

ing down houses and slaughtering cattle. In the end, the Algonquin were outnumbered by the well-armed Dutch, under constant threat of attack from the neighboring Iroquois, and riddled with European diseases.

The tribes were muscled out of their own territory. The Indians' fate had been sealed the moment that Europeans set eyes on it. In 1524 Giovanni da Verrazano sailed into the Lower Bay and remarked on its "commodiousness and beauty," which he believed was "not without some properties of value." Verrazano took glowing descriptions back to his patrons in France, but no one in Europe paid much attention to the new land until 1609, when Henry

LEFT: immigrants arrive in the "home of the brave."
RIGHT: detail from the painting *Purchase of Manhattan by Pieter Minuit, 1626*, by Alfred Friedericks.

Hudson sailed into the natural harbor of the future port of New York under a Dutch flag.

English by birth, Hudson was hired by a Dutch trading company to trace the elusive Northwest Passage. He didn't have much luck finding the legendary short-cut. After tangling with a group of Indians, he pointed his ship, the *Half Moon*, up the river that would later bear his name, and sailed to the site of Albany before realizing he wasn't headed for the Pacific Ocean. The voyage wasn't a total loss, though. Along the way, he discovered a woodland brimming with commercial possibilities. He was especially interested in the pelts worn by local Indians. Fur meant big money in a cold country

to settle tiny Nut Island (Governor's Island) just off the tip of Manhattan. Within a few months, late arrivals crowded the camp, and the group moved to Manhattan. They planted their new settlement at the southern end of the island, naming it New Amsterdam.

Peter Minuit was one of the first men the company appointed to govern the small village. He arrived in 1626 and immediately made his fateful deal with the Indians, probably at the site of Bowling Green, plunking down a chest of beads, knives and hatchets in exchange for the entire island. Unaccustomed to the European idea of private property, the Indians probably didn't understand the deal. On the other hand,

like the Netherlands, so he sent samples back to his trading company, explaining there were plenty more where they came from.

Trading posts

Hudson's employers were unimpressed, but when word of his discovery leaked out, merchants made for the New World seeking fortunes in pelts. In 1621 The Dutch West India Company acquired exclusive trading rights to New Netherland, a territory stretching from Cape May (New Jersey) into New England.

To seal its claim, the company established trading posts along the coast and rivers, and sent about 50 French-speaking Walloon Protestants

Minuit didn't understand the division of tribal territory and may have paid off a group who had no claim to Manhattan in the first place.

Life in tiny New Amsterdam was tumultuous, to say the least. There were Indian raids, and fears of English imperial ambitions in the New World. Drinking seems to have been the favored pastime of the lustier sorts, boozy knife-fights running a close second. The town itself was little more than a cluster of wood houses and mud streets huddled around a rude fortification. In its first few years, the Walloons and Dutch were joined by a motley collection of convicts, slaves, religious zealots and profiteers with nowhere else to go, with occasional groups of Indians wandering in to trade. In all, the people of New Amsterdam represented four continents and at least eight nationalities, with as many as 15 languages. It was an explosive mix, made all the more volatile by the short-sightedness of Dutch leadership.

In 1647 the company decided to put New Amsterdam back on the straight and narrow, and they had just the man to do it. Peter Stuyvesant was a hard-bitten soldier who had served as governor of Curaçao, where he lost his right leg in a tussle with the Portuguese.

"Peg Leg" Pete's rule was iron-handed; he cracked down on smuggling and tax evasion, and made much use of the whip and branding

Between the Brits

With the English on either side, it was only a matter of time before the thriving Dutch town came under pressure, and in 1664, King Charles II dispatched Colonel Richard Nicholls with four warships to seize New Amsterdam.

Stuyvesant was ready for war, but the townspeople refused to fight. They were hopelessly outnumbered by Nicholls' men, and glad of the opportunity to get out from under Stuyvesant's rule. Without a single shot fired, the English raised the Union Jack over Fort Amsterdam and renamed the town New York in honor of the King's brother. The Dutch recaptured the town about 10 years later in the Second Anglo-Dutch

iron on the town's rowdier citizens. Stuyvesant made few friends in New Amsterdam, but he got things done.

During his 17-year rule, he established the town's first hospital, prison, school and post office. To keep both the English and Indians at arm's length, he built a wood barricade from river to river at the present site of Wall Street (hence the name). And his New Amsterdam attracted settlers, doubling the population to about 1,500 people.

LEFT: a fanciful view of a meeting between Native Americans and European colonists.
ABOVE: lower Manhattan in the 1730s.

War, but swift negotiation returned it to British hands, again without a drop of blood shed.

The British didn't fare much better than the Dutch at keeping a lid on the possession. In 1712, a group of slaves set fire to a house, and nine whites died trying to put it out. Rather than face the cruel colonial court, six of the would-be revolutionaries committed suicide.

Others were banished, burned alive or tortured to death. Anger over the incident lingered until 1741, when a series of mysterious fires ignited a shameful anti-slave hysteria. Under the pretense of a bizarre black-Catholic conspiracy, white New Yorkers executed more than 30 slaves. The British were also struggling to control trade between the mother country and the colonies. Pirates and smugglers – including the infamous Captain Kidd – swarmed to New York in order to fence their ill-gotten merchandise and avoid the hefty customs taxes.

Stirrings of independence

The signal of New York's independence came in 1765 with the passage of the Stamp Act. After a 100-year struggle for supremacy in North America, King George III launched a battery of legislation to assert his authority over the colonies and stuff the royal coffers.

The new laws prohibited colonial currency, curtailed trade, and the Stamp Act levied tax on

King George didn't take the defeat lightly, and in 1767, through his new prime minister, Charles Townshend, lashed out with a tax on imported items like paper, lead and tea. This time the King backed the levy with an extra contingent of redcoats.

The Sons of Liberty despised the soldiers and took every opportunity to make their lives miserable. They erected a symbolic Liberty Pole and taunted the troops.

The year-long battle of nerves finally exploded in January 1770, when the rebels and the redcoats faced each other at the Battle of Golden Hill. Although casualties were light, this was one of the first significant armed encoun-

everything from tobacco to playing cards. To the feisty colonials, these restrictions were worse than the old Navigation Acts and smacked of the same arbitrary wielding of power. The rallying cry rose up, "No taxation without representation" – and New Yorkers hit the streets with a vengeance.

Spurred on by agitators known as the Sons of Liberty, angry mobs stormed a government stronghold and terrorized the officials. By the time the stamps actually arrived in New York, there wasn't a bureaucrat in town brave enough to distribute them. Heavily pressured by a colonial boycott, the British relented, and the volatile and hated Stamp Act was repealed.

ters between colonists and British soldiers.

Following the example from Boston, New Yorkers protested against the hated Tea Tax with their own "Tea Party." On April 22, 1774, a mob of angry citizens boarded an English cargo ship and dumped the tea into the harbor.

A year later, the "shot heard 'round the world" was fired at Lexington, Massachusetts, and the American Revolution was off and running. When the Declaration of Independence was read to crowds in New York, a mob raced down Broadway to topple the statue of King George III in Bowling Green. According to legend, the statue was melted down into musket balls, and fired at British troops.

Washington in New York

After General George Washington chased the British out of Boston, he came down to New York for a rematch against General Howe, but this time he fared badly. British troops beat back Washington's fledgling army from Brooklyn through Manhattan, to a resounding defeat at White Plains. The battle at Fort Washington was especially tragic. While Washington led his men across the Hudson River, a single regiment defended them from Washington Heights. But, rather than follow the rest of the army, the commanding officer dug in at Fort Washington to face the British head-on. Watching from New Jersey, Washington wept as more than 5,000 men were slaughtered by the superior British force. A brutal seven-year occupation followed.

When Washington eventually returned to New York in 1785 it was to celebrate America's victory and to bid farewell to his officers. He meant to retire to Virginia, and not serve again, but four years later he was back in New York, his hand on a Bible, taking the oath of office at Federal Hall. New York was the nation's first capital for a total of 18 months.

Still a small town at the turn of the 19th century, New York's population stood at about 35,000. Although an outbreak of yellow fever scared some residents off to the open spaces of Greenwich Village, most stayed huddled in the crooked lanes south of Canal Street.

After the Revolution, there was plenty to keep New Yorkers busy. Public debate raged over the new Constitution; brokers hammered out the New York Stock Exchange in the shade of a buttonwood tree on Wall Street; five people were killed in a riot against Columbia University doctors who were robbing graves to supply their anatomy labs; and occasional buffalo hunts were held, with animals shipped in from the western territories.

Politically, the town was split between Democrats and Federalists, represented by the city's two most prominent lawyers: Aaron Burr, who would serve as vice-president under Thomas Jefferson, and Alexander Hamilton, the nation's first Secretary of the Treasury. After

LEFT: the Battle of Saratoga against the redcoats.
RIGHT: George Washington en route to New York to fight the British; by 1789, New York would be the nation's first capital and Washington its president.

years of feuding, the two schemers settled their differences on the field of honor. In 1804, Aaron Burr shot and killed his rival in a duel at Weehawken, New Jersey.

The Erie Canal stretched over 350 miles (565 km) from Buffalo to Lake Erie, and took 12 years to build. With it, New York was transformed into a maritime giant, ships from all over the world jamming into the East River Harbor (now South Street Seaport) with goods for the heartland. Fueled by cheap immigrant labor, the city became an industrial dynamo, too. Business boomed, the population soared to 312,000 (1840), and real-estate prices went through the roof. Wheeler-dealers like John Jacob Astor and

1770.

Cornelius Vanderbilt made killings in property and shipping, and the banking business rose to national prominence. In 1835 the city celebrated its new affluence with the World's Fair at the magnificent, though short-lived, Crystal Palace.

Immigrant labor

While businessmen "lapped up the cream of commerce," the people who did most of the work – immigrants from Ireland and Germany – struggled to survive. Irish immigrants arrived in time to build the Erie Canal, but the floodgates didn't open until the 1840s, when "Potato Blight" in Ireland and a failed revolution in Germany sent thousands to the New World.

The immigrants crammed into the overcrowded tenements of slumlords like John Jacob Astor, who grew fat on exorbitant rents. The dilapidated Five Points district – the largest Irish community outside Ireland – was particularly rancid, with frequent outbreaks of cholera and yellow fever, and gangs like the Bowery Boys and Plug Uglies marauding the streets.

So-called native Americans organized against the immigrants, declaring that Americans could never allow the government "of our Revolutionary forefathers to pass into the hands of foreigners." The highly secretive nativists, called "know-nothings" by newspaper editor Horace Greely because they answered every question with, "I know nothing," focused their bigotry on a trumped-up Irish "Catholic conspiracy" against god-fearing Yankees.

Not all New Yorkers scorned the Irish, though. Democratic politicos at Tammany Hall saw a keg of electoral power waiting to be tapped: if an immigrant needed naturalization papers, if someone got in trouble, a Tammany man was there to pull the right strings. All the Irish need do was vote Democrat.

Slavery

By the 1850s, however, it seemed less likely that the country would be overrun by foreigners than split apart by domestic conflicts. Thanks largely

THE GREAT FIRE OF 1835

On the night of December 16th, 1835, fire tore through New York's downtown business district and burned for more than 15 hours. Raging from the East River almost as far as Broad Street, 674 buildings, including the Merchant's Exchange, the Post Office and, ironically, more than half of the city's insurance companies, were destroyed at a cost of over $20 million. The blaze spread in 15 minutes to 50 timber buildings, propelled by fierce wind. The volunteer fire department was disorganized and unequal to the challenge, handicapped by lack of wells, hoses and the East River being frozen. Fortunately, only two people died in the conflagration.

to a Bostonian named William Lloyd Garrison, slavery was becoming the live issue of the day. Disparaged as fanatics and demagogues, New York abolitionists tried to bring their message to the people, only to find themselves facing bankers and businessmen who were heavily invested in the Southern agricultural economy.

"The city of New York belongs almost as much to the South as to the North," the *Evening Post* reported. Even Mayor Fernando Wood supported the "continuance of slave labor and the prosperity of the slave master." When civil war seemed inevitable, he proposed that New York City declare itself independent in order to protect its business with the South.

In February 1860, a dark-horse candidate by the name of Abraham Lincoln spoke at Cooper Union, a free college established one year earlier by philanthropist Peter Cooper. Despite an ill-fitting suit, painfully tight shoes and an initial touch of stage fright, Lincoln's reasoned words and powerful delivery riveted the audience. Copies of the Cooper Union address were distributed throughout the country, and Lincoln himself recognized that it was a critical turning point in his bid for the US presidency.

In November, Lincoln was elected without a single Southern electoral vote, and five months later Fort Sumter was bombarded by Confederate artillery. At the Plymouth Church of Brook-

Brothers churned out uniforms. As the war dragged on and hope of a speedy victory faded, however, New York's fighting spirit started to sag. Among the war-weary lower classes, defeatism turned to rage when Lincoln pushed for a conscription law in 1862. It was bad enough that Lincoln had dragged them into a war. But a draft? That was outrageous. When it was then learned that wealthier young men could buy their way out of the army for $300, the poverty-stricken masses were unable to contain themselves.

On a steamy July morning a mob of several thousand stormed the Third Avenue draft office, routed police, and set fire to the entire block.

lyn, abolitionist minister Henry Ward Beecher shrieked for "war redder than blood and fiercer than fire." And that's exactly what he got.

The Civil War

In April 1861, Lincoln called for volunteers to put down the rebellious Southerners, and New York responded dutifully, producing 8,000 soldiers, including Irish and German regiments. Patriotism was suddenly in vogue, and even local businesses got in on the act. Tiffany's started crafting military regalia, and Brooks

Their appetite for carnage whetted, the mob rampaged for three more days while what little was left of the civil guard tried to cope. Apparently unsatisfied with beating policemen to death, the mob turned its attention to the few blacks who hadn't escaped. An orphanage for children was burned on Fifth Avenue, and 18 black men were lynched, their mutilated bodies left hanging from lampposts. The Draft Riots brought the most barbaric violence New York had ever seen, and in the end, armed regiments were recalled from the Union Army to quell them. The Civil War ended two years later. Within months, Abraham Lincoln's body lay in state at New York's City Hall. ❑

LEFT: the Great Fire of 1835 destroyed 674 buildings.
ABOVE: New York sent 8,000 troops to the Civil War.

THE MODERN AGE

From Manhattan's Big Bang after the Civil War, to
the World Trade Center tragedy early in the new millenium,
New York is the capital city of comeback

Although the founding of New York was in 1625, when the Dutch settled on lower Manhattan, the familiar financial giant of today – bristling with skyscrapers, the dreamhaven of immigrants – didn't begin to take shape until after the Civil War.

The late 19th century was Manhattan's Big Bang, a time of explosive growth and wondrous achievements. The American Museum of Natural History was established in 1877, and the Metropolitan Museum of Art in 1880. The Metropolitan Opera opened in 1883, as did the Brooklyn Bridge. A few days later, a dozen people were trampled to death, panicking that the span of the bridge would collapse. Three years after, in 1886, the city of Paris' gift of the Statue of Liberty was dedicated in New York Harbor.

Tammany Hall

Mass immigration continued after the Civil War, although new arrivals were now coming from southern and eastern Europe, and China. Italians – most from the southern provinces – crammed into the dilapidated tenements around Mulberry Street or in Greenwich Village. Jews forced out of Russia by anti-Semitic "pogroms" flooded into the Lower East Side, and Chinese immigrants settled around Mott Street. In 1898, the unification of the five boroughs under a single city government brought New York's population to 3.4 million people – half foreign-born, and two-thirds living in tenements. The city was

LEFT: Twin Towers of the World Trade Center, completed in 1973.
RIGHT: Empire State Building under scaffolding, 1930.

run by Tammany Hall, and Tammany Hall was run by William Marcy Tweed. A 300-pounder of voracious appetites, "Boss" Tweed started out as a chairmaker, worked his way up the ranks of the Democratic machine, and landed a position on the County Board of Supervisors. Within a few years, he was the most powerful politician in New York City, if not the entire state.

Tweed established his influence the old-fashioned way – by patronage, graft and kickbacks. The foundation of Tammany power was the loyalty of the lower classes, who saw Tweed as a type of Robin Hood figure, stealing from the rich and cutting the poor in for a slice of the booty, however small. One observer called it,

A Day in the Life

The Lower East Side went by many names: the typhus ward, the suicide ward, the crooked ward, or simply Jew-town. It was the New World ghetto, an irregular rectangle of tenements and sweatshops crooked between the Bowery and the East River, an energetic Babel crammed with Russian, Polish and German Jews.

Between 1880 and 1920, more than 2 million eastern European Jews came to the United States and over 500,000 settled in New York City, mostly on the Lower East Side.

With 330,000 people per square mile, sanitation was primitive; yellow fever and cholera were a constant threat, and child labor and exploitation were everyday facts of New York life. It was not uncommon for families of six or seven to live in one small room; some in hallways, in basements, in alleyways – anywhere they could squeeze themselves in. And the rents were extortionate.

A family often slept, cooked and ate in the same room where they worked, and from the youngest to the oldest, everyone did their part. The "needle trade" was a keystone of the economy, and rooms were often cluttered with half-sewn clothes piled on the floor. The more a person produced, the more he or she was paid. As a result, the hours were long and the pace grueling. The whine of sewing machines started no later than 6am and continued into the night.

For the sweatshop toilers, things were no better. Not only were working conditions appalling, but employees were charged for needles, thread and other supplies, for their lockers and chairs, and fined for damaged material at twice or three times its value. Wages were minimal – maybe $8 or $10 a week for a family of five or six, $14 or $15 for those doing exceptionally well. With so little coming in, survival was often hand-to-mouth, with every penny precious.

As writer Michael Gold remembered, "On the East Side people buy their groceries a pinch at a time; three cents' worth of sugar, five cents' worth of butter, everything in penny fractions." There was no margin for error. A family's survival could ride on a few cents. Compassion for one's friends had a high personal cost. "In a world based on the law of competition," Gold noted, "kindness is a form of suicide."

The center and heart of the neighborhood was Hester Street market, and Jews not in the needle trade sold meats, produce or cheap clothing from pushcarts. The area was nicknamed the Pig-Market, as photo-journalist Jacob Riis said, "probably in derision, for pork is the one ware that is not on sale."

Eastern European Jews put high value on learning and political organization, and community members with left-leanings were active in the labor movement. Rudimentary unions were organized and strikes launched, but "strike-busters" were hired to intimidate them with threats and violence.

Despite the efforts of Tammany Hall to woo their votes for the Democratic Party, East Side socialists eventually saw their candidates in Congress. Meanwhile, organizations such as the Educational Alliance sponsored lectures and demanded libraries; Yiddish theater blossomed on the stages of Second Avenue; and religious observances continued as they had in the old country. ❑

LEFT: portrait of an East Side immigrant by photo-journalist and reformer Jacob Riis.

"The government of the rich by the manipulation of the vote of the poor." Although Tweed did his share of do-gooding for the poor, most of his energy was spent lining his own pocket.

City contracts, for example, were commissioned on a simple percentage basis. Jobs were padded with extra funds, and a percentage of the total – sometimes the largest percentage – wound up fattening Tweed's wallet. One spectacular morning, Tweed and his cronies raked in a cool $5.5 million. Ironically, the contract in question was for the New York City Courthouse (a.k.a. the "Tweed Courthouse") immediately behind City Hall. As far as opposition went, Tweed simply bought off anyone who stood in

and was spirited away to Spain. He was recaptured, thrown back into jail, and died of pneumonia less than two years later.

Tweed's corrupt empire had little if any effect on the new breed of "social Darwinists" who pulled in money hand over fist. Cornelius Vanderbilt consolidated his vast railroad empire; the Astor family continued to rake in rents from hundreds of tenements, and financier Jay Gould cornered the gold market, precipitating the Panic of 1869. By the end of the century, J. P. Morgan was well on the way to creating the first American company to hit the billion dollar mark (US Steel); John D. Rockefeller struck pay dirt with Standard Oil, and Andrew Carnegie

his way. He kept the police department in his back pocket and had a number of judges on the payroll. And if money wasn't enough to cool the fires of reform, a visit from the police, health inspector or local Plug Uglies gang did the trick. But after 17 rowdy years as New York's unofficial monarch, Tweed's reign came to an end.

He was sent to the Ludlow Street Prison, which he had been responsible for building, after three years' litigation. Tweed hardly led the life of a typical jailbird, though. During one of his frequent visits to his Madison Avenue brownstone, Tweed ducked out the back door

ABOVE: men on the unfinished Brooklyn Bridge, 1872.

plunked down a tidy $2 million for a brand-new concert hall, named after himself, of course. He had Tchaikovsky conduct at the opening gala.

March of the upper crust

Abandoning their downtown haunts to the immigrants, the upper crust began a 50-year march up fashionable Fifth Avenue, leaving a trail of extravagant mansions as they moved farther uptown. It was at this time that the elite came to be known as the "Four Hundred," said to be because of Mrs Astor's habit of inviting 400 guests to her annual ball. "There are only about four hundred people in fashionable New York society," an insider explained. "If you go outside the number, you strike people who are either not at ease in a ballroom or else make other people not at ease. See the point?"

While the Four Hundred gorged themselves at lavish parties, downtown New York was as wretched as ever. Two thousand immigrants poured into the new Ellis Island Immigration Station every day, cramming tenements and sweatshops with more people than they could house. Despite the work of reformers like photojournalist Jacob Riis, it took a tragedy for people to take notice of the horrid conditions.

On March 25, 1911, as the five o'clock bell sounded, fire broke out on the top floors of the Triangle Shirtwaist Company near Washington Square. Around 600 workers were inside. With stairways locked or barred by flames and only a few slow elevators, many were trapped. Spectators wept aloud as girls jumped from the eighth and ninth floors, thudding on the sidewalk. The blaze lasted only about 10 minutes, but over 140 workers were killed, most of them Jewish and Italian women no more than 20 years old. Although the two owners of the company were acquitted, the tragedy stimulated sweeping labor reforms.

World War I came and went with minimal impact on New York. Doughboys, as the US infantrymen became known, returned home to find business still booming, the population still

THE JAZZ AGE

In the early years of the 20th century, the black community started moving into the failed developments of Harlem. By the 1920s, a blossoming of black culture known as the Harlem Renaissance gave a forum to writers like Zora Neale Hurston and the poet Langston Hughes *(see page 129)*, while the innovative big bands of Count Basie and Duke Ellington gave swinging soundtracks to the white audiences of the Cotton Club, Small's Paradise and other ritzy after-hours clubs. Presiding over the festivities was the prince of Jazz-Age New York, Mayor James Walker. The high-living playboy – a former Tin Pan Alley songwriter – was the embodiment of the freewheeling Roaring Twenties. He was a gambler, a lady's man and a fashion plate. Loose with money and light on Prohibition, Walker wasn't keen on administration, preferring to act as a figurehead and leave the running of the city to the hacks at Tammany Hall. He played craps with reporters, hobnobbed with the stars, and flaunted his affair with a Broadway actress. He had his own booth at '21' (a speakeasy then, an important restaurant now), drinking downstairs while raids were taking place upstairs. When Walker raised his own salary by $10,000, his response to critics of this extravagance was, "Think what it would cost if I worked full-time."

growing, and an era of good feelings taking hold of the city. Prohibition kicked off the "Roaring Twenties" on a dreary note, but somehow the good times seemed better and the parties wilder now that drinking was taboo.

Prohibition backfired

In fact, Prohibition backfired in New York even more than in other cities. The liquor trade turned into a gold mine for organized crime, especially the mafiosi around Mulberry Street. Some estimates put twice as many speakeasies in New York City after Prohibition as there were legitimate bars before. A well-known madam is supposed to have said, "They might as well try to

knocking 'em back with his hoodlum buddies, the Hudson Dusters, at a speakeasy called the Hell Hole, and blowing the lid off the theater world at the Provincetown Playhouse.

The city may have been going to Hell in a handbasket, but most New Yorkers kept right on partying. And they kept right on spending too. In the 1920s the city went on a stock-buying binge that sent the daily numbers through the roof – and it didn't look like they were ever coming down. It didn't matter that stocks were being bought on credit, or that the city was being bilked of millions by Tammany Hall. As long as the money kept rolling in, the lights burned on Broadway, and Mayor Jimmy Walker *(see box*

dry up the Atlantic with a post office blotter."

The free-spirited Twenties had its share of free-thinkers, too. Cheap rents and a certain "old quarter" atmosphere attracted writers, artists and radicals to Greenwich Village, much to the chagrin of the Italian and Irish families in the neighborhood. People like John Reed, Emma Goldman, Louise Bryant and Edna St Vincent Millay advocated everything from communism to free love. All the while Eugene O'Neill was

LEFT: the Cotton Club: epitome of the Jazz Age.
ABOVE: writer Dorothy Parker and cartoonist James Thurber (far right) with members of the Round Table, which first assembled at the Algonquin Hotel in 1919.

opposite) was smiling, everything was all right. As gossip columnist and broadcaster Walter Winchell said, "In the 1920s the American people were hell-bent for prosperity and riches. And they wanted a politician who would be hell-bent only for reelection… a man who would respect the national rush to get rich, who would accept greed, avarice and the lust for quick gain as a legitimate expression of the will of the people… Walker knew what the people wanted."

Black Thursday

When the bottom fell out of the stock market on Black Thursday – October 24, 1929 – Walker's reign of good feelings crashed with it. The Great

Depression hit New York hard; total income was slashed by more than half, and unemployment soared to 25 percent. People were robbed of their livelihoods, their homes and their dignity. Makeshift "Hoovervilles" sprang up in Central Park, and breadlines became common. As Groucho Marx put it, he knew the city was on the skids "when the pigeons started feeding the people in Central Park."

Before Walker could ride out his second term, his administration started to unravel. An investigation into city government uncovered a pile of corruption second only to the Tweed Ring. Walker was hauled up to the town of Albany where Governor Franklin D. Roosevelt

reviewed the charges against him. Walker knew there was no way he was going to walk away without a political, and personal, skinning. He resigned his office in 1932, and caught the next ship to Europe.

Fiorello LaGuardia

About a year later, a new mayor moved into City Hall. Fiorello LaGuardia was a small, plump man with an animated face and a line in rumpled suits. He had none of Walker's finesse, but he was quick-witted, savvy, and determined to whip the city back into shape. He could be hard-nosed, almost ruthless, but still paternalistic and warm. The man who ordered Lucky

Luciano off the streets also read out the comics over the radio every Sunday. LaGuardia had his critics, but for a city ravaged by the Depression, he was the closest thing they had to a savior.

LaGuardia was elected in 1933 and immediately got on board Franklin Roosevelt's New Deal, launching massive relief and construction programs to revive the economy. His administration swung into action, building bridges, highways, housing, even finding work for artists and writers with the Works Progress Administration. At the same time, large-scale projects launched in the 1920s came to completion. Art deco burst into town with the opening of the Chrysler Building in 1930, the Empire State Building and Waldorf-Astoria Hotel in 1931, and the Rockefeller Center in 1933.

Then, in 1941, the US entered World War II, and the city was swept into the war effort. German spies were arrested; Japanese families were incarcerated on Ellis Island, and blackouts were ordered – even the torch of the Statue of Liberty was turned off. In the basement of a Columbia University physics lab, Enrico Fermi and Leo Szilard were experimenting with atomic fission, groundwork for the atomic bomb, known later as the Manhattan Project.

Sleek New York

With the United Nations moving into the city in 1947 and Idlewild Airport (now Kennedy) opening in 1948, New Yorkers were flush with a sense of possibilities. World peace, a healthy economy, the riches of technology all seemed within reach. The glass-walled UN Secretariat Building brought a sleek look to Midtown and kicked off the 1950s with a fitting sense of modernity. A new generation of glass-box skyscrapers lined Park and Madison avenues, eventually spreading to the West Side and the Financial District. Birdland, the be-bop nightclub named after saxophonist Charlie Parker, opened on Broadway, and Franklin National Bank issued the world's first credit card.

Then, as in many other northeastern cities, the post-war years brought decline. The middle class moved out to the suburbs, corporations relocated, and poor blacks and Hispanics flooded into the city. By the mid-1970s, New York's budget was so stressed the city was on the verge of bankruptcy. It seemed as if the glory days were gone for good.

The trouble had started in 1946 when William O'Dwyer took over the mayor's office. Although never charged with any crime, O'Dwyer presided over an administration thick with underworld connections. A change had come over Tammany Hall. After Fiorello LaGuardia broke the old Democratic machine, Tammany was infiltrated by organized crime – "Murder Inc." as the papers called it. Tammany politicos were involved in gambling, prostitution and the "waterfront rackets," and made substantial political inroads, especially at the police department, to protect their interests.

In the 1950s, Mayor Robert Wagner oversaw a gradual political healing, but by then a social civil rights movement taking shape across the nation, they began to demand their slice of the political and economic pie.

Racial tensions

As the black power and anti-war movements gained momentum in the 1960s, the tensions became volatile. Intended to enhance the city's international reputation, the 1964 World's Fair was a staging ground for one demonstration after another. Bitter questions were raised over the segregation of New York schools, police were accused of brutality against minorities, and demonstrators grew militant. Mayor Wagner ordered the police to clear protestors after a 44-

transformation was under way, with repercussions up to the present day. In the late 1940s, a wave of Puerto Rican immigrants came to New York and the influx continued through the 1950s. Some of the resulting tensions were dramatized in the 1957 musical *West Side Story*.

Attracted by war-time jobs, the black community also grew during and after World War II. Like immigrants before them, the black and Hispanic communities faced a wall of opposition. Equality in jobs, housing, city services and education were denied them, and with the

day sit-in at City Hall, starting a minor riot.

In the summer of 1964, the black communities of Harlem and Bedford-Stuyvesant (Brooklyn) stirred with anger and a new spirit of activism. When a young black man was shot by police under questionable circumstances, Harlem erupted. Two days later, on July 18, 1964, several thousand assaulted the 123rd Street police station. Rioters raged in Harlem for six days, burning white-owned buildings, looting stores that refused to hire blacks, and assaulting passersby. All the while, Mayor Wagner tried to assure black New Yorkers that "Law and order are the Negro's best friend."

Wealthier whites found something to protest

LEFT: Fiorello LaGuardia, Depression-era mayor.
ABOVE: the UN building under construction, late 1940s.

about, too. The demolition of Penn Station in 1965 strengthened the preservation movement. Surely not all of New York's heritage should fall so readily to the developer's dollar? Other significant social battles of the time involved gays and women. In 1969, the gay rights movement gained momentum when police raiding the Stonewall Inn in Greenwich Village encountered fierce resistance. The following year, the legendary McSorley's Old Ale House was forced to admit women.

Although the Harlem riots passed, the bitterness behind them was unresolved. In the late 1960s and early 1970s, a liberal Republican, John Lindsay, sought progressive solutions to

mayor and another effort was launched to buoy the city budget with borrowing – this time the Federal government provided a loan guarantee of $1.65 billion. A resurgence of corporate development fed capital into the economy, and the city began to get back on its feet. Half-empty since their opening in 1973, the 110-story twin towers of the World Trade Center sprang to life, their gravity-defying prominence marked in 1974 when a tightrope walker strolled between them at a dizzying height. Three years later, George Willig illegally scaled one of the towers and was fined one penny per story.

Nearby in Lower Manhattan, Battery Park City and the South Street Seaport were devel-

New York's problems, first in the House of Representatives and then as mayor (1966–74). With the tax base eroding and calls on public services at an all-time high, New York was in a financial stranglehold that constant labor disputes did nothing to ease.

Near bankruptcy

By 1975, the city was on the verge of bankruptcy. The banks refused to lend more money and, when the city went cap in hand to the Federal government, President Gerald Ford's response was summed up by the *Daily News* thus: "Ford to City: Drop Dead."

In 1976, the feisty Edward Koch was elected

oped. In Midtown, the Citicorp Building opened in 1977, sparking the development of One UN Plaza, the AT&T (now Sony) and IBM buildings, and other skyscrapers.

Internationally, New York sustained its reputation as a place of excess. In 1977, Studio 54 opened, symbolizing an era of sybaritic, cocaine-driven culture. A power failure the same year was accompanied by widespread looting – in marked contrast to the community spirit that had prevailed during a previous major blackout in 1965. In 1980, former Beatle John Lennon was murdered outside the Dakota apartment building where he lived, by the deranged Mark Chapman. Broadway theatres began their shows an hour earlier to give tourists and out-of-towners a chance to get clear before the late-night muggers moved in.

The haves and have-nots

The most worrying trend was the widening gap between rich and poor. While gentrification swept through the neighborhoods, the under-class grew more entrenched. Ronald Reagan entered the White House in 1980, promising "trickle-down" economics to ensure that the poor would benefit from concessions given to the rich. But the new wealth didn't seem to trickle down very far. The legacy of homeless-ness was evident on almost every street corner;

of conspicuous consumption was celebrated in the pages of *Vanity Fair*, a long defunct maga-zine revived by Condé Nast in 1983. By 1987, the good times had turned sour, with two of Wall Street's biggest share dealers heading for jail and the market taking a record one-day plunge of 508 points.

In 1989, David Dinkins became New York City's first African-American mayor – appro-priately enough since a census of the city's res-idents showed that whites had become a minority. But his term was not a success. The annual murder rate peaked at 2,245 and the number of citizens on welfare reached a new high. Domestic violence was accompanied by

Aids and drug abuse pushed the health-care sys-tems far beyond their capacity; and racial con-flicts erupted with alarming regularity. Compounding the problems, many Manhattan businesses and middle-class workers fled to the suburbs or New Jersey, further eroding New York's tax base.

All the while, super-rich moguls like Donald Trump gobbled up New York real estate like squares on a Monopoly board, and the glitziness

international terrorism when a car bomb exploded in the World Trade Center in 1993, killing six people.

The Giuliani years

To many, the city seemed ungovernable – an attitude which partly explains the victory in the 1993 mayoral election of Brooklyn-born Rudolph ("Rudy") Giuliani, an abrasive former prosecutor with the Department of Justice, and a New York district attorney who promised to get tough on crime. The first Republican mayor for two decades in what is essentially a Democ-rat stronghold, he more than kept his promise, extending "zero tolerance" to law-breaking,

LEFT: New York's largest ticker-tape parade was held in 1962 for the *Apollo 11* astronauts.
ABOVE: Donald Trump (here with *Playboy*'s Christie Hefner and ex-wife Ivana) symbolized the 1980s.

encompassing not only criminals and police corruption, but also jaywalkers, beggars, graffiti vandals and people who didn't sort their garbage properly for recycling. It wasn't a policy that endeared him to liberals, but it won respect, especially when the crime rate fell dramatically, turning New York into one of the safer big cities in the US. By 1997, the murder rate had dropppped by two-thirds from its 1990 high to an average of 2.1 killings a day.

Business Improvement Districts (BIDs) sprang up across the city, construction boomed, and seedy areas like Times Square were cleaned up. The economy rebounded wildly from a 1987–92 slump, and unemployment fell. With

two Boeing 767s, each laden with 10,000 gallons of fuel, into both of the World Trade Center's towers. As New Yorkers and television viewers around the world looked on in horror, the towers collapsed, killing nearly 3,000 people, including hundreds of policemen and firefighters who raced to the scene.

The smoke at "Ground Zero" took three weeks to subside, and the wreckage smouldered for weeks after. More than 20,000 New Yorkers were displaced from their apartments near the 16-acre (6.5-hectare) disaster area. Even criminals were subdued; the week following the attack, crime in Manhattan fell 59 percent.

The resilience of New Yorkers showed

much fanfare, Giuliani was elected to a second term in 1997 and turned his ambitions to the US Senate. But in 2000 his luck ran out: the combination of a prostate cancer diagnosis and a messy separation from his second wife forced him to pull out of the contest, which was won by the high-profile Democratic candidate, Hillary Rodham Clinton. Giuliani seemed a beaten man, destined to serve out his last months as a lame-duck mayor.

Terrorism hits the Twin Towers

On the morning of September 11, 2001, terrorists hijacked five passenger planes and, in a meticulously planned suicide mission, crashed

WORLD TRADE CENTER SITE

In the immediate aftermath of the destruction of the Twin Towers, some people felt the site should become an open space, to commemorate the dead. Others advocated rebuilding the 110-story towers as a gesture of defiance to terrorism. A competition was held, but the outcome was not without controversy. The winning entry, Daniel Libeskind's Freedom Tower, is currently under construction. It is 1,776 feet (541 meters) in height – 1776 being the date of America's Declaration of Independence from England – and is 30 percent higher than the Twin Towers. The site will also include a reflective hanging garden, a cultural center and a memorial to those who perished.

through, cued by Mayor Giuliani, whose trademark abrasiveness gave way to a straight-talking compassion that avoided hysteria and earned the citizens' trust. These qualities were called on again just nine weeks later when an American Airlines Airbus crashed in the Rockaway district of the borough of Queens. Terrorist action was not blamed, but in a bitter irony, the crash site was home to many emergency workers who bore such a toll on 9/11.

Giuliani's popularity was such that he only had to endorse Michael Bloomberg as his successor to ensure the self-made media mogul won the November election for the Republicans. A political ingenue, and a billionaire who

been ruthlessly pruned. Fears of economic recession combined with the effects of the terrorist attack to swell the ranks of the jobless.

The future is back

As ever in New York, fresh ideas came to the fore. Transportation links have seen improvments, including express cross-streets and better bus services, and the neglected Hudson River waterfront is being revived and regarded as a huge success. The future is back on the agenda.

In 2004, New York hosted the Republican National Convention amid extraordinary security. Governor's Island became a retreat for visitors; the spectacularly rebuilt Museum of

put $41 million of his own money into the campaign, Bloomberg had previously been well-known on Wall Street for his financial data empire, as well as in the gossip columns for the series of glamorous women he escorted after his 1993 divorce. Bloomberg inherited a daunting set of problems. As well as the massive rebuilding program in Lower Manhattan, the city faced an $8.7 billion budget shortfall, even though New York's social services budgets had already

LEFT: the remains of the World Trade Center after the terrorist attacks of September 11, 2001.
ABOVE: the spectacularly renovated Museum of Modern Art opened on November 20, 2004.

Modern Art returned from Queens and opened to great acclaim. A new Time-Warner building stood tall over Columbus Circle, with a soaring Hearst Tower scheduled to join it in 2006. Architect Daniel Libeskind continues with his plan to replace the Twin Towers of the World Trade Center, though not without controversy, of course. This is Gotham City, after all; a city of change, struggle, joy and ambition, where anything can happen.

It's a place where traffic, noise and outrageous street life keep up a frenzied, non-stop rhythm. One thing is certain, though; by the time you think you understand New York, your understanding will already be obsolete. ❏

Decisive Dates

1524 Italian explorer Giovanni da Verrazano, under the patronage of Francis I of France, sights the territory but doesn't land.

1609 Englishman Henry Hudson weighs anchor on the island, then sails the *Half Moon* up the river that now bears his name.

1624 The Dutch West India Company establishes a trading post on the southern tip of the island at the current site of Battery Park.

1626 The provincial director general of the New Amsterdam settlement, Peter Minuit, purchases Manhattan from the Algonquin Indians for 60

guilders' worth of trinkets – the equivalent of $24 in today's currency.

1630s Dutch farmers settle land in what is now Brooklyn and the Bronx.

1643 Conflict with local Algonquin tribes leaves at least 80 Indians dead at what became known as the Panovia Massacre.

1647 Peter Stuyvesant becomes director general and soon suppresses political opposition.

1653 Stuyvesant builds a fence along what is now Wall Street to protect New Amsterdam from British incursion.

1664 In the first year of the sea war between England and Holland, Stuyvesant is forced to surrender the town to the British without a fight.

New Amsterdam is renamed New York, after King Charles II's brother, James, Duke of York.

1673 The Dutch recapture New York and rename it New Orange, again without fighting.

1674 New York is returned to the British as a result of the Anglo/Dutch Treaty of Westminster.

1690 With a population of 3,900, New York is now the third-largest town in North America.

1735 Newspaper publisher Peter Zenger is tried for slandering the British crown. He is acquitted, establishing the precedent for press freedom.

1765 In accordance with the Stamp Act, unfair taxes are levied against the colonists.

1770 A series of skirmishes between the Sons of Liberty and British soldiers culminate in the Battle of Golden Hill.

1776 The Revolutionary War begins and the colonies declare their independence from England. George Washington, in command of the colonial troops, loses the Battle of Long Island. British troops occupy New York until 1783.

1789 New York becomes the capital of the newly-founded United States of America, but only retains this status briefly.

1789 George Washington is inaugurated at the site of the Federal Hall, Wall Street.

1790 A first official census reveals that New York now has a population of 33,000.

1792 An open-air money market is founded beneath a buttonwood tree on Wall Street.

1807 Robert Fulton, sailing along the Hudson River, establishes the first successful steamboat company.

1811 An important decision is made affecting the city's future appearance: all streets are to be laid out in the form of a grid.

1820 An official Stock Exchange replaces the outdoor money market on Wall Street.

1825 The economic importance of New York increases sharply as a result of the construction of the Erie Canal, connecting the Hudson River with the Great Lakes.

1830 Irish and German immigrants begin arriving in great numbers. The city's population soon tops 200,000.

1835 Manhattan, between South Broad and Wall Street, is ravaged by the "Great Fire."

1857 William Marcy "Boss" Tweed, elected to the County Board of Supervisors, launches a career of notorious corruption.

1858 Calvert Vaux and Frederick Law Olmsted submit plans for the city's Central Park.

1860 New York City becomes the largest metropolis in the US; in the previous 30 years Brooklyn's population increased 10 times.
1861 The Civil War begins.
1863 The Draft Riots rage for three days. It is thought that around 100 people are killed.
1870s William Marcy "Boss" Tweed is arrested; he later dies in jail.
1877 The Museum of Natural History opens.
1880 The Metropolitan Museum of Art opens.
1883 The Brooklyn Bridge opens, and there is a first performance by the Metropolitan Opera.
1886 The unveiling of the Statue of Liberty, a gift from France, on Liberty Island.
1892 Ellis Island in New York Harbor becomes the point of entry for immigrants to the US.
1898 New York's five boroughs are united under one municipal government.
1902 The Flatiron Building is completed.
1904 A subway system is established.
1911 The Triangle Fire alerts the public to the appalling living conditions of immigrants.
1913 Construction of the world's tallest sky-scraper, the Woolworth Building, begins. It is superseded in 1930 by the Chrysler Building.
1929 Wall Street crashes, and with it comes the start of the Great Depression.
1931 The Empire State Building opens.
1933 Fiorello LaGuardia is elected mayor and uses federal money to fight the devastating effects of the Depression.
1939 Ten years after its foundation by Abby Aldrich Rockefeller, the Museum of Modern Art moves into its new home on 53rd Street.
1941 The United States enters World War II.
1946 The United Nations begins meeting in New York. The permanent buildings on East 42nd–48th streets are completed 6 years later.
1959 The Guggenheim Museum opens for the first time. Work begins on the Lincoln Center.
1965 A 16-hour power cut paralyzes the city.
1970 Economic decline sets in, which contin-ues until around 1976.
1973 The World Trade Center opens, with its 110-story Twin Towers.
1975 Impending bankruptcy is avoided only via a bridging loan from the Federal government.

1977 A second power cut occurs, this time 27 hours long. Widespread looting and vandalism.
1982 The IBM Building opens, followed by the AT&T Building in 1983.
1986 Battery Park City opens.
1987 "Black Monday" on Wall Street. Shares suffer a sudden 30 percent drop in value.
1990 David Dinkins becomes the city's first African-American mayor.
1993 A bomb explodes below the World Trade Center. Many are injured.
1997 Mayor Rudolph Giuliani's "get tough on crime" campaign is effective, with declines in crime transforming the Big Apple into one of the safer large cities in the United States.

1998 The city celebrates the Centennial of Greater New York, marking the amalgamation of the five boroughs in 1898.
2001 Terrorists crash two planes into the World Trade Center; nearly 3,000 people are killed. Michael Bloomberg is elected mayor.
2003 Mayor Bloomberg's law to ban smoking in bars, clubs and restaurants is implemented. New York suffers another power cut.
2004 The Museum of Modern Art reopens in Manhattan. The soaring Time Warner Center in Columbus Circle opens.
2005 Artists Christo and Jeanne-Claude erect "The Gates" in Central Park, 7,500 "gates" of saffron-colored fabric panels. ❏

LEFT: among the early inhabitants of Manhattan Island were the Algonquin Indians.
RIGHT: Towers of Light, the temporary World Trade Center memorial created after September 11, 2001.

NEW YORK, NEW YORKERS

A place of high culture
and low-brow burlesque, the migrant melting
pot of New York has given creative refuge to
artists and thinkers of every kind

The first thing about New Yorkers that strikes visitors is the talk. They talk a mile a minute, to everybody. They could talk for their country – they often seem as though they *are* talking for their country, although, of course, their country is New York. In such a fast-moving, densely packed metropolis, there's a loud background to speak above, but more surprising is the range and depth of discourse. On the bus or in an elevator, casual conversations are as likely to strike up about the Austro-Hungarian pact as they are over the Yankees' recent play-offs.

This intellectual diversity is evident in the rows of chess tables outside so many cafés, and the range of literature being read on the subway. A visible part of New Yorkers' widely encompassing inclusivity is the sheer intellectual hunger. Just heft the weight of the Sunday *New York Times* to feel it.

Stock market and sculpture

Certainly, there is a public face to intellectual accomplishment in this city. The intellectual life here has its rituals, like museum openings, and its own venues. There are professional philosophers and critics who by their presence give definition to the proper noun New York Intellectual. Intellectual life in New York is not a cerebral speakeasy where a panel slides open in a door and you whisper "Kierkegaard sent me." Rather, it is a range of mental

PRECEDING PAGES: Lincoln Center.
LEFT: noontime crowds on Fifth Avenue.
RIGHT: lounging in NoLita.

endeavor – the stock market and sculpture, poetry and particle physics – and it is a rich and polyglot marketplace of lectures, galleries, museums, plays, concerts, libraries, films and, of course, dinner parties. It is the casual way great minds have always moved through the landscape: Thomas Wolfe stalking the streets of Brooklyn, Sonny Rollins sitting and practicing the saxophone on the Williamsburg Bridge.

Culture and intellect not only transform the individual, they give identity to the mass, to the city as a whole. In his book *The Art of the City: Views and Versions of New York,* Peter Conrad writes, "Every city requires its own myth to justify its presumption of centrality," and he then goes on to cite artistic annotators of New York, from the songwriter George M. Cohan to the painter Saul Steinberg, whose famous cover for the *New Yorker* suggests an earth largely occupied by Manhattan.

Alexander Alland, Jr, former chairman of the anthropology department at Columbia University, puts the myth into words: "The intellectual life is why I am a New Yorker. It's why I stay here. I spend my summers in Europe, and when they ask me if I'm an American, I say, 'No, I'm a New Yorker.' I don't know about everyone else, but for me that's a positive statement."

Gravitational tilt

New York began its rise to intellectual primacy in the 1850s. It is easy now to forget that throughout the colonial era and the early 19th century New York was at best the third city of the nation, behind Boston and Philadelphia. What shifted the gravity was the migration of the publishing industry from Boston to New York. Initially, the publishers were simply seeking more customers – New York had the largest population – but their relocation set off a chain reaction that altered the city. With publishing houses came writers and editors and illustrators.

Meanwhile, the city had begun to change in

FACTS THAT FIT

Biggest: the biggest meteorite to hit the earth weighed 34 tons (31,000 kg), and is on display at the American Museum of Natural History.

Longest: after Broadway leaves the city, it becomes the Albany Post Road, and travels all the way to New York's state capital – a distance of 175 miles (282 km).

Oldest: the oldest grave in New York is located in Lower Manhattan's Trinity Churchyard.

Most clogged: according to the Bureau of Traffic, the city's most congested area is along 42nd Street, between Third and Madison avenues.

Waterlogged: it takes an average of seven hours and 15 minutes to swim around the island of Manhattan.

Making the switch: Radio City's Rockettes make nine costume changes during their annual Christmas show.

Flipping the switch: Thomas Edison turned on New York's first public electric lights on Wall Street, 1882.

City shore: New York has 15 miles (24 km) of beaches.

City core: how New York got the nickname "the Big Apple" is open to debate. Some say it came from a 1920s newspaper column about horse racing called "Around the Big Apple." Others say it was used by jazz musicians to indicate getting to the top of their profession, or reaching "the Big Apple."

other ways. At the top of the New York economic scale, the captains of commerce and industry began to endow museums and to support individual artists; at the bottom, each wave of immigrants enriched and diversified the intellectual community. City College, established in 1849, acted as the great pedagogue for those without wealth, and later came to be known as "the poor man's Harvard."

Immigrants

The German influx of 1848, the Irish flight from famine, migrations of Jews, Italians, Greeks, Chinese, Koreans and Vietnamese – all brought knowledge and culture from

Never closely associated with the American mainstream, New York is one of the few American cities where 'minorities' (including American-born blacks, Hispanics and Asians) comprise the majority of the population. Multiculturalism and multiracialism have long been an integral part of the city's color, complexity and problems. The people of New York have learned to be accepting, if not always enthusiastic, about the difficulties and responsibilities that a large immigrant community inevitably entails.

Public schools offer bilingual instruction. Traffic signs, advertisements and subway signs are commonly printed in two or three

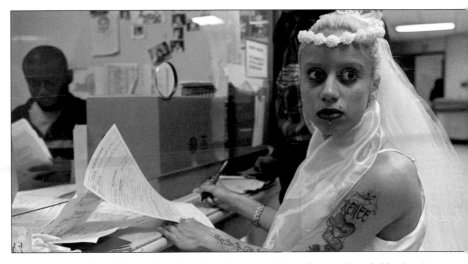

abroad to New York, making an American city cosmopolitan. In 1933, the New School for Social Research acknowledged that rich resource by founding the University in Exile (now the Graduate Faculty of Political and Social Science) as a graduate school to be staffed by European scholars who escaped the Nazi regime. The international dynamic continues today, with the Soviet Jews of Brighton Beach, with the West Indians of Jamaica in Queens, with the Southeast Asians of Queens' Elmhurst district.

LEFT: this is a city where the majority are minorities.
ABOVE: marriage, Manhattan-style.

languages depending on the neighborhood, but most often in Spanish or Chinese, the city's unofficial second and third languages. There are at least a dozen non-English newspapers published in the city itself and countless others imported from their countries of origin. Immigrants can take driving tests in other languages, and do business at foreign banks. Even automatic cash machines can "talk" in Spanish, Chinese or French.

Although there are other cities in the US with a high percentage of foreign-born residents, none can match the diversity of New York's ethnic communities, or the cultural depth of even the smallest groups.

A quick run-down of nationalities makes it quite clear that New York is the home-away-from-home for people from every continent. As demographers are fond of pointing out, there are more Greeks in New York than in any city but Athens; more Dominicans in New York than in any city but Santo Domingo. And that's only scratching at the surface.

The attraction for immigrants, of course, is New York as a land of opportunity. Some variation of the American dream is still alive on these streets, and immigrants seem eager to share it. Once a migrant group gets its hooks into a line of work, others follow in the same trade. Although there are always exceptions,

Stieglitz, composer Duke Ellington and film makers Woody Allen and Martin Scorsese. These artists have drawn on New York for subject matter, and their work, in turn, has informed the world's impression of the city.

Artists also pioneer the resurgent neighborhoods of the city. When creative people moved to Soho in the 1970s, it was hard to get cabs to go there. When that neighborhood became too expensive, the artists moved on to new frontiers. They colonized the area known as Alphabet City (Avenues A, B, C and D) on the Lower East Side of Manhattan, or across the East River to Greenpoint and Williamsburg, or to a part of Brooklyn they simply call

in recent years Koreans have tended to dominate the grocery business, Chinese workers have flooded the garment industry, and Indians or Pakistanis own newsstands. Greek coffee shops and Latino *bodegas* have become part of the New York landscape.

Rampant creativity

If immigrants define much of the New York mix, then so, emphatically, do artists. From the time Walt Whitman published *Leaves of Grass* in 1855, artists have been the bards of New York. Whitman is the common ancestor in an artistic family that includes novelist Theodore Dreiser and photographer Alfred

DUMBO, for Down Under Manhattan Bridge Overpass. Trendy stores, bars and restaurants then follow, rents soar, and artists go back on the lookout for new territories to occupy.

As more and more creative people inhabited New York, even more were drawn to it. Scale is the key word: the number of college graduates in New York today collectively would make up a very large city.

With size comes sustenance for all sorts of specialized intellectual communities. Greenwich Village became an urban version of the artists' colony, a home to creators of all stripes, the place that gave Eugene O'Neill one of his early stages in the 1920s (at the Provincetown

Playhouse) and Bob Dylan a bandstand in the 1960s (at Folk City). Miles uptown, Harlem was home to a black intelligentsia that included the writers Langston Hughes *(see page 129)*, James Weldon Johnson and James Baldwin; the political theorist W.E.B. Du Bois, and the photographer James Van Der Zee, whose record of his era appeared decades later in the album *Harlem on My Mind.*

Pop culture

The notion of pop culture versus high culture is almost meaningless, because the esoteric can enjoy a mass audience: such demanding playwrights and composers as Tom Stoppard

rigor. There are almost a dozen Roman Catholic colleges in New York City; there is an Islamic Seminary on Queens Boulevard. And in the *shtibels* – houses of study – Hasidim gather to progress centuries-old theological debates.

The intellectual force of New York sends ripples far beyond the city. The principal network news in the United States originates not from the nation's capital but from New York. Two major news magazines, *Time* and *Newsweek*, and two national newspapers, the *New York Times* and the *Wall Street Journal*, are published here. Most of the leading critics of theater, film, art, dance and music make

and Stephen Sondheim can have hits on Broadway, while a gospel version of *Oedipus at Colonu*s – could anything seem more unlikely? – can be a sell-out at the Brooklyn Academy of Music. Intellectual life also interacts with political life. From A. Okey Hall, the hack figurehead for Boss Tweed, to Rudolph Giuliani, New York's mayors have often doubled as writers. Like politics, religion is a matter of passion, but also of intellectual

LEFT: Wollman Rink, Central Park, where over 4,000 New Yorkers a day take a glide.
ABOVE: Tibetan monks stroll past the famous bull near Wall Street.

their pronouncements from Manhattan, the town where many of the artistic activities they review were created originally.

But the point here is not name-dropping. Without any of those figures, important as they are, intellectual life in New York would proceed with just as much vigor. It is, remember, largely a private and a personal affair. Manifested in individual taste and style, at its heart it has little to do with celebrity or vogue. The intellectual sweep of New York allows almost unparalleled opportunity for eclecticism, for search and discovery. New Yorkers differ from one another in myriad ways, but so many share the same autobiographical tale that it has become mythic itself. With endless variations, the story goes something like this:

An able young man (or a young woman) feels the need to leave home. Perhaps he feels misunderstood and unappreciated, surrounded by what playwright Eugene O'Neill called "spiritual middle-classers." He yearns to escape these small-town minds and to be among people with a broader vision. Perhaps he simply wants to reinvent himself by shedding the identities and labels of his childhood and later youth. Or perhaps he has a dream, an aspiration too great or too strange to be realizedat home.

He feels imprisoned, be it in the Bronx or

Iowa. He believes that only in a great urban center like Manhattan will he find people who can understand his strivings and applaud who he is and what he has to offer.

So he comes, and whether or not his dreams are realized even partially, he eventually feels the city has spoiled for him any other place in the world. Despite the pressure, the pace, and the grime of New York, he has a tremendous sense of being alive.

Aiming for the top

"New York draws the cosmopolite, the person who wants to be challenged the most, who needs the most varied and rich stimulation," said a well-known Jungian analyst, Dr James Hillman. "It is the person who is full of possibilities, but who needs New York to draw them out of him. You come to New York to find the ambience that will evoke your best. You do not necessarily know precisely what that might be, but you come to New York to discover it.

"If there were a god of New York it would be the Greeks' Hermes, the Romans' Mercury. He embodies New York qualities: the quick exchange, the fastness of language and style, craftiness, the mixing of people and crossing of borders, imagination."

A public hub of imaginative and intellectual activity is a great bookstore, and in New York the Strand is arguably the best. In a former clothing store at Broadway and East 12th Street in Manhattan, the Strand carries some 2 million volumes of such vast variety that on a single table the tomes might range from *The Sonata Since Beethoven* to *Civil Aircraft of the World*. Over the years, the Strand has counted among its regular customers writers Anaïs Nin and Saul Bellow, the painter David Hockney and poet/rock singer Patti Smith. Smith also worked at the store, which gave her the creative stimuli she craved.s

The complete city

So what, then, knits the city together, stringing the fabric of reinvention and the rigors of intellectual life? What leads immigrant film makers, flower vendors and restaurateurs to pack their belongings and move here, and intellectuals to end their days here?

Back to the Jungian Dr James Hillman, "New York is the city of rampant creativity, of abundant imagination, whether in advertising or the theater or the stock market. They are all fields built on imagination, the spinning of ideas and creations, of fantasy becoming reality. It is everything.

Any syndrome that might characterize another city is found in New York: manic energy, depression and hopelessness, the extreme excitement of the hysteric, the anger of the paranoid. Psychologically, New York is the complete city." ❑

LEFT: it's a dog's life in Washington Square Park.
RIGHT: sybaritic style in Soho.

CULTURE AND THE CITY

New York is both a breeding ground and an international showcase for art and artists of every kind. If you can make it here, you can make it anywhere

Broadway, Lincoln Center, Carnegie Hall and Madison Square Garden are among New York's world-class venues for the performing arts. Outside, on every corner and subway platform, dreamers and talented students lean on the "if I can make it here, I can make it anywhere" refrain. Still, that short jazz-step indoors from the mean city streets is not an easy one.

As New Yorkers are so hard to impress, the cultural benchmarks are high. Big-ticket theater clusters around Broadway, but the "off-Broadway" scene has blossomed far enough to spawn a lively "off-off-Broadway" family. Parks across the city host opera and concerts, and outdoor performances of the New York Philharmonic, the Metropolitan Opera and the New York Shakespeare Festival offer free, fresh-air culture.

Movies by the dozen are made in Manhattan, great jazz toughened up in a club called Birdland, and artists of all kinds have fed in the Big Apple, from Edward Hopper in his studio on Washington Square, to Andy Warhol's divas and prima donnas at the Factory, to Jimi Hendrix, who was "discovered" by British bass player Chas Chandler in a Greenwich Village bar.

Live music

New York is famous for great jazz clubs, including the Blue Note and the Village Vanguard in Greenwich Village. The best of up-

LEFT: detail from *Twenty Marilyns*, Andy Warhol, 1962.
RIGHT: cool sounds in a hot Village club.

and-coming music of any kind can be heard at BAM (Brooklyn Academy of Music), home to the innovative Next Wave Festival since 1982. Most New York rock music is a more peripatetic scene, navigated by the *Village Voice, Time Out New York*, and other listings publications. CBGB's Lower East Side stage launched 1970s groups like Talking Heads and the gritty Ramones, and still does brisk business. The Knitting Factory in Tribeca has avant-garde sounds; Sounds of Brazil (SOB) in Soho is a lively venue for world music; the Mercury Lounge is popular for up-and-coming groups, and clubs like the Bottom Line still folk-rock-on in the Village.

Cultural centers

In the 1960s, the Upper West Side was revitalized when tenement buildings were replaced by the Lincoln Center for the Performing Arts. The Metropolitan Opera and New York City Opera, and the Philharmonic dwell here, and Avery Fisher Hall and Alice Tully Hall hold concerts and recitals. The Vivian Beaumont and Mitzi E. Newhouse theaters mount theatrical productions, and each September, the New York Film Festival opens at the Lincoln. Jazz at Lincoln Center has a facility at the new Time Warner complex, under the artistic direction of Wynton Marsalis. The center is also one of New York's

great meeting places, especially at night, by the computer-controlled fountain.

The Lincoln Center's cultural range is matched by Carnegie Hall, which opened in 1891 with Tchaikovsky's American debut; it has hosted guests from Albert Einstein, Amelia Earhart, and Winston Churchill, to Frank Sinatra, the Beatles and Elton John. Charles Dana Gibson drew the Gibson Girls and established the first *Life* magazine in a studio on the premises, and dancer Isadora Duncan lived at the hall. In the late 1950s, developers wanted the hall demolished, but violinist Isaac Stern led a group of outraged citizens, saving the site from turning into an office block. In Studio

1011–12, Baroness Hilla von Rebay convinced Solomon Guggenheim to aid struggling artists, and the Guggenheim Foundation was established, with Alexander Calder and Wassily Kandinsky among the beneficiaries. The baroness's acquisitions became the core of the Guggenheim collection, housed in the Frank Lloyd Wright building on Madison Avenue.

Visual arts

Prices at art auctions have brought the art trade to public attention. In the early 1990s a Renoir fetched $78.1 million at Sotheby's, and a Van Gogh sold for $82.5 million at Christie's. Van Gogh once wrote that he wished his paintings were worth what he had spent on the paint. Art experts called the auction frenzy a blip, but the Metropolitan Museum of Art purchased Jasper Johns' *White Flag* for around $20 million. In 2004, Picasso's *Garcon a la Pipe* fetched $104 million at Sotheby's, New York.

The Metropolitan, the Guggenheim, the Jewish Museum and others line "Museum Mile" along Fifth Avenue between 82nd and 104th streets (*see page 114*). The Metropolitan and the recently reopened Museum of Modern Art on West 53rd Street (*see page 100*) are the biggest and best. The Frick, once a private Fifth Avenue mansion, has a fine collection of Rembrandts and Vermeers. The New York Public Library on 42nd Street exhibits art in a majestic setting, while the grand reading room serves as an office for many writers.

Moving pictures

Once upon a time in New York, Radio City Music Hall was to movies what the Lincoln Center is to ballet and opera. Now it's a spectacular art deco throwback; even the ladies' powder room is worth a visit. Designed by S.L. "Roxy" Rothafel, a showman known for lavish silent-film theaters, Radio City opened in 1932 for vaudeville. The idea apparently came in a dream Roxy had watching the sunrise on the deck of an ocean liner. The annual Christmas show with the Rockettes doesn't draw sophisticated New Yorkers, but even these jaded souls occasionally succumb to the glitz and nostalgia, and it's still an exciting place to see a movie.

For TV art, classic episodes of *Star Trek, I Love Lucy* and other vintage shows are kept at the Museum of Television and Radio in Midtown. For a sight of the live workings of television, join the audience for *Late Show with David Letterman*, *Satuday Night Live*, or one of the dysfunctional daytime shows *(see Travel Tips, page 235 for details.)*

Space is precious in the city and the multiplex movie theater rules, which can make movie-going seem like standing in line just to watch a TV screen. However, the Angelika Film Center on West Houston Street in Soho has six screens and an espresso bar with an atmosphere as good as the coffee. On West Houston Street, the Film Forum highlights particular genres and directors, as do the Museum of Modern Art and the American Museum of the Moving Image, aptly located in the Kaufman Astoria film studio complex in Queens.

As well as hosting the New York Film Festival, the Lincoln Center's Walter Reade Theater shows foreign and independent films, as do the Brooklyn Academy of Music's BAM Rose Cinemas, with the bonus of Digital Surround Sound. The Tribeca Film Festival, launched by actor Robert De Niro several years ago, is now a regular hot-ticket each August. Movie lines that wind around the block are a common occurrence in Manhattan, and provide ample opportunities for eavesdropping and people-watching.

And the unobtrusive guy waiting ahead of you just could be Woody Allen.

Dance

New York's dance boom began in the 1960s, with an infusion of funding and the defection of Russian superstars Rudolf Nureyev, Mikhail Baryshnikov and Natalia Makarova.

The legendary George Balanchine created the New York City Ballet, a hand-picked company of dancers put through almost superhuman training. "Dancers are like racehorses; they need a jockey on their backs," "Mr B" was known to say. Balanchine, who died in 1983, designed much of the performance space at the Lincoln Center's New York State Theater (which the ballet shares with the New York City Opera), with a basket-weave dance floor to provide elasticity and minimize injury.

The American Ballet Theater performs at the Lincoln Center's Metropolitan Opera House when the opera's not in season. ABT began with a more classical repertory than the New York City Ballet but, under Mikhail Baryshnikov's artistic direction, opened up to contemporary choreographers like Twyla Tharp.

The Dance Theater of Harlem, founded in 1969 and often performing in Harlem itself, also has both classical and contemporary repertoires. Other venues for dance, particularly modern dance (Garth Fagan, Merce Cunningham) range from the Brooklyn Academy of Music to the Joyce Theater in Chelsea.

Theatrical stories

In 1901, the glare of electric signs earned the theater district of Broadway the name of the Great White Way. Taking in Seventh Avenue and several side streets, its heyday was before talking pictures, in 1927, and long before television. Declining in the 1970s and '80s, when staged drama was overshadowed by drugs, pornography and prostitution on the streets, Times Square today is lined with shiny theaters, hotels, megastores and restaurants.

The Shubert Theatre opened in 1913 between Broadway and Eighth Avenue, and was separated by an alley from the Hotel Astor. This was a private passage for the Shubert

LEFT: aiming for the Lincoln Center – a student at the Juilliard School of Music next door.
RIGHT: *Brief Fling*, choreographed by Twyla Tharp.

brothers, who built dozens of theaters, and the thoroughfare is still famous as Shubert Alley.

After a rocky start, the evergreen Palace, on West 47th Street, was rescued by Sarah Bernhardt's 1913 appearance and became America's foremost vaudeville theater from 1910 to the 1930s. Now it's a prime venue for lavish musicals like *Beauty and the Beast*.

The Belasco Theatre, between Broadway and Sixth Avenue, was founded by flamboyant playwright-actor-director David Belasco in 1907. Known as the bishop of Broadway because he dressed like a priest – though he was said not to live like one – after his death his ghost famously haunted the theater, but

hasn't been seen since the nudity in the 1970s' production of *Oh! Calcutta*. Maybe he was a closet bishop after all.

Off-Broadway

Throughout Manhattan, off-Broadway venues are a feeding ground for Broadway stages, and a cultural force in themselves, offering diversity and lower prices. Off-Broadway dates from Eugene O'Neill's presentations of one-act plays after World War I at the Provincetown Playhouses on Cape Cod and downtown in Greenwich Village. It came of age in the late 1940s and early 50s, with Geraldine Page's performance in Tennessee Williams' *Summer and Smoke* and O'Neill's *The Iceman Cometh*, directed by Jose Quintero.

Downtown today, the Lucille Lortel and the Cherry Lane theaters and others in Greenwich Village fly the off-Broadway flag. In the East Village, Joseph Papp's Public Theater offers sometimes experimental, always quality productions, while P.S. 122, the Kitchen in Chelsea, and LaMama are ultra-casual spots offering off-off Broadway productions with a performance-art edge. Comedy also keeps theaters lit, and it's possible to catch Chris Rock or Modi dropping in at Caroline's, Stand-up New York, Stress Factory or the Comic Strip.

Today, Broadway is in reasonable shape. Although it stages some excellent drama, the big noise is the musicals. Successful musicals often have longer runs than plays. *A Chorus Line* gave an astounding 6,137 performances, before being overtaken by *Cats,* which yowled on the stage here for more than 20 years. ❑

BUYING BROADWAY TICKETS

A Chorus Line may be returning to Broadway in 2006 – 16 years after it folded – but with a few useful tips you don't have to wait as long to find good Broadway tickets. The **TKTS booth**, at Broadway and 47th Street, just north of Times Square, has discounted seats (25–50 percent off) for that night's performances. It's open Monday through Saturday 3pm to 8pm for evening performances, Saturday and Wednesday 10am to 2pm for matinees, and Sunday 11am to 7.30 pm for both shows. Near South Street Seaport in Lower Manhattan, a booth at 186 Front Street sells tickets for the following night's shows.

Lines form early and are very long, so take a book to read. TKTS booths don't take credit cards, so be sure to have travelers' checks or cash.

● Unsold tickets can often be bought at theater box offices an hour or so before show time.

● Numerous (expensive) ticket brokers can be contacted via hotel concierges.

● The Times Square Visitor Center in the historic Embassy Theater, Broadway between 46th and 47th streets, also sells theater tickets.

● www.broadway.com is a useful website to visit for the latest theater information.

Regards to Broadway

The New York theater, like Miss Jean Brodie, has been going through a prime period for a while now. Broadway's 45 theaters sell more than 11 million tickets annually, earning upwards of $558 million. Sir Andrew Lloyd Webber's imported musical megahits – *Phantom of the Opera*, *Cats* – dominated the box office for more than a decade, but American dramas and comedies (often lumped together as "straight plays") are also produced with reassuring regularity. In an average season of 35 new productions, roughly half will be new plays.

In the early days of the 20th century over 100 new plays were staged each season. Playwrights and composers like Eugene O'Neill, Lillian Hellman, Cole Porter, Irving Berlin, Rodgers and Hart, Arthur Miller and Tennessee Williams all made their names in New York, and their work is often revived. Contemporary American playwrights, including David Mamet, Wendy Wasserstein, Sam Shepard and John Guare, have also seen revivals in recent years, both on- and off-Broadway.

Of the 45 theaters known as "Broadway," only a handful are on the Great White Way itself, including the Broadway Theatre, the Palace and the Winter Garden. The rest are on the side streets from 41st Street as far north as 65th Street.

One of the oldest, and one of the most beautiful theaters, the Lyceum (1903), is a neo-baroque beauty on West 45th Street, east of Times Square. The New Victory on 42nd Street is even older. Built by Oscar Hammerstein in 1890 as the Theater Republic, its name was given a patriotic boost during the 1940s. Thirty years later it was reduced to showing porno movies, but now the New Victory presents colorful and imaginative productions, often aimed at children.

Broadway may make the headlines, but off-Broadway is considered by many to be the true soul of New York theater. Some playwrights bypass Broadway altogether in favor of the smaller venues. Off-Broadway is also where plays that are unsuitable for the mainstream are staged, either for their content, or for reason of cost. A hit in an off-Broadway theater like Playwrights Horizons or the Public Theater, provides the confidence backers need to move Uptown. *Rent*, *Bring In 'Da Noise, Bring In 'Da Funk* and *A Chorus Line* started this way.

With limited time on a New York visit, it can be better not to fixate on a particular show, but to have a number of options,

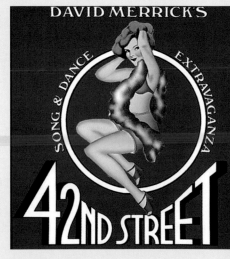

then choose the one that offers the best ticket deal. It can also be rewarding to play a hunch and try something relatively unheard of. A surprise can offer the most memorable kind of New York theater experience, as well as giving the chance to see something spectacular before the critics and the audiences make ticket prices soar.

Glittering stars, luscious musical productions and ground-breaking, often controversial drama can all be found any night in New York. Whether it's the glamorous, dressy occasion of Broadway or the intimate interiors of challenging off-Broadway drama, the play's the thing. ❑

LEFT: Joseph Papp's The Public Theater was a godsend to off-Broadway productions.
RIGHT: a tribute to the street *and* the musical.

HOLLYWOOD ON THE HUDSON

From the early days of the silver screen, New York has glittered on film

Ever since *The Lights of New York* was released in 1927, the city and its landmarks have been illuminating the big screens of the world's celluloid consciousness. King Kong atop the Empire State Building is an enduring image – although the 1976 remake was so bad it's remarkable that actress Jessica Lange's fledgling career survived the premiere. The Empire struck back when New York writer-turned-director Nora Ephron made *Sleepless in Seattle,* itself a pastiche of the 1957 three-hankie weepie *An Affair to Remember.* Director Spike Lee vividly conveyed contemporary life Uptown in *Mo Better Blues,* while Greenwich Village has featured in everything from Fonda and Redford going *Barefoot in the Park* to Scorsese's *Raging Bull* (the swimming pool by St Luke's Place). *How to Marry a Millionaire* was set in between the two areas; the classy apartment rented by those sassy dames Monroe, Grable and Bacall is 36 Sutton Place South in Midtown. Over 200 films are made here each year, many at the Kaufman Astoria Studios *(see page 204),* and the number rises annually; no Escape from New York to Hollywood just yet.

RIGHT: King Kong takes charge. Kong hit the screens in 1933, only two years after the Empire State Building was finally completed.

ABOVE: *Manhattan:* Critic Andrew Sarris described Allen's 1979 homage to New York as "a masterpiece that has become a film for the ages by not seeking to be a film of the moment."

ABOVE: *Breakfast at Tiffany's:* George Peppard and Audrey Hepburn's search for love, diamonds and breakfast in the classic 1961 comedy was based on Truman Capote's darker book.

WOODY ALLEN

From *Annie Hall* to *Manhattan* to *Hannah and Her Sisters*, no filmmaker has portrayed modern New York (and his own personal neuroses) with more acuity and affection than Woody Allen. Born Allen Stewart Konigsberg in Brooklyn in 1935, he started his career as a comedy writer, later became a successful stand-up comic, and segued to writer/director with *Take the Money and Run* in 1969. The city has played a pivotal role in almost all his movies since then, including *Broadway Danny Rose*, *Crimes and Misdemeanors*, *Manhattan Murder Mystery*, *Bullets over Broadway* and *Celebrity*. Today, after a high-profile court case, he lives quietly on the Upper East Side and plays the clarinet with the New Orleans Jazz Band on Monday nights at Cafe Carlyle where, according to *People* magazine, he turned down a request for an encore because he was coming down with a cold, noting: "People are always saying I'm a hypochondriac, but they're all wrong. I'm more of an alarmist."

ABOVE: *The Godfather:* Things get gritty in Little Italy in Francis Ford Coppola's 1972 tale of the Mafia. The late Marlon Brando *(above)* won an Academy Award for his portrayal; the film was voted best picture and was the first in a trilogy that confirmed Coppola's reputation.

BELOW: You talkin' to me? Director Martin Scorsese's *Taxi Driver* *(below)* starred Robert de Niro as a lonely and obsessed New York cabbie, defining both a city and a genre. Also featuring Cybil Shepherd, the movie catapulted the careers of Shepherd, Harvey Kietel and Jodie Foster. Ironically, Foster was herself the object of obsession for John Hinkley, motivating his later attempt to assassinate President Ronald Regan in 1981.

MEDIA IN MANHATTAN

All the news that's fit to print, and then some:
New Yorkers can't get enough information – from the
printed page, computer LCD screens,
or the multitude of TV channels

Media in New York is a physical force, and its people are driven by the intensity of their information addiction. For New Yorkers, knowledge is power.

In the "city that never sleeps," New Yorkers who aren't sleeping are surfing around 50 radio stations, up to 1,000 television stations, over a dozen daily and weekly newspapers, hundreds of magazines, not to mention the global library of the Internet. Is it possible to process all this information? Addicted to the Internet and Bloomberg TV as previous generations were to their newspapers and morning coffee, New York media-maniacs are probably too busy to ponder the question.

Read all about it

New York has the oldest continuously published daily newspaper in the country, the *New York Post* (founded by Alexander Hamilton, the first Secretary of the Treasury). Voracious readers browse hundreds of local, national and international periodicals at the Eastern Newsstand in the MetLife Building above Grand Central Terminal, or at Universal News on West 42nd Street, between Seventh and Eighth avenues. Both stock publications like the *Sydney Morning Herald*, *Jerusalem Post*, British tabloids and publications representing New York's diverse nationalities, like *The Irish Voice*, *La Stampa*, or *El Diario*. Not to be overlooked is the national edition of the *Wall Street Journal* – much thicker than its

international cousin. As stylish men and women know, the Big Apple is the fashion capital of the US, and *Women's Wear Daily* proves it. For a more gossipy and glamorous read, *WWD*'s sister publication, *W*, is for the oh-so-social set. The best local magazines are *New York*, the *New Yorker* and *Time Out New York*. Others committed to "being on top of things" read free weekly papers like the *Village Voice* and *New York Press*.

The pale-peach *New York Observer*, another well-known weekly, has a loyal following; the *New York Daily News* claims to have the largest circulation in the country; and, of course, there's the immmense "gray lady" her-

LEFT: mass media is the subject of three city museums.
RIGHT: New York is the publishing capital of America.

self (now with parts in glorious color), the *New York Times*.

New York seems to be where every book in the world originates – or at least where authors and agents lunch, at the Four Seasons on East 52nd Street. The city has hundreds of bookstores, and smaller venues like the cozy Gotham Book Mart on East 46th Street or dusty, second-hand emporia like the Strand in Greenwich Village provide musty havens for kindred spirits.

Radio

Readers and radio listeners remain friendly relatives, since they espouse the well-turned

phrase and articulate debate. Radio lends itself to busy city life as, day or night, listeners can multi-task. Very New York.

News and information on the AM dial comes from WINS at 1010 or WCBS at 880, and Bloomberg Radio at 1130 AM airs nonstop business updates. WFAN (660 AM) is all-sports radio. Call-in radio shows are as popular as ever, especially if the host insults the audience. This type of programming may be a reaction to easy listening, but it has a large and fiercely vocal following.

Classical, rock, jazz, country and other music genres found a home on the FM radio dial over the years, and each corresponding

notch has a permanent setting on New York car radios. Early on summer mornings, the outrageous cackle of "shock jock" Howard Stern, or the indomitable Don Imus, blast out through jazzy sound-bites and traffic news from taxis hustling on the avenues.

Television

Radio's link to TV is through sports; many New York fans turn the sound down on the television to get the play-by-play commentary from their preferred radio sportscaster.

The late media guru Marshall MacLuhan saw TV replacing fireplaces in the home, becoming glowing, electronic light to read by. The practice has extended far beyond reading – and for TV etiquette, frequent channel zapping is a necessity, not an option.

When CBS' *Late Show with David Letterman* (taped at the Ed Sullivan Theater on Broadway) goes to commercials, alternative viewing options range from NY-1, a cable station with nonstop New York news – to the always intriguing, often wacky world of Public Access. Here, the home-grown untelegenic astrologers and big-earringed numerologists take viewers' calls. Here, too, is the *demimonde* of cable-porn and lusty Robyn Byrd's strip-show. Cable is always fascinating, if only in a highway accident kind of way.

Mainstream appetites are fed by commercial television's prime-time fare of national morning shows, including *Today* (broadcast from the NBC Studios at the Rockefeller Center), *Good Morning America* and the local *Good Day New York* (on Rupert Murdoch's Fox Network), and the magazine-format evening news programs.

Global news junkies have CNN. Insomniacs have C-Span for coverage of Congressional activities and the Weather Channel for the rainfall in Madagascar. Nostalgia nuts can tune into TCM or AMC for movie classics. Rock fans migrate to MTV (headquartered in Times Square); and decades after they first aired, Nick at Night brings vintage American sitcoms to generations of fans, from baby-boomers to their children and grandchildren. Some shows now multi-task themselves. CNBC, for instance, simulcasts real-time stock quotes at the bottom of the screen while interviewing CEOs about corporate mergers above.

Wired

Long gone is the era of 12 television channels, when the daily newspaper and evening newscast were the limit of information overload. Today, local news can be accessed online at *Crain's New York Business* (www.crains newyork.com) and from the websites of the major daily newspapers.

Each media development confirms New York's media imprint more indelibly. Add the Big Apple need-to-know-*now* to the multiple media sources and communications tools, and you have a formula for obsessive-compulsive behavior. (Witness the city-suited, cellphone addicts striding the streets, networking, an

Search at www.newyork.citysearch.com; www.nypl.org for everything you ever wanted to know about (and from) the New York Public Library; and the online sister to *Time Out New York* at www.timeoutny.com.

Customized environments

Increasingly, local office space and residential apartments entice would-be tenants with built-in communications features. Ads in the Sunday *New York Times* offer apartments wired for multiple phone lines, high-speed Internet access and TV with 200 channels.

All this is fitting in the town where the literary Round Table of *New Yorker* editors and

iPod earphone in the other ear, sipping coffee.)

If TV built the global village, the Internet transformed it into a metropolis. Many cafés offer wireless broadband access as, courtesy of *Wired* magazine, does the whole of Union Square. Not to be outdone, the Downtown Alliance has organized free wireless Internet "hotspots" all over Lower Manhattan, including South Street Seaport and City Hall Park. Good New York websites include the official visitor's website at www.nycvisit.com; City-

LEFT: Manhattanites are major news junkies.
ABOVE: the Museum of Television and Radio on West 52nd Street has vintage TV shows to rent.

writers hobnobbed at the Algonquin Hotel in the 1920s, which saw the birth of national television networks in the 1940s and '50s, and introduced the world to MTV in the 1980s. Website content providers and software mavens in Union Square keep the city at the media's cutting edge.

New Yorkers embody Alvin Toffler's *Future Shock* forecast of decades ago: "The mass media instantly and persuasively disseminate new images, and ordinary individuals... coping with an ever more complex social environment, attempt to keep up... Racing swiftly past our attention screen, they wash out old images and generate new ones." ❏

NEW YORK'S GREEN SPACES

**Pocket parks in Alphabet City,
sunset walks along the Hudson River,
and the deep, green expanses of the Outer Boroughs offer
tranquillity far from Manhattan's madding crowds**

Alligators may not lurk in the city's subways, as the urban myth says, but peregrine falcons nest on ledges of Midtown skyscrapers, jackrabbits have settled beyond the runways of Kennedy Airport, and coyotes do wander down from Westchester County into the Bronx.

From the ocean breezes of Battery Park, where a broke and homesick Noel Coward watched ships sail for England in the 1920s, to the forest of oak, hemlock and tulip trees at Manhattan's northern tip, New York City sprouts wildlife and open spaces. Urban gardens bloom, from community efforts in Alphabet City – complete with colored lights in the summertime – to the Brooklyn Botanic Garden, where Japanese cherry trees explode in clouds of riotous pink every spring. Pocket parks all over town, many so tiny you could miss them as you pass, have lately been lovingly spruced, mostly by passionate volunteers. Some New York graveyards offer a scenic detour: Green-Wood in Brooklyn, where Boss Tweed and Lola Montez lie, and Woodlawn in the Bronx, both date from the late 1800s when rolling fields, woods and streams gave rest to the recently deceased.

Despite the Bush administration's wish to hand it to private developers, Governor's Island transferred to the National Park Service in 2003. It opened to the public in 2004, for the first time since the American Revolution. New York has over 28,000 acres (11,300

hectares) of parks, of which 10,000 acres (4,000 hectares) or so are more or less in their natural state.

Autumn in New York

In 1609, when Henry Hudson sailed the *Half Moon* up the North River, later renamed the Hudson, his first mate, Robert Juett, wrote: "We found a land full of great tall oaks, with grass and flowers, as pleasant as ever has been seen." His words echo when strolling in Central Park. To landscape architect Frederick Law Olmsted, its designer with Calvert Vaux in the 1850s, the purpose was to "supply hundreds of thousands of tired workers, who have

LEFT: Battery Park, the perfect place for sunset.
RIGHT: Union Square has grass *and* internet access.

no opportunity to spend summers in the country, a specimen of God's handiwork."

Central Park includes the largest stand of American elms in the country (in the middle of the park, at 65th Street) as well as the North Woods, a remote overgrown forest between 102nd and 106th streets that seems more like Minnesota than Manhattan. Trails run through a deep ravine, a mossy loch, and waterfalls tumble between a pair of rustic stone bridges.

Past the narrow beauty of Riverside Park on the Upper West Side and the fragrant herb gardens of The Cloisters in Fort Tryon Park, is one of the most isolated places on the island of Manhattan, Inwood Hill Park, a 196-acre

(79-hectare) expanse of trees and meadows. Wolves roamed free and Native Americans ranged here, and about 100 acres (40 hectares) form Manhattan's last native forest.

Flying squirrels and a family of screech owls nest in a grove of 100-ft-high (30- meter) tulip trees. This part of the park is known as the Shorakapok Natural Area, after an Indian village that stood between what is now 204th and 207th streets.

Outer Boroughs outlook

Van Cortlandt Park in the Bronx is New York City's third-largest green space. Despite its 1,146 acres (446 hectares) being crossed by three major thoroughfares, parts of it feel as far removed from the rest of the city as, well, New England. One trail passes through a centuries-old hardwood forest with skunks, pheasant and racoons; another meanders along Van Cortlandt Lake into a freshwater marsh with swans, egrets and snapping turtles. The *pièce de résistance* for walkers is the route north along the overgrown tracks of the Old Putnam commuter train line.

Where the Bronx meets Long Island Sound, Pelham Bay Park's 2,764 acres (1,118 hectares) encompass two golf courses, a riding stable, the city's Mounted Police School and a large glacial rock. Religious refugee Anne Hutchinson, of the Massachusetts Bay Colony, who settled in 1642, hid here from Indian attacks. The Split Rock remains a natural monument to the virgin forest and wetlands. Past Goose Creek Marsh is a wildlife sanctuary for wading herons, sandpipers and lazy woodcocks.

Queens is New York City's greenest borough, with more than 7,000 acres (2,833 hectares) of parkland and over half of the city's trees, including Kissena Park's vintage arboretum (the remains of a 19th-century nursery), Forest Park's stand of native red and white oaks, and the stately Weeping Beech Tree. Planted in 1847; in 1966 it became the first tree designated as a New York City historic landmark.

Wedged between the Long Island Expressway and Grand Central Parkway in northeastern Queens, about two thirds of 324-acre (131-hectare) Cunningham Park is natural forest, ponds and fields. Nearer the shore, Alley Pond Park borders the marshlands of Little Neck Bay, with parcels of woods (interrupted by highways) totalling more than 600 acres (243 hectares).

The Old Vanderbilt Motor Parkway was built by a scion of the illustrious Vanderbilt family in 1908 so he could race his motorcars, and an overgrown stretch connects the two parks. The narrow dirt drive to the Queens County Farm Museum in Floral Park really feels like country. A 47-acre (19-hectare) working farm, the museum has a farmhouse built in 1772, a stand selling homegrown vegetables and a farmyard with geese, sheep, cows and pigs.

A tree grows in Brooklyn

The oldest farmhouse in New York, and its first officially designated landmark, lies in Brooklyn's Flatlands. Built in 1652 by Pieter Claeson Wyckoff, an indentured servant who became one of the settlement's most prominent citizens, the simple house was the heart of a farm carved from salt marsh formerly owned by Canarsie Indians. Now a museum, it's surrounded by a small park with foliage the Wyckoff family would find familiar, including a kitchen vegetable and herb garden, and a spring garden of daffodils and tulips.

Brooklyn's most famous park is 526-acre (212-hectare) Prospect Park, designed, like Staten Island. Traditionally more rural than other parts of New York, the borough changed forever when the Verrazano-Narrows Bridge opened it to tri-state traffic in 1964. The commuters whooshing by are missing 28 miles (45 km) of gorgeous trails from High Rock Park to La Tourette Park, part of the Greenbelt's 2,500 acres (1,011 hectares) of rocky outcrops and tangled woods, winding past suburban ranch homes and turn-of-the-20th-century mansions.

Emerald necklace

For years the dream of conservation groups has been to ring Manhattan in an "emerald

Central Park, by Frederick Law Olmsted and Calvert Vaux. From the entrance at Grand Army Plaza a path leads to the peaceful expanse of Long Meadow, a rolling green stretching to a dark ridge of distant trees, part of the Ravine at the park's wild heart. Olmsted wrote, "the contemplation of natural scenes… is favorable to the health and vigor of men."

When he wasn't designing parks for other boroughs, Olmsted cultivated pear trees and vegetables at his farm off Hylan Boulevard on

LEFT: community garden in Alphabet City.
ABOVE: the 1907 beaux arts boathouse in Brooklyn's Prospect Park is now a nature education center.

necklace" of parks and tree-lined walkways. In 1998, legislation was finally signed that created a joint city-and-state "public benefit corporation" and a continuous riverfront walkway and bike path that stretches along the Hudson River most of the way to 155th Street. Almost every inch of it is used by New Yorkers, and people from all parts of the city head for Battery Park, overlooking the Statue of Liberty, to walk, rollerblade and enjoy the wonderful sunsets.

In the words of the late poet and museum curator Frank O'Hara, "One never need leave the confines of New York to see all the greenery one wishes." ❑

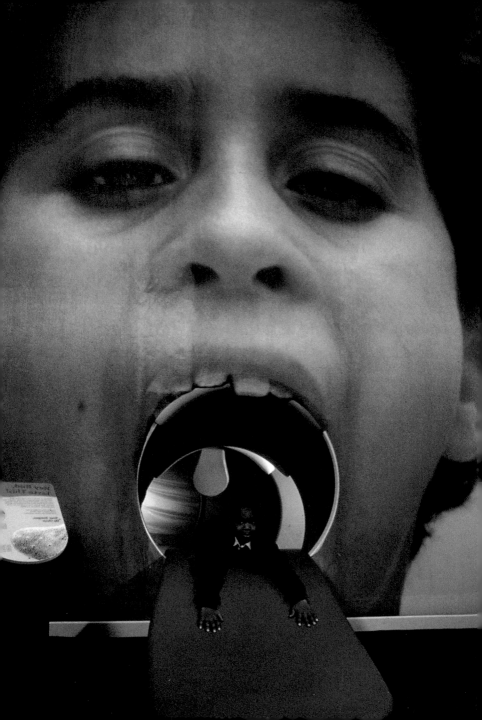

PLACES

A detailed guide to the Midtown and Uptown
neighborhoods of New York, with principal sites
cross-referenced by number to the maps

New York is where I *have* to be," said a character in Jack Olsen's *The Girls in the Office*. "I wish I knew why." The people who live here, and the ones who visit here, could tell her why. New York's industrial resources are vast. So is its cultural life – witness the fact that the Metropolitan Museum has more than 2 million works of art in its permanent collection. The city's cultural vigor is matched, perhaps, only by its culinary awareness. Take your choice of more than 17,000 eating establishments, from coffee shops to *bijou* bistros to soul food in Harlem. And that doesn't include the hundreds of hot dog vendors.

There's a mix of freedom and foreignness in New York that is unsurpassed anywhere. You want to go dancing, when the moon is high and the mood overtakes you? You want to go rollerblading, ice skating or take in that hot new movie? You want to get a bite to eat 24 hours a day? You've come to the right town.

New York has energy to spare, along with clutter, confusion and great charm. Much of that is evident in its residents' pace of life and cost of living. It's the ultimate competitive city and the lyrics of the song *New York, New York* "if you can make it here, you can make it anywhere" ring true.

If there are more ways of making it here, there are also more ways of spending it. FAO Schwarz, on Fifth Avenue, sells every kind of toy, while Zabar's, on Broadway, is an West Side institution. Tiffany & Co. is where you'll find the bauble of your dreams, while the upscale stores lining Madison Avenue are stocked with high-ticket, high-fashion wardrobe additions. Then, there's always Macy's and Bloomingdale's.

But not all of New York comes with a hefty price tag. On sultry summer nights, free operas and concerts are held on the Great Lawn in Central Park. Pack a picnic and take advantage of Shakespeare in the outdoors, or even the Philharmonic Orchestra. You can visit botanic gardens, historic buildings and the Rockefeller Center, without disposing of a penny. The best of everything is here for the taking. Cop an attitude and check it out. ❏

PRECEDING PAGES: a view of Midtown, looking north; Halloween in Greenwich Village.
LEFT: kids get an inside look at the human body when they visit the Children's Museum of Manhattan on the Upper West Side.

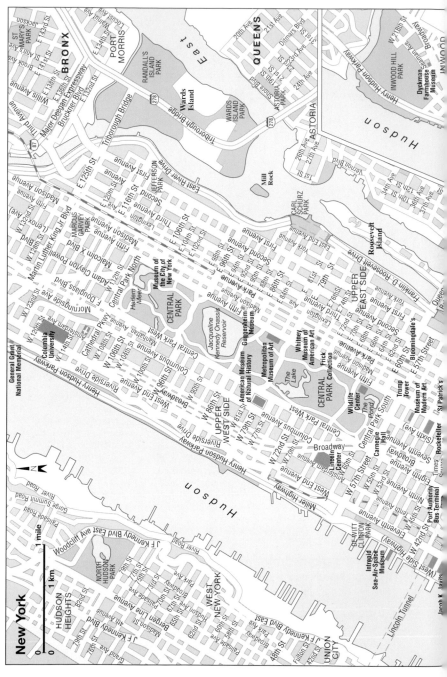

New York

0 ___ 1 mile
0 ___ 1 km

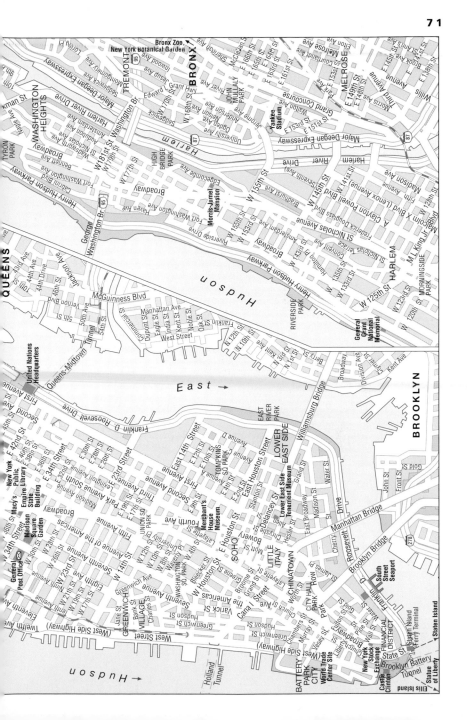

FIFTH AVENUE

Paris has the Champs Elysées,
London has Bond Street, Rome has the Via Veneto,
but only New York has Fifth Avenue

There are few streets that evoke the essence of the city as powerfully as Fifth Avenue. It's all here – the audacity of the Empire State Building, the ambition of the Rockefeller Center and the old-world elegance of the Plaza Hotel. Fifth cuts through the heart of midtown Manhattan, dividing the island into East and West. It's a timeline, chronicling Manhattan's northward and economic growth.

Fifth Avenue begins at Washington Square, near the crooked streets of Greenwich Village. Past the Flatiron Building to Madison Square Park, between 23rd and 26th streets – site of the original Madison Square Garden – the avenue marches by the Empire State Building and Rockefeller Center, hugs Central Park for 26 scenic blocks, before plunging into "Museum Mile" *(see page 114)*, which plays host to some of the city's most important collections.

Continuing past the mansions and embassies of the Upper East Side, Fifth runs a sketchy course through Harlem, bisecting Marcus Garvey Park, and finally comes to a halt just before the Harlem River. South to north, culturally, socially and economically, few streets in the world can provide a more varied tour of extremes.

The empire strikes back

The **Empire State Building** ❶ (tel: 212-736 3100; last elevator 11:15pm; charge) rises like a rocket from the corner of 33rd Street. When it was completed in 1931, this was the tallest structure in the world. It remains the city's tallest building – but, at 1,454 ft (443 meters) and 102 stories, it now ranks behind buildings in Kuala Lumpur, Taipei and the Sears Tower in Chicago. When it comes to the view, however, the Empire State can't be

Map on page 74

LEFT: the Empire State Building changes color depending on the occasion; check the website for a schedule.
BELOW: St Patrick's, framed by a statue of *Atlas* holding up the world.

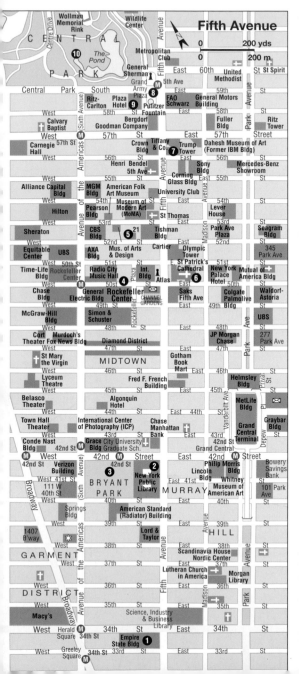

beaten. On a clear day you can see as far as 80 miles (130 km). At night, Manhattan spreads out below, a floating sea of twinkling lights.

You can catch the elevator to the 86th-floor observation deck at the concourse level. From here, a second elevator goes up to the smaller observatory on the 102nd floor (closed to the public), which is just about where Fay Wray had her fateful rendezvous with the "tallest, darkest leading man in Hollywood," a 50-ft (15 meters) ape by the name of King Kong.

They're not the only ones who met their fates up here. Of the 16 people who have jumped off the building, only two were wearing parachutes, and both were arrested as soon as they hit the ground.

Ride the sky

The Empire State Building's upper floors are illuminated at night, and special light displays are put on for festivals like the Fourth of July, Christmas and Hanukkah. **New York Skyride** (tel: 212-279 9777; charge) is a popular tourist attraction in the building and offers a simulated flight through and above the city (not recommended for those who suffer from motion sickness).

Back on earth and across the street, the **Science, Industry and Business Library** (enter at 188 Madison Avenue, tel: 212-592 7000) is a good place to get online if you left your laptop at home, since it's well-stocked with computers available for public use. Five blocks north at Fifth and 39th Street, **Lord & Taylor** is one of New York's most enduring department stores, and famous for its extravagant holiday displays. People have been known to line up on a cold winter day just to peer into the windows.

Right across the street, office workers and tourists can be found lounging in front of the main branch

of the **New York Public Library** ❷
(tel: 212-661 7220), under the
watchful gaze of two stone lions that
flank the marble steps. Stretching
between 40th and 42nd streets, this
1911 beaux arts monument is one of
the world's finest research facilities,
with some 88 miles (141 km) of
bookshelves and a vast archive collection that includes the first book
printed in the US, the *Bay Psalm
Book* from 1640, and the original
diaries of Virginia Woolf.

In addition to a fine permanent
collection of paintings, the library
has a third floor space for exhibits,
most but not all relating to books.
The biggest treasure of all, however,
may be the main reading room, a
vast, gilded gem where windows
overlook adjacent **Bryant Park** ❸.
Ask inside about joining one of the
twice-daily tours (11am and 2pm) of
the entire building. Also at the rear
is the delightful Bryant Park Grill
(see page 79).

Bibliophiles can continue the tour
opposite the park at **Coliseum
Books** or a few blocks north at the
Gotham Book Mart (16 East 46th

Street). Gotham is located in a townhouse that was once home to the
antiquarian bookseller who opened
the original store in 1920. The late
Frances Stelloff, GBM's founder,
held court over a comfortable clutter of books, and found time to
champion and lend a hand to writers
like Eugene O'Neill, Tennessee
Williams and James Joyce, whose
monumental tome *Ulysses* Stelloff
defended at a censorship trial.

Rockefeller Center

At 49th Street, Fifth Avenue lives up
to its famous legend, thanks in large
part to the **Rockefeller Center** ❹,
one of the world's biggest business
and entertainment complexes and an
absolute triumph of art deco architecture. The Rockefeller Center has
been called a "city within a city,"
and it's got the numbers to prove it.

The center's daily population
(including visitors) is about 240,000
– greater than many American
cities. It has more than 100,000 telephones, 48,758 windows and 388
elevators that travel a total of 2 million miles (3.2 million km) per year

*The New York Public
Library's stone lions
are called Patience
and Fortitude.*

BELOW:
Rockefeller's Channel
Gardens at Christmas.

Festivites on Fifth: famous parades include the October Columbus Day Parade, the Easter Parade and the St Patrick's Day Parade, when the center stripe is painted green.

BELOW: the
Rainbow Room evokes
starlight memories of
sleek, sophisticated
nights on the town.

– about 40 times around the planet. Add to this a 2-mile (3.2-km) underground concourse, stores and restaurants, four major subway lines, a Post Office, several foreign consulates and airlines, and you've got quite a little metropolis.

The **Channel Gardens** – so named because they separate La Maison Française on the left and the British Building on the right, just as their two countries flank the English Channel – draw visitors into the center of the **Plaza**. It's dominated by the soaring **GE Building**, which is fronted by a sunken courtyard used as a restaurant and a sometimes drive-in cinema in summer, and an ice rink in winter.

This is where the famous Christmas tree, lit with countless bulbs, captivates holiday visitors. The *Today* show is broadcast from a glassed-in studio here, too. The **NBC Studio Experience** has TV exhibits as well as many shops. Tours of both NBC and Rockefeller Center depart every 60 minutes, every day of the week.

If there were a restaurant situated in heaven, it might well look like the **Rainbow Room**, on the GE Building's 65th floor. The view to the horizon would no doubt be similar – thousands of twinkling lights stretching out as far as the eye can see in every direction. With its revolving dance floor and art deco architecture, an evening here is a quintessential New York experience. The Rainbow Room has varying opening times (tel: 212-632 5000) but is only open for dinner or Sunday brunch. The **Rainbow Grill** next door costs less and comes with the same panoramic views.

As both are owned by the Cipriani family of Venice (Harry's Bar), a certain decorum is encouraged, implying a jacket and tie for men, and appropriate attire for ladies.

Classic dining is also the keynote at **21 ⑤** (21 West 52 Street, tel: 212-582 7200, *see page 78*), where every president since Roosevelt has been elegantly entertained. Now owned by Orient Express Hotels, the atmosphere is hushed, the lighting is low, and everyone looks like a movie star – and might well be.

BELOW: the Rainbow Room evokes starlight memories of sleek, sophisticated nights on the town.

Saks and St Pat's

Back on Fifth Avenue, **Saks Fifth Avenue**, across the street from the Rockefeller Center, is the flagship department store for Saks Fifth Avenue stores stretching from Dallas to St Louis. On the next corner up is the **International Building**, with Lee Lawrie's monumental figure of *Atlas*, crouching under the weight of the world, at its entrance. Although the bronze figure is over 25 ft (7.6 meters) tall, it is dwarfed by **St Patrick's Cathedral** ❻ directly across the way.

St Pat's is the largest Catholic church in the country. Opened in 1879, the cathedral is a formidable Midtown landmark, its Gothic facade working an intriguing counterpoint against the angular lines and smooth surfaces of the skyscrapers around it. And yet St Pat's is unmistakably New York: where else would one need tickets to attend midnight Mass? Look around the cathedral's interior, where F. Scott Fitzgerald married his Southern belle, Zelda, before going on to literary fame and domestic hell.

Beyond St Patrick's, Fifth Avenue returns to its more worldly concerns, namely, commerce and upscale shopping. **Tiffany** and **Cartier**, Gucci and Pucci are a few that contribute to the avenue's elan.

At 57th Street, fashionable folk stroll between **Hermès**, **Dior** and the expensive emporia within the **Trump Tower** ❼. While part of Fifth Avenue has undergone a mall-like transformation with big, neon logos, shopping is still a leisurely pursuit at **Henri Bendel** and **Bergdorf Goodman**. Located on the former site of the Cornelius Vanderbilt mansion, Bergdorf is more like a collection of small boutiques than a department store. Exquisite, and expensive.

Grand Army Plaza ❽ on 59th Street punctuates Fifth Avenue and marks the boundary between Midtown and the Upper East Side. It borders the **Plaza Hotel** ❾ *(see page 216),* a 19th-century home-away-from-home for Mark Twain. The views of **Central Park** ❿ *(see page 80)* are worth the prices in the Plaza's wood-paneled Oak Bar. ❑

Tiffany's – meet here for breakfast.

BELOW: St Patrick's Cathedral is the largest Catholic church in the country.

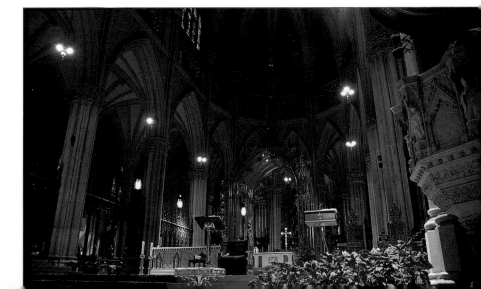

RESTAURANTS, BARS AND CAFÉS

Restaurants

21

21 W. 52 St (between 5th and 6th aves). Tel: 212-582 7200. Open: L & D Mon–Fri, D only Sun. **$$$$**
This former speakeasy will never be out of style with the movers and shakers of Manhattan. Miniature jockeys line the exterior, while other corporate toys hang from the Bar Room ceiling. A plaque over Table 30 reads "Bogie's Corner." Sip his favorite tipple, Ramos Gin Fizz, and order the Chicken Hash.

Alain Ducasse at Essex House

155 W. 58th St (between. 6th and 7th aves). Tel: 212-265 7300. Open: Mon–Sat D, Thur–Fri L. **$$$$**

How much is a meal worth? The place to research the question is this haughty French gastro-temple, one of the most expensive restaurants in town, where the namesake chef delivers the heavenly goods to an appreciative audience.

Aquavit

65 E. 55th St (between Park and Madison aves). Tel: 212-307 7311. Open: L & D Mon–Sat, Br & D Sun **$$$**
This is a new location, but it's the same sublime Scandinavian cuisine of gifted chef Marcus Samuelson.

Benihana of Tokyo

47 W. 56 St (between 5th and 6th aves). Tel: 212-581 0930). Open: L & D daily. **$$**
An entertaining meal for all the family – food is cooked tableside – in an area of Manhattan where that can be a difficult experience to find.

Bice

7 E. 54 St (between 5th and Madison aves). Tel: 212-688 1999. Open: L & D daily. **$$$**
Northern Italian cuisine, and pretty pricey, but apparently not for the high-end Euro crowd that frequents the place.

La Bonne Soupe

48 W. 55 St (between 5th and 6th aves), Tel: 212-586 7650. Open: L & D daily. **$$**
An old standby that serves up lots more than just soup in the cheap and cheerful category. Hands down, the best vinaigrette salad dressing anywhere.

Burger Heaven

20 E. 49th St (between. 5th and Madison aves). Tel: 212-755-2166. Open: B, L & T Mon–Sat, Br & L Sun. **$**
Midtown workers are willing to put up with the hellish noontime crush at this burger joint, which can't be beaten for big juicy burgers at good, even bargain, prices.

Harry Cipriani

Sherry Netherland Hotel, 781 5th Ave (at 59th St). Tel: 212-753 5566.Open: L daily. **$$$$**
Posh, expensive, of the famed Venice bellini; high-fashion types always welcome here.

DB Bistro Moderne

55 W. 44th St (between 5th and 6th aves). Tel: 212-391 2400. Open: L and D Mon–Sat, D only Sun. **$$$$**
So *moderne* that the menu is organized by ingredients. Chef Daniel Boulud's bistro is awash in art deco glitz and culinary surprises, with a clientele to match the atmosphere.

La Grenouille

3 E. 52 St (between 5th and Madison aves). Tel: 212-752 1495). Open: L & D Mon–Sat. **$$$$**
The last of the great French, Midtown establishments, where a quenelle is still a quenelle and the flowers have rarely been more beautiful. A classic.

Keen's Steakhouse

72 W. 36 St (between 5th and 6th aves). Tel: 212-947 3636. Open: L & D Mon–Fri, D only Sat–Sun. **$$$**
Vintage Americana dating back to 1885, a stone's throw from the Empire State Building.

Hale & Hearty Soups

55 W. 56 St (between 5th and 6th aves). Tel: 212-245 9200; 22 East 47 St (between Fifth and Madison). Tel: 212-557 1900). Open: L only, Mon–Sat. **$**
A chain of good, reliable eateries that serves the basics on the run.

Katsuhama

11 E. 47 St (between 5th

LEFT: catering to the hungry crowds.

and Madison aves). Tel: 212-758 5909. Open: L & D daily. **$$**
No frills here, but an affordable sushi spot that's always good to known about.

Michael's
24 W. 55 St (between 5th and 6th aves). Tel: 212-757 0555. Open: B, L & D Mon–Fri, L only Sat. **$$$**
Media and publishing movers and shakers sign deals here; now open for power breakfasts, too.

Osteria al Doge
142 W. 44th St (between 6th Ave and Broadway) Tel: 212-944-3643. Open: L and D Mon–Sat, D only Sun. **$$–$$$**
Dinner at this bustling pre-theater favorite is a show in itself. Take a seat on the balcony and watch the crowds.

Plantain Café
20 W. 38th St (between 5th and 6th aves) Tel: 212-869 8601. Open: L and D Mon–Sat. **$–$$**
Doing its part in bringing innovative, affordable Caribbean cuisine into vogue, this café serves delicious new takes on Latin staples.

Rock Center Café
20 W. 50th St (between 5th Ave and Rockefeller Pl) tel: 212-332 7620l **The Sea Grill**, tel: 212-332 7610. Open: B, L & D daily. **$$$**
Both are at the Rockefeller Center with views of skaters or fun seekers. The first has a general ringside menu; the second has excellent fish.

Town
15 W. 56th St (between 5th and 6th aves) Tel: 212-582 4445. Open: B, L and D Mon–Fri, D only Sat, Br only Sun. **$$$**
Grown up and glamorous, this striking yet subdued room in the Chambers Hotel is well suited to its range of dishes, that are solid enough to be classics yet exciting enough to be memorable.

Trattoria Dopo Teatro
125 W. 44th St (between 6th Ave and Broadway). Tel: 212-869-2849. Open: L and D Mon–Sat, D only Sun. **$$–$$$**
Unlike the "wolf-it-down" experience found in many Theater-District chow houses, a meal of Italian basics in this plain, high-windowed dining room or rear garden is always relaxing.

Virgil's Real BBQ
152 W. 44th St (between Broadway and 6th Ave). Tel: 212-921 9494. Open: L and D daily. **$$**
Forget the diet at this fun Southern restaurant serving some of the best brisket in New York City. The hickory smoke from the grill hanging in the air adds to the barbeque experience.

Wolf's Deli
41 W. 57 St (between 5th and 6th aves). Tel: 212-888 4100). Open: L & D daily. **$$**
The real thing in a sleek, modern room with great garlic pickles and stacked sandwiches.

Bars and Cafés

Bryant Park Grill, 25 W. 40 St (between 5th and 6th aves), has a busy lunch scene at this terraced eaterie behind the New York Public Library; it's a great place for a drink and meeting spot in the early evening, and there's an attractive after-work crowd.

Coliseum Books Café, 11 W. 42nd St (between 5th and 6th aves). Go for coffee or light snacks at this good, independent bookstore. Free WiFi.

Cosi Sandwich Bar 38 E. 45 St (between 5th and Madison aves). Freshly baked Italian flatbread sandwich joints with many other locations to choose from.

King Cole Bar (2 E. 55th St). Sipping a drink with the gorgeous Maxfield Parrish mural at the St Regis Hotel as a backdrop simply can't be beaten. Tea, coffee and light snacks, too.

Morrell Wine Bar & Café at 1 Rockefeller Plaza, has a noisy, fun, warm-weather crowd spilling over on a sidewalk café.

Oak Bar at The Plaza, 5th Ave at 59 St, has wonderful views of Central Park.

Rainbow Grill, 30 Rockefeller Plaza. Food is served here, too, but drinks afford an incomparable sunset view.

RIGHT: would-be chefs at work.

CENTRAL PARK

Stretching from Harlem to the Ritz-Carlton, Central Park is the playground and meeting place of the metropolis

Central Park is a great recreation area to explore, in addition to providing an oxygenating green space in the middle of this crowded, towering city. Frederick Law Olmsted and Calvert Vaux designed "Greensward," as they called it, in 1858. Olmsted's aim in creating the 843-acre (340- hectare) park was, in his words, to "supply hundreds of thousands of tired workers who have no opportunity to spend summers in the country with a specimen of God's handiwork."

The Central Park Dairy, in the middle of the park, around 65th Street, was built in 1870 to provide fresh milk and toys to the city's children. The fairytale structure, restored in 1979, now serves as a visitor information center.

Modern facilities of the park include 21 playgrounds, 26 baseball diamonds and 30 tennis courts, plus miles of bridle paths (horses can be rented, *see page 120*) and jogging tracks. This is in addition to a zoo, a theater and the Great Lawn for outdoor concerts and opera.

BELOW: by West 72nd Street, across the street from John Lennon's former New York home in the Dakota building, is "Strawberry Fields." This little area is adorned with flowers most of the time, but especially on his birthday, October 9th, and the anniversary of his senseless murder, December 8th.

ABOVE: taking a boat on the lake affords serene views of the Majestic Apartment building's post-art deco twin towers, which are next to the darker, Gothic gables of the famous Dakota building. It also provides an afternoon's gentle exercise; rent boats from the Loeb Boathouse, near East 75th Street.

ABOVE: Bethesda Fountain was designed with a surrounding terrace to be the park's architectural centerpiece. Along with wonderful views of the lake, the fountain provides a perfect spot for romantic meetings.

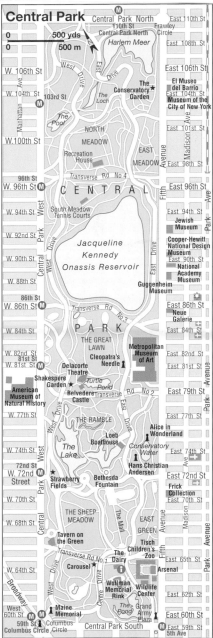

Central Park

0	500 yds
0	500 m

Central Park North
110th St
Central Park North
Harlem Meer
East 110th St
Frawley Circle
East 108th St
West Drive
East Drive
W. 106th St
East 106th St
W. 104th St
103rd St
The Loch
The Conservatory Garden ★
El Museo del Barrio
East 104th St
Museum of the City of New York
Manhattan Ave
The Pool
NORTH MEADOW
East 101st St
W.100th St
Recreation House
EAST MEADOW
East 98th St
Fifth Avenue
Transverse Rd No 4
96th St
W. 96th St Ⓜ
C E N T R A L
East 96th St
W. 94th St
South Meadow Tennis Courts
East 94th St
Jewish Museum
W. 92nd St
Cooper-Hewitt National Design Museum
East 90th St
Jacqueline Kennedy Onassis Reservoir
W. 90th St
National Academy Museum
W. 88th St
East Drive
Guggenheim Museum
Central Park West
86th St
W. 86th St Ⓜ
Transverse Rd No.3
East 86th St
Neue Galerie
W. 84th St
P A R K
East 84th St
THE GREAT LAWN
Cleopatra's Needle
Metropolitan Museum of Art
East 82nd St
W. 82nd St
81st St
W. 81st St Ⓜ
Delacorte Theatre
Shakespere Garden ★
Turtle Pond
East 81st St
American Museum of Natural History
Belvedere Castle
Transverse Rd No 2
East 79th St
Park Avenue
W. 77th St
THE RAMBLE
East 77th St
Alice in Wonderland
Loeb Boathouse
Conservatory Water
East 74th St
The Lake
Hans Christian Andersen
Madison Ave
W. 74th St
72nd St
W. 72nd Street Ⓜ
Strawberry Fields
Bethesda Fountain
East 72nd St
Frick Collection
East 70th St
W. 70th St
THE SHEEP MEADOW
The Mall
EAST GREEN
Tisch Children's Zoo
W. 68th St
Tavern on the Green
Fifth Avenue
Madison Avenue
Park Avenue
Transverse Rd No 1
The Dairy
East 65th St
W. 64th St
Carousel
Arsenal
Broadway
Centre Drive
Wollman Memorial Rink
Wildlife Center
East 62nd St
West 60th St Ⓜ Ⓜ
Maine Memorial
Columbus Circle
The Pond
Grand Army Plaza
East 60th St
59th St
Columbus Circle
Central Park South Ⓜ
East 59th St
5th Ave

RIGHT: in the heart of the section of the park that Frederick Law Olmsted designated the "children's area," and providing visitor information, the Central Park Dairy also has a permanent exhibit on the park's history. The wooden loggia overlooks the Wollman Ice Rink.

Central Park Information

LEFT: Hans Christian Andersen offers a story-telling knee to lucky youngsters. Among the statues to delight the kiddies are Mother Goose, Humpty Dumpty, Little Jack Horner and Little Bo Peep.

MIDTOWN EAST

The Chrysler Building,
Grand Central and the East River –
Midtown East is the perfect example of
quintessential New York

Midtown East covers much of what Manhattan conjures when people think of New York. This is where the city's corporate heart beats loudest, where power-lunching, power-shopping and sidewalk power-phoning is a way of life.

Like its counterpart to the west, Midtown East begins above 34th Street, and rises to a bustling climax between 42nd Street and the Queensboro (59th Street) Bridge, beyond which lies the calmer Upper East Side. Stretching east of Fifth Avenue over to the East River, it's a compact, energetic microcosm of Manhattan, encompassing steel and glass office towers, expensive stores and restaurants, familiar historic landmarks and some very exclusive neighborhoods.

Hills and bays

Along 35th Street, you'll come to the border of **Murray Hill ❶**, a residential area in the shadow of sleek Midtown office buildings, and where cross streets are lined by brownstone relics of a more genteel era. A plaque on the south side of 35th Street and Park Avenue marks the center of an 18th-century farm owned by Robert Murray, "whose wife, Mary Lindley Murray (1726–82) rendered signal service in

the Revolutionary War." Close by, on Madison Avenue, the fascinating **Church of the Incarnation**, built in 1864, exhibits stained-glass windows executed by Tiffany, LaFarge and Burne-Jones, among others.

The **Morgan Library ❷** (29 East 36th Street, tel: 212-685 0610; charge), also called the Pierpont Morgan Library, was opened to the public by financier J.P. Morgan in 1924. The Morgan Library is undergoing extensive renovation and will reopen at the beginning of 2006.

Map on page 84

LEFT: the Chrysler Building's spire was designed in secret and lifted swiftly into place in one piece.
BELOW: beaux arts Grand Central.

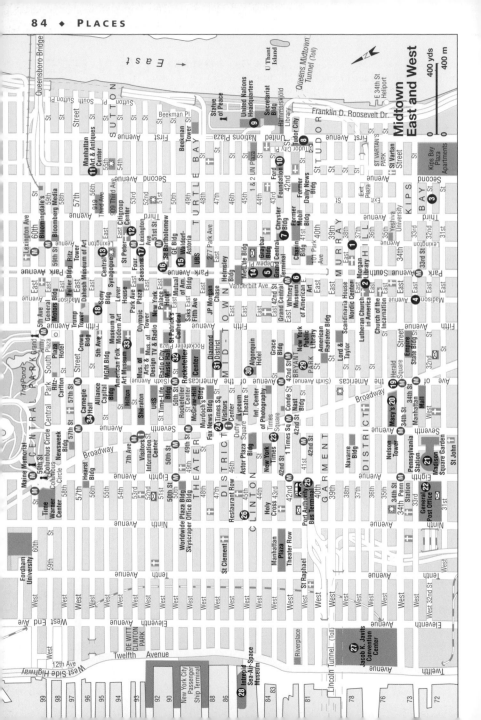

Midtown
East and West

Map on page 84

From here, walk back to 36th Street and east across Park and Lexington avenues, to reach one of the city's tiniest and most charming historic districts. The rowhouses of **Sniffen Court** were constructed in Romanesque Revival style at the time of the American Civil War, and were originally stables for Murray Hill's grander residences (now, of course, they are very expensive and highly desirable real estate).

East of here is **Kips Bay ❸**, a mainly residential area of high-rise apartment buildings, medical offices affiliated with **New York University Medical Center**, restaurants and – at 34th Street – movie theaters, which are increasingly hard to find.

The area is named for Jacob Kip, a Dutch settler whose farm overlooked a bay, long-since filled-in, at the present day intersection of Second Avenue and 35th Street. Nearby **St Vartan's Armenian Church** was modeled after a 5th-century house of Eastern Orthodox worship and stands at the corner of 34th and Second. It features a small collection of Armenian antiquities.

Advertising industry

Historically, **Madison Avenue ❹** has been spiritual home to the advertising industry, especially the blocks between 42nd and 57th streets. This is one of the city's commercial hearts, where sharp-suited men and women buy their clothes at Brooks Brothers on 44th Street and stop off for cocktails at the Yale Club one block east on Vanderbilt, before running to catch their trains home to the suburbs from **Grand Central Terminal ❺**.

With entrances at Vanderbilt and 42nd Street, as well as Park and Lexington avenues, Grand Central is the hub in a spoke of Metro-North commuter lines reaching deep into the suburbs of Westchester County and neighboring Connecticut, and is used by almost half a million passengers each day, on more than 550 trains. Unlike the old Pennsylvania Station, Grand Central was saved from demolition by the city's Landmarks Preservation Commission, and thus this 1913 beaux arts reminder of days when travel was a gracious experience remains almost

Grand Central's renovation makes the station a delight to visit; try the food hall for delicious, last-minute purchases.

BELOW: a culinary landmark – Grand Central's famous Oyster Bar.

intact. More importantly, it's undergone a $200 million restoration to renew its former glory. Advertising signs were removed, dozens of new restaurants and stores opened, including an indoor food hall for last-minute purchases, and the glorious illuminated zodiac on the vaulted ceiling of the main concourse – one of the world's largest rooms – gleams like new.

The UN flags along First Avenue are those of its original member nations. In alphabetical order, the first flag is Afghanistan (48th Street), while the last flag is Zimbabwe (42nd Street).

Tours are available on Wednesdays (inquire at the main information booth or call the Municipal Art Society on 212-935 3960). Before leaving, don't miss the lower-level **Oyster Bar**, a culinary landmark in its own right.

Across 42nd Street is a branch of the **Whitney Museum of American Art ❻** (120 Park Avenue, tel: 917-663 2453; closed Sun; free) in the Altria Building lobby.

Jewel of the skyline

On Lexington Avenue, the famed **Chrysler Building ❼** is one of the jewels of the Manhattan skyline. Erected by auto tsar Walter Chrysler in 1930, its art deco spire rises 1,000 ft (305 meters) into the city air like a stainless-steel rocket ship. Stop in and admire the lobby's marble-and-bronze decor, enhanced by epic murals depicting transportation and human endeavor.

Back on 42nd Street, walk east past the glass and glitz of the **Grand Hyatt Hotel** (which adjoins Grand Central, and was built over the old Commodore Hotel), to the former *Daily News* building, between Third and Second avenues.

This art deco structure, though no longer home to the newspaper, looks so much like the headquarters for the fictional *Daily Planet* that they used it in the *Superman* movies. Check out the gigantic globe in the lobby before continuing east toward First Avenue, past the steps leading up to **Tudor City ❽**, a private compound of Gothic brick high-rises. These date from the 1920s, when land along the East River was filled with slums and slaughterhouses; one reason why all the windows face west toward the Hudson River.

The busy main entrance of the **United Nations ❾** building is at

BELOW:
the UN's
symbol of peace.

The United Nations

The name "United Nations" was devised by United States' president Franklin D. Roosevelt, and was first used in the "Declaration by United Nations" of January 1, 1942, during World War II, when representatives of 26 nations pledged their governments to continue fighting the war in Europe and Asia together.

The UN charter was drawn up in 1945 at a conference in San Francisco and signed by delegates from 50 countries; in the new millennium, membership has risen to over 190 countries. The institution has won many Nobel Peace Prizes.

Just like a foreign embassy, the United Nations' grounds, which cover 18 acres (7.2 hectares) of land along the East River, are not considered a part of the United States, and are outside the jurisdiction of city, state and federal laws.

The complex consist of four main buildings: the Secretariat, the General Assembly, the Conference area, and the Library. The UN maintains its own independent police force, fire department and post office. Guided tours last about 45 minutes and in English, leave every half an hour from the lobby. Tours are also available in 16 other languages, including Mandarin and Hebrew.

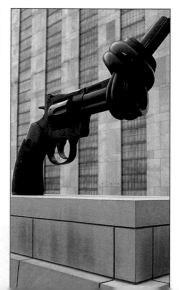

46th and First, and it's well worth stopping here to observe the workings of international diplomacy. Guided tours are offered almost every half hour from the lobby (tel: 212-963 8687). Don't miss the moon rock display just inside the entrance, the Chagall stained-glass windows or the lower-level gift shop, which sells inexpensive handicrafts from all over the world.

On weekdays, the surprisingly inexpensive Delegates' Dining Room is often open to the public for lunch: jackets are required for men, and reservations must be made a day in advance. The view of the river is almost as interesting as the multilingual eavesdropping.

Historic districts

Back on 42nd Street, the lobby garden of the **Ford Foundation** ❿ (glass-enclosed, all lush trees and flowers) is considered one of the city's most beautiful institutional environments. This part of town is also home to three of the city's classiest addresses. **Turtle Bay**, once home to such privacy-loving celebrities as Katharine Hepburn, conductor Leopold Stokowsky and author Kurt Vonnegut, is an historic district between 48th and 49th streets where 19th-century brownstones share a garden hidden from the public.

Beekman Place, just east of First Avenue, is a two-block enclave of elegant townhouses (one once the home of famed songwriter Irving Berlin) and apartments set along the East River. **Sutton Place** is an oft-used synonym for luxury in books and movies. Starting above 54th Street and stretching north for five blocks, its high-rises are filled with dowagers and poodles, and visual relief is provided by the occasional quaint cul-de-sac of townhouses, gardens and promontories offering views of the river.

You'll find more than enough shopping opportunities nearby, starting with the **Manhattan Art and Antiques Center** ⓫ on Second Avenue between 55th and 56th streets. Over 100 small shops sell everything from antique clocks to jewelry. On the lower level, you'll find that increasingly rare city

Map on page 84

The MetLife Building was constructed in 1963, 50 years later than Grand Central, in the foreground of the picture.

BELOW: flying the flag: United Nations' Day is on October 24.

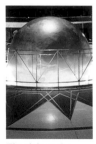

The globe in the lobby of the former Daily News *building featured in the* Superman *movies; these real-life premises were the offices of Clark Kent's paper, the* Daily Planet.

BELOW: homeless people are much less visible now, but New York is still a city of haves and have-nots.

amenity, public restrooms. Or stop in the **Citigroup Center** , on 54th Street between Third and Lexington avenues. Its slanted roof makes this a skyline standout, while the indoor atrium lined by shops and cafés make a pleasant stopping place.

Before exiting onto Lexington Avenue, drop by the adjoining **St Peter's** church, which includes a chapel designed by artist Louise Nevelson. St Peter's is famous for its weekly jazz eucharists; it also has frequent concerts. The York Theater, where plays by authors both known and unknown are presented, is on the church's lower level.

Walking north, note the landmark **Central Synagogue**, at the corner of 55th Street. Built in 1872, it adds a note of exotic, Moorish-style grace to an otherwise ordinary block; it was rebuilt and reopened in September 2001 after being severely damaged by fire.

There are boutiques and galleries in both directions on 57th Street, generally growing pricier the closer you get to Fifth Avenue. Toward Third, expensive gadgets galore are

displayed at Hammacher Schlemmer, while continuing west on 57th you'll find such fashion fortresses as Turnbull & Asser, Chanel, Hermès, and Burberry. Along the way to these stores, be sure to note the elegant, *circa* 1929 **Fuller Building** (41 East 57th Street), home to numerous art galleries where exhibitions are open to the public.

Above Grand Central

The view down Park Avenue stops abruptly at the **MetLife Building** (formerly the Pan-Am Building), which was plonked on top of Grand Central Terminal in the early 1960s, but fortunately, this part of the avenue still retains some of its original glamour. The **Waldorf-Astoria**, between 49th and 50th *(see page 216)*, is one of the city's grandest hotels, and has attracted guests of the royal and presidential variety since opening here in 1931. The Duke and Duchess of Windsor and Cole Porter were only some of the "permanent residents" who lived in the hotel's exclusive towers. The original Waldorf Hotel, on Fifth Avenue, was torn down to make way for the Empire State Building.

St Bartholomew's Church opened its doors on Park and 50th Street in 1919, and is a fine example of neo-Byzantine architecture. One block west, on Madison, the opulent **New York Palace Hotel** *(see page 215)* incorporates as part of its public rooms two of the **Villard Houses**, 19th-century mansions once used as offices by the Archdiocese of New York. Built in 1884 by the architectural firm McKim, Mead & White, these half-dozen houses were designed to look like one large Italian palazzo. The owner was the noted publisher Henry Villard, after whom the houses are named.

Almost 100 years later, when two of the mansions were sold to provide a lavish interior for the Palace, New

York historians took exception to the sale. Today, the hotel serves afternoon tea beneath a vaulted ceiling designed by Stanford White.

Picasso for a season

You'll see lines of limos waiting in front of the **Four Seasons** ⑰, on East 52nd Street between Park and Lexington, a restaurant so important that its interior has been declared an historic landmark. Picasso's 22-ft (6.7-meter) painted curtain from a 1920 Diaghilev ballet hangs inside, and luminaries from the worlds of politics and publishing do likewise.

The restaurant is within the distinctive **Seagram Building**. The tycoon Samuel Bronfman, head of Seagram Distillers, had planned to erect an ordinary office block until his architect daughter introduced him to Mies van der Rohe. The result is one of the best of the Modernist constructions of the 1950s period.

In the 1980s, some of New York's biggest corporations created public spaces, and contributed significantly to the quality of crowded Midtown life. One of the first was tiny little **Paley Park**, at 3 East 53rd Street, built on the site where the glamorous Stork Club once stood.

A short walk away, Philip Johnson's mammoth **Sony Building** ⑱ (originally built for AT&T), on Madison Avenue between 55th and 56th streets, includes a public arcade squeezed between shops displaying the latest Sony equipment. Drop into the adjacent **Sony Wonder Technology Lab** for demonstrations of how all this super-tech stuff works (tel: 212-833 8100; closed Mon).

On the corner of 56th Street is the former IBM building, a sharply angled tower designed by Bauhaus-inspired architect Edward Larrabee Barnes. The below-ground concourse houses exhibitions, while above is the **Dahesh Museum of Art** (tel: 212-759 0606; closed Mon; charge), with a collection of 19th-century European art. Alternatively, head for the atrium, where there's casual dining on the mezzanine, and relax before heading back into the adrenalin-pumping Midtown madness outside. ❑

The most remarkable modern art at the Four Seasons is a huge Picasso (see photo on page 91), a stage curtain designed for the 1920 production of Le Tricorne.

BELOW: the Duke and Duchess of Windsor lived here.

RESTAURANTS, BARS AND CAFÉS

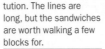

Restaurants

Asia de Cuba
Morgan Hotel, 237 Madison Ave (between 37th and 38th sts). Tel: 212-726 7755. Open: L & D Mon–Fri, D only Sat & Sun. **$$$**
A gorgeous room designed by Phillipe Starck attracts pretty people and serves a very fancy form of Asian-Latin cuisine to devotees.

Burritoville
866 Third Ave. (entrance on 52nd St. between 3rd and Lexington aves). Tel: 212-980 4111. Open: L & D daily. **$**
A great little Mexican chain that's a real step above normal fast food. In fact they call it "mex-cellent." There are other Burritoville branches around town.

Café Centro
MetLife Bldg, 45th St and Vanderbilt Ave. Tel: 212-818 1222. Open: L & D Mon–Fri, D only Sat. **$$**
There's a busy office lunch crowd near Grand Central, but it's great for light dinner and drinks.

Café St Bart's
109 E. 50 St (at Park Ave). Tel: 212-888 2664. Open: L only Mon–Fri. **$$**
Tucked into a terrace between St Bart's Cathedral and The Waldorf Astoria is an affordable spot on Park Avenue best for lunch.

Carnegie Deli
854 7th Ave (at 54th St). Tel: 212-757 2245. Open: B, L & D daily. **$**
You won't find a more authentic deli experience than this New York insti-tution. The lines are long, but the sandwiches are worth walking a few blocks for.

Counter @ The Oyster Bar
Grand Central Terminal, Lower Level, Tel: 212-490 6650. Open: L & D Mon–Sat. **$$**
The Oyster Bar's Main Dining Room will deliver a much heftier bill of fare than the counter seats, where chowders and pan roasts hit the spot but not the wallet.

Dawat
210 E. 58th St (between 3rd and 2nd aves). Tel: 212-355-7555. Open: L and D Mon–Sat; D only Sun. **$$$**
The cuisine of the sub-continent goes haute amid elegant surround-ings at what is arguably the finest Indian eatery in New York City.

Four Seasons
99 E. 52nd St (between Lex-ington and Park aves). Tel: 212-754 9494. Open: L and D Mon–Fri, D only Sat. **$$$$**
Since opening 40 years ago, the Four Seasons has had a clientele that rivals any *Who's-Who* listing. The decor is priceless *(see page 89)* and the seasonal clas-sics served in the ele-gant pool room or the grill room impeccable.

Grand Central Terminal
42nd St and Vanderbilt Ave, Lower Level. Open: B, L & D daily. **$**
A noisy collection of restaurants of ethnic variety where food can be taken away to eat on the train or consumed on the premises: Asian, Mexican, Jewish deli, pastries – something for every taste.

Guastavino's
409 E. 59 St (between 1st and York aves). Tel: 212-980 2455. Open: L & D Mon–Fri, Br & D Sat–Sun. **$$$**
Terrence Conran's brasserie-under the-bridge attracts a young crowd for drinks and serves a tasty and extensive menu.

Le Perigord
405 E. 52 St (East of 1st Ave). Tel: 212-755 6244. Open: L & D Mon–Fri, D Only Sat–Sun. **$$$$**
French classic serving a well-heeled Sutton Place clientele for years.

L'Impero
45 Tudor City Place (east of Third Ave, between 42nd and 43rd sts). Tel: 212-599 5045 Open: L & D Mon–Sat. **$$$$**
Stylish Tuscan, very pop-ular with trendy foodies.

March
405 E. 58th St (between 1st Ave and Sutton Pl). Tel: 212-754-6272. Open: D daily. **$$$$**
In the pretty garden and intimate, two-level dining room, Asian and Latin

LEFT: Carnegie Deli is a real New York experience.

touches transform simple ingredients into culinary delights.

Montparnasse
230 E. 51st St (between 3rd and 2nd aves). Tel: 212-758 6633. Open: L and D daily. **$$–$$$**
A somewhat undiscovered gem of a bistro that feels like Paris. A wide selection of wines available by the glass, excellent service, and hearty but refined classic bistro dishes.

Oceana
55 E. 54 St (between Park and Madison aves). Tel: 212-759 5941. Open: L & D Mon–Fri, D only Sun. **$$$$**
Exquisite seafood in beautiful surroundings. It's something special, as are the prices.

The Palm
837 2nd Ave (between 44th and 45th sts). Tel: 212-687 953 plus branches. Open: L & D Mon–Fri, D only Sat. **$$$$**
Huge steaks and lobsters in small, narrow room filled with regulars.

Pershing Square
90 E. 42 St (at Park Ave). Tel: 212-286 9600. Open: B, L & D Mon–Fri, Br & L Sat–Sun. **$$**
A step away from Grand Central, reasonably priced American fare.

P.J. Clarke's
915 3rd Ave (at 55th St). Tel: 212-317 1616. Open: L & D daily. **$$**
Many think P.J. Clarke's serves the best hamburger on the East Side. Certainly the historic

saloon, dating from the late 1800s and popular in Sinatra's time, has undergone a renaissance. A bonus: serves food after 11pm.

Rosa Mexicano
1063 1st Ave (at 58 St) Tel: 212-753 7407. Open: D daily. **$$$**
The Rosa is famous for table-side guacamole, as well as an excellent and imaginative modern Mexican menu.

Ruth's Chris Steakhouse
885 2nd Ave (at 47th St). Tel: 212-759 9496. Open: L & D Mon–Fri, D only Sat–Sun. **$$$**
Fans swear by this format, which originated in New Orleans: the steaks are big and buttery.

San Martin
143 E. 49 St (between Lexington and 3rd aves). Tel: 212-832 0888. Open: L & D daily. **$$$**
Tasty Spanish cuisine in a warm, attractive room.

Smith & Wollensky
797 3rd Ave (49th St). Tel: 212-753 1530. Open: L & D Mon–Fri, D only Sat–Sun. **$$$**
This NY institution is usually packed with a boisterous crowd of stockbrokers and Midtown executives. For a less expensive food option, try the adjacent Wollensky's.

Water Club
East River (at 30th St). Tel: 212-683 3333. Open: L & D Mon–Sat, Br & D Sun. **$$$**
Reservations are a must

at this floating restaurant with great fish and even better views.

Zarela
953 2nd Ave (between 50th and 51sts).Tel: 212-644 6740. Open: L & D Mon–Fri, D only Sat–Sun. **$$**
Mexican regional cooking never tasted this good. Share space with the faithful following.

Bars and Cafés

Bogarts, 99 Park Ave (at 39th St), is popular with the young after-work crowd, and a stone's throw from the train.
Bull & Bear, in the Waldorf Astoria, has a long mahogany bar and a masculine mood, but patrons love the clubby atmosphere.
Campbell Apartments at Grand Central Terminal is a popular hideaway with the after-work,

before-train "suit" crowd as well as for an after-dinner drink – or two.
Juan Valdez Café, 140 E. 57th St, has Columbian coffee and great pastries for anyone shopping at Bloomies.
Le Colonial, 149 E. 57 St (between Lexington and Third aves), has a good bar. A romantic meeting spot, then stay for Vietnamese cuisine.
Monkey Bar in Hotel Elysee (between Madison and Park aves). Stylish but noisy, great decor. Think Banana Daquiris.

PRICE CATEGORIES

Prices for a three-course dinner per person with half a bottle of wine:
$ = under $20
$$ = $20–$45
$$$ = $45–$60
$$$$ = over $60

RIGHT: the Picasso stage curtain at the Four Seasons.

MIDTOWN WEST

The lights of Broadway shine most brightly here, glittering off tourist-friendly Times Square, the Museum of Modern Art and the dancing girls of Radio City

The West Side shines as brightly as the east, at least in terms of sheer neon wattage, and what Midtown West lacks in finesse it makes up in tenacity. This is where billboards vie with world-class art, and where, as the old saying goes, there's a broken heart for every light on Broadway.

At the center of it all, Times Square has donned new neon baubles like an aging beauty queen with a facelift – stretched end to end, the neon in Times Square would extend from New York City to Washington D.C. Flash and frenzy dazzle the eye. New NASDAQ headquarters in the Condé Nast Building dominate with a huge LED display teeming with the latest quotes. And Broadway – the glamorous Great White Way – has been rejuvenated.

But then, that's the story of Midtown West. It's been bruised, but it's never gone down for the count. The lights that burn on Broadway, and a bevy of new hotels, restaurants, stores and other businesses here, make sure that the West Side is alive and booming.

Starting at 34th Street, the transition from East to West Midtown begins at **Herald Square ⑲**, where Broadway intersects Sixth Avenue. Named for the *New York Herald* newspaper, whose headquarters once stood here, today this chaotic intersection is best known for its retail temples.

Macy's

Immediately south of Herald Square is the **Manhattan Mall**, where nine floors are occupied by nearly a dozen eateries and roughly 50 (and growing) retailers. The big draw, however, is **Macy's ⑳**, a New York institution for more than a century. Like the sign says, Macy's is the

Map on page 84

LEFT: looking down on Midtown.
BELOW: your Point & Shoot Agent awaits.

Search out sample sales and factory floor bargains in the Garment District around busy Seventh Avenue.

BELOW: be alert: these Seventh Avenue fellas with their clothes racks are in a hurry.

biggest department store in the world, and it's worth seeing for its size alone. In the past, Macy's was a staple for middle-class shoppers, but these days it's got panache and designer labels. Don't leave without visiting the "Cellar," a gourmet emporium with gadgets that even the most creative chef would covet.

Exiting Macy's on Seventh Avenue puts you right in the middle of the **Garment District**, a jangly, soot-covered workhorse that still turns out much of America's fashion. There's not much to do or see here, although dedicated bargain-hunters have been known to walk away with first-class deals from the factory floor or sample sales.

Showrooms, too, dot the area, where you can find the latest, if not always the greatest, fashions, although you may have to shop around a little, both for the bargains and the showrooms themselves. Keep an eye out for the young men pushing clothing racks through the streets; they're definitely not looking out for you.

The structure at Seventh Avenue

and 33rd Street is Madison Square Garden, disliked by purists not only for its functional, clumsy design but also for replacing McKim, Mead and White's magnificent Pennsylvania Station, demolished in 1963. The "new" **Penn Station** is now 50 ft (15 meters) beneath it, where it shuttles a quarter-million commuters daily to Long Island and elsewhere.

Once located between Madison and Fifth avenues – that is, Madison Square itself – **Madison Square Garden ㉑** is one of America's biggest entertainment arenas, where rock shows, ice hockey, basketball games, tennis matches and even circuses are held. Whatever your feelings about the building, there's no denying it fulfils its function, and the behind-the-scenes tour is surprisingly interesting, even visiting the locker rooms of the NY Knicks (tel: 212-465 6741).

If you're a Glenn Miller fan, you may want to check out the venerable **Hotel Pennsylvania** *(see page 216)*, across Seventh Avenue at 33rd Street. This used to be the Big Band era's hottest ticket, immortalized by Miller's hit *Pennsylvania 6-5000* – still the hotel's phone number.

Directly behind Madison Square Garden, the **General Post Office ㉒** is hardly a favorite tourist attraction, although it is impressive, with a monumental Corinthian design that makes your average Greek temple look like a tiki hut. There are plans to redevelop the building so that the US Postal Service shares space with AMTRAK's rail service. There's also that terrific slogan inscribed on the frieze: "Neither snow nor rain nor heat nor gloom of night stays these couriers from the swift completion of their appointed rounds." The motto was actually stolen from Herodotus, who obviously never mailed a letter in Manhattan.

Heading back to Herald Square, Broadway slices through the Mid-

town grid to 42nd Street. This is the Downtown end of Times Square, the garish heart of Midtown West, and one of the city's most dramatic success stories.

Times Square

Stretching along Broadway to 48th Street, with the **Theater District** sprawled loosely on either side, the long awaited renovation of **Times Square** ㉓ has again made this the "crossroads of the world" *(see photo feature on page 102)*.

Whether you're here for a show or not, be sure to take a stroll down **Shubert Alley**, a busy walkway that runs behind the Booth and Shubert theaters, from 45th to 44th Street. **Sardi's** is a venerable Broadway landmark. In addition to its fabled dining rooms with star-caricatures galore, there's a great bar, abuzz with show talk before or after the theater. Nostalgia-buffs should head for the **Lyceum Theatre**, a block east on 45th Street, which is one of the oldest on Broadway and – with its elaborate baroque facade and dramatic mansard roof – probably the most

beautiful. The **Times Square Visitors Center** ㉔ (daily 8am–8pm), is a walk-in facility in the landmark **Embassy Theater**, on Broadway between 46th and 47th streets, across from the half-price TKTS booth.

The square is changing all the time: recent 42nd Street attractions include the **Ford Center for the Performing Arts** and the **E-Walk** entertainment complex, as well as **Ecko Unlimited**, a high-flying hip-hop store.

At the corner of 44th Street is the Viacom building, where the **Times Square Studio** and headquarters of **MTV** is located. Despite the square's transformation, however, there's still an old-fashioned sleaze-factor seeping over from the few remaining sex shops on Eighth Avenue, where the **Port Authority Bus Terminal** ㉕ (between 40th and 42nd and now cleaned up) is a major commuter hub.

Hell's Kitchen

Heading north on Eighth or Ninth avenues, things get interesting in the old **Hell's Kitchen** neighborhood,

If all the neon lights in Times Square were laid end-to-end, they would stretch from New York City to Washington, D.C. See page 102 for a glimpse of this neon nirvana.

BELOW: Macy's Thanksgiving Day parade is broadcast to the nation.

The Jacob K. Javits Center will soon be bigger and better than ever, thanks to state funds granted for expansion.

BELOW: Radio City's Rockettes dance for Santa, baby.

now known as **Clinton** ㉖. At the start of the 20th century, Hell's Kitchen was one of the most notorious slums in the country. Immigrants were crammed into unsafe and insanitary tenements, and Irish gangs governed the streets like petty overlords. Even the police were afraid to venture into the neighborhood alone.

There's still a certain gut-level edginess to the area and a new generation of immigrants, but there are also artists and actors, as well as culinary discoveries to be made. Ninth Avenue from 57th Street to 42nd Street is a globe trot for diners, with reasonably priced restaurants geared to an atlas of international cuisines.

A stretch of West 46th Street from Eighth to Ninth avenues – known as **Restaurant Row** – is a solid block of eateries popular among the pre-theater crowd. During the annual Ninth Avenue Food Festival (May), thousands of New Yorkers flock to gorge themselves on an astonishing variety of ethnic delicacies. If you love to eat, this is an event that you shouldn't miss.

There's also an active off-Broad-way theater scene on 42nd Street between Ninth and Tenth avenues, where the block of small, experimental or low-budget venues here are known collectively as **Theatre Row**. This makes an attractive pairing with Restaurant Row for a good evening out.

West of here, the main attraction is the **Jacob K. Javits Convention Center** ㉗. Located at Twelfth Avenue and 34th Street, this is one of the country's largest exhibition spaces – home to the National Boat Show and other events. At the end of 2004, the state of New York allocated massive funds to expand the Javits Center, eager to take advantage of the more than $1.1 billion said to be spent by delegates, exhibitors and event organizers every year.

Intrepid

For non-delegates and those not convening, farther Uptown from the Javits Center at Pier 83 on 43rd Street, **Circle Line** boats depart for delightful cruises around Manhattan. At Pier 86, the *USS Intrepid* is a decommissioned World War II aircraft carrier that's now the **Intrepid Sea-Air-Space Museum** ㉘ (West 46th Street and Twelfth Avenue, tel: 212-245 0072; charge), where fighter jets are strewn across a deck the size of a few football fields. The *Intrepid*'s newest non-military exhibition aircraft is perhaps the most beautiful airplane in aviation history, the *Concorde*. The museum is open Wednesday to Sunday, with last admission at 4 pm. Farther along, cruise ships and transatlatic liners, like the *QE II* and *Queen Mary II* berth alongside the Hudson piers.

For an alternate tour of Midtown West, walk east instead of west from Times Square to **Sixth Avenue**. Signs will announce the **Avenue of the Americas**, but don't be fooled. To New Yorkers, Sixth Avenue is

Sixth Avenue, no matter how many flags hang from the lampposts. At the corner of 42nd Street is the lovely **Bryant Park ㉙**, where fashion shows, summer concerts and sometimes outdoor movies are held. At the next corner up is the **International Center of Photography** (1133 Sixth Avenue, tel: 212-768 4682; closed Mon; charge).

A right turn at 44th Street leads to the neighborhood of the **Algonquin Hotel ㉚** *(see page 214)*, where Dorothy Parker, Robert Benchley and other distinguished *literati* traded wit at the famous Round Table. West 44th Street has quite a clubby atmosphere, in fact. No. 27 is the premises of the **Harvard Club**, whose interior can more easily be observed by peering into a back window, rather than shelling out for four years' education; No. 37 houses the distinguished **New York Yacht Club**, with a 1899 nautical beaux arts facade.

Another right leads to the block-long **Diamond District ㉛**, an enclave at 47th Street where close to $500 million in gems is traded every day. Most of the diamond merchants are Hasidic Jews, distinguished by black suits, wide-brimmed hats and long beards. From 47th Street north, corporate monoliths march up Sixth Avenue. Names change, but the structures stay the same. This is actually the Rockefeller Center's backyard.

Radio City

Relief from this chilly modernism comes at **Radio City Music Hall ㉜**, gracing the corner of Sixth Avenue and 50th Street. Radio City is the world's largest indoor theater and the Rockefeller Center's crowning glory. Both the outside and the interior are magnificent, and the guided tours (inquire at the box office or call 212-307 7171) are recommended. From the massive chandeliers in the Grand Lobby to the plush, scalloped auditorium, Radio City was the last word in art deco extravagance; the acoustics are excellent and even the restrooms were custom designed. The Stuart Davis mural that graced the men's smoking lounge was considered so important it was acquired by the Museum of Modern Art.

Map on page 84

TIP

Big spenders should head straight for the Algonquin dining room, where a $10,000 martini is on the menu. Why does it cost so much? There's a loose diamond at the bottom of each glass.

BELOW: the tour of dazzling, art deco Radio City is one of the best in town.

Map on page 84

The American Folk Art Museum has two branches, both on Manhattan's West Side.

BELOW: Tchaikovsky conducted at the opening gala of Carnegie Hall.

The **Museum of Television and Radio** (25 West 52nd Street, tel: 212-621 6600; charge) is a feast for committed couch potatoes. The vast archive of vintage radio and TV programs can be rented for an hour at a time. It's a perfect rainy day activity, any day except Mondays, when the museum is closed, rainy or not.

MoMA

The **Museum of Modern Art** ❸ (11 West 53rd Street, tel: 212-708 9400; closed Tues; large charge), known to culture vultures as MoMA, has been completely rebuilt *(see page 100)*, and offers one of the world's most exciting and provocative art collections. Don't miss the much-loved sculpture garden.

In the same block as MoMA, the **American Folk Art Museum** (45 West 53rd Street, tel: 212-595 9533; closed Mon; charge) is home to traditional art from the 18th and 19th centuries. The Folk Art museum has also retained its small, Lincoln Center branch *(see page 120)*.

The **Museum of Contemporary Arts and Design** (40 West 53rd Street, tel: 212-956 3535; charge) has works in glass and paper. It moves to Columbus Circle soon.

From Seventh Avenue and 55th Street, you're two blocks away from **Carnegie Hall** ❸. As every American knows, there's only one way to get to Carnegie Hall – practice, practice. The joke is about as old as the hall itself, which was built in 1891 by super-industrialist Andrew Carnegie. Ever since Tchaikovsky conducted at the opening gala, Carnegie Hall has attracted the world's finest performers, including Rachmaninov, Toscanini and Sinatra; it would be pleasant if the hall's architecture was as inspiring as its history or acoustics.

Midtown West wraps up with a sophisticated flourish just two blocks away on **Central Park South**, famed for luxury hotels and lines of sleek limousines. It's a good place to catch one of the touristy **horse-drawn carriages** that clip-clop around the park. A ride is expensive, but worth it once in a lifetime – especially in December, when Midtown glistens with holiday lights. ❏

RESTAURANTS

Restaurants

Algonquin Hotel, Blue Bar & Lobby
59 W. 44 St between 5th and 6th aves). Tel: 212-840 6800. Open: B, L, T & D daily. $$$
Whether it's martinis at the Blue Bar or afternoon tea in the wood-paneled lobby, there's a sense of literary history in the air once shared by Dorothy Parker and other members of the Round Table. The people behind a recent renovation have worked hard to change nothing at all.

Angus McIndoe
258 W. 44th St (between Broadway and 8th Ave). Tel: 212-221 9222. Open: L & D Mon–Sat, Br & D Sun. $$
Newer than Joe Allen's and Sardi's, the latest drop-in place provides three levels for various theater stars to unwind after a show.

Barbetta
321 W. 46th St. Tel: 212-246 9171. Open: L & D Tues–Sat. $$$
The grande dame of "Restaurant Row" has been doing uninterrupted business since 1906. An elegant townhouse plus dreamy backyard garden make for a grand experience of delicious Italian food.

Becco
355 W. 46th St. Tel: 212-397 7597. Open: L & D daily. $$
A fixed price, all-you-can-eat pasta paradise. It's moderate in price with wine, extremely inexpensive without it.

Café Un Deux Trois
123 W. 44th St (between Broadway and 6th aves). Tel: 212-354 4148. Open: L & D daily. $$
Midtown madness, but with a pre-theater or lunchtime brasserie menu. The *pommes frites* are perfect.

Carmine's
200 W. 44th St (between 7th and 8th aves). Tel: 212-221 3800. Open: L & D daily. $$
Theater District Italian eatery with big portions. It's absolutely perfect for big families, too.

China Grill
CBS Building, 60 W. 53rd St. Tel: 212-333 7788. Open: L & D Mon–Fri, D only Sat–Sun. $$–$$$
Fabulous Asian-nouvelle restaurant which can be reasonably priced after careful study of the creative menu.

Cite
120 W. 51st St (between 6th and 7th aves). Tel: 212-956 7100. Open: L & D Mon–Fri, D only Sat–Sun. $$$
A chophouse popular for years for its all-you-can-drink wine dinner.

Firebird
365 W. 46th St. Tel: 212-586 0244. Open: L Wed, Sat & Sun, D Tues & Sun. $$$$
Opulent, exotic Russian restaurant fit for a tsar.

Gallagher's Steakhouse
228 W. 52nd St between Broadway and 8th Ave). Tel: 212-245 5336. Open: L & D daily. $$$
A sometime celeb hangout and New York tradition since 1927. It's easy to spot; look for beef in the windows.

Hourglass Tavern
373 W. 46th St. Tel: 212-265 2060. Open: D daily. $$
The gimmick here (a formula that has been popular for years) is that diners must be in and out in 60 minutes.

Joe Allen
326 W. 46th St. Tel: 212-581 6464. Open: L & D daily. $$
Long-time theater hangout serves basic American food with the added bonus of frequent celebrity sightings.

John's Pizzeria
260 W. 44th St (between Broadway and 8th Ave). Tel: 212-391 7560. Open: L & D daily. $
Quality, thin-crust pizza, plus much more on the menu in this former church. What's better, the stained glass or the low prices?

Le Bernardin
155 W. 55th St (between 6th and 7th aves). Tel: 212-554 1515. Open: L & D Mon–Fri, D only Sat. $$$$
Top-of-the-line for fish lovers who are willing to pay the price.

Molyvos
871 7th Ave (at 55th St). Tel: 212-582 7500. Open: L & D daily. $$$
A lush *taverna* that serves up Greek food in a style all its own. Perfect for pre-Carnegie Hall lunch or dinner.

Ruth's Chris Steakhouse
148 W. 51st St (between 6th and 7th aves). Tel: 212-245 9600. Open: L & D Mon–Fri, D only Sat–Sun. $$$
Scrumptious steaks + loyal customers = winning formula.

Trattoria Dell'Arte
900 7th Ave (at 56th St). Tel: 212-245 9800. Open: L & D daily. $$$
Look for the fabulous antipasti bar that doubles as a popular main course. This trattoria is always buzzing with cogniscenti from every profession you could hope to meet.

The View
1535 Broadway (at 45th St). Tel: 212-704 8900. Open: D daily, Br Sun only. $$$
High atop the Marriott Marquis Hotel in Times Square is a revolving restaurant with a wonderful panoramic view of the skyline. Closed lunchtimes, but Sunday brunch and dinner are served, with early dinner (great for sunsets) at a slightly reduced cost.

PRICE CATEGORIES

Prices for a three-course dinner per person with half a bottle of wine:
$ = under $20
$$ = $20–$45
$$$ = $45–$60
$$$$ = over $60

MUSEUM OF MODERN ART

After more than two years in Queens, MoMA is back in Manhattan – and it's bigger and better than ever

ABOVE: *The Starry Night*, 1889, Vincent van Gogh. "Looking at the stars," he said, "always makes me dream."
BELOW: *The Bather*, ca. 1885, by Paul Cézanne, the painter whom Henri Matisse described as "the father of us all."

After a 30-month stay in Queens, MoMA has returned home to 11 West 53rd Street, between 5th and 6th avenues. John Updike said in the *New Yorker* of the new 630,000-sq-ft (58,000-sq-meter) space, "It feels breathless with unspared expense. It has the enchantment of a bank after hours." Much more of the museum's painting and sculpture, prints and illustrated books, drawings, architecture and design, photography, and film and media are on display than before. The much-loved sculpture garden has been enlarged to the original 1953 design, setting Rodin, Picasso and Tony Smith pieces among trees and reflecting pools.

ABOVE: MoMA's new gallery, designed by Japanese architect Yoshio Taniguchi, opened in November 2004 and gives the collections nearly 50 percent more space than previously.

BELOW: *La Clowness assise (The Seated Clowness)*, 1896, Henri de Toulouse-Lautrec. Diminutive Lautrec is best known as poster-maker and chronicler of the *belle époque*, and the girls of Paris's *fin de siecle* Moulin Rouge nightclub in particular.

MoMA IN THE MAKING

Abby Aldrich Rockefeller, Mary Quinn Sullivan and Lillie P. Bliss started the Museum of Modern Art's collection in 1929 with eight prints and a single drawing. Abby's enthusiasm for the works of modern artists like Matisse, van Gogh and Chagall was not shared by her husband, John D. Rockefeller, who decried the work as "unintelligible," and unfit for public viewing. The opening show of works by Cézanne, van Gogh, Gauguin and Serrat was held on the 12th floor of a building on 57th Street and 5th Avenue. After three moves to larger premises, MoMA took up its present location in 1939.

The museum's most recent incarnation showcases about as broad an interpretation of modern art as the term will stretch to include: ball-bearings, cars, motorcycles and the popular Bell helicopter share gallery space with architecture, furniture and movies, in all chronicling over 100,000 creative highlights of the 20th century.

In keeping with MoMA's tradition, the newly remodeled gallery is almost as controversial as the art the museum has exhibited. The huge space has been variously described as corporate and cavernous, as well as breathtaking and inspired.

ABOVE TOP: *The False Mirror*, 1928, René Magritte.
ABOVE: *Side 2*, 1970, by Shiro Kuramata: innovative storage from MoMA's architecture and design collection.

Times Square Then and Now

How often do you have to change a light bulb in Times Square? Every 2¹/₂ years. For more facts about the "Crossroads of the World," read on...

In the late 1800s, the harness shops and stables around 42nd and Broadway began to give way to an entertainment district which came to be known as Times Square. Theaters sprouted up all around the area, and hotels and restaurants soon followed. During the Golden Age of the Theater District in the 1920s, big-name producers like the Shubert Brothers and song-and-dance man George M. Cohan staged as many as 250 shows a year. That same decade, Prohibition brought speakeasies, gangsters and gritty Damon Runyon stories to the square.

The 1930s saw the premieres of such classic plays as *Our Town*, although many of the old vaudeville theaters were being replaced by burlesque or movie emporiums. At the end of World War II, more than two million people crowded into the square to celebrate VJ Day. By the 1960s, Times Square was in a decline that lasted another few decades, its image linked with sleaze, crime and pornography.

In one of the great revivals of the 20th century, a public and non-profit private-sector effort in the 1990s transformed the area back into a tourist mecca. New and face-lifted hotels, restaurants and entertainment now bring more than 20 million visitors a year, and the biggest draw is still the incomparable Broadway plays and musicals.

The Times Square Visitors Center at 1560 Broadway, between 46th and 47th streets, has multi-lingual facilities in addition to maps, brochures, ATMs and free internet terminals. *(See page 95 for more about Times Square.)*

ABOVE: the Great White Way: free walking tours of the area depart from the Times Square Visitors Center at 1560 Broadway between 46th and 47th streets. The center, in the historic Embassy Theater, is open daily 8am–8pm.
BELOW: Broadway babe: 1942's Miss Greenwich Village, Lauren Bacall, 21 years later at Loew's State Theatre for the world premiere of the movie *How to Marry a Millionaire.*

THE *NEW YORK TIMES*

Times Square takes its name from the *New York Times*, which used have its headquarters at the Times Tower at the intersection of 42nd Street and Seventh Avenue, now called One Times Square. Founded in 1851 as the *New-York Daily Times*, in 1896 the paper was purchased by Tennessee newspaperman Adolph S. Ochs, who in 1904 moved its offices from downtown Manhattan to what then went by the name of Longacre Square (the poster detail above is *circa* 1900.) In 1913, it relocated around the corner to 229 West 43rd Street where today, headed by Ochs' great-grandson, chariman Arthur Sulzberger, Jr, the paper continues to follow its mandate as "an independent newspaper... devoted to the public welfare" under the slogan: "All the News That's Fit to Print." Despite some recent setbacks, the *New York Times* has a weekday circulation of around 1.1 million (around 1.7 million on weekends), at least 50 percent of whom do not live in Gotham. It has also received the most awards for journalistic excellence of any newspaper in the world.

BELOW: breadlines on Broadway: during the Great Depression in the 1930s, a city newspaper opened a relief kitchen in Times Square to feed the poor and the desperate.

ABOVE: a Manhattan bargain at the TKTS booth near the Embassy Theater: discount tickets go on sale in the morning for that day's Broadway shows *(see page 52).*

LEFT: Times Square may have been cleaned up, but pickpockets and con-artists are still drawn to the big crowds on the small side streets especially. Watch your wallets.

UPPER EAST SIDE

Old, opulent, moneyed New Yorkers
glide from Millionaires Row to Museum Mile
before indulging in retail therapy
on Madison or at Bloomies

The Upper East Side's romance with wealth began in the late 1800s, when the Four Hundred – so-called because a contemporary social arbiter decreed that in all of New York there were only 400 families that mattered – moved into Fifth Avenue to cultivate roots alongside Central Park.

The homes they built were the most luxurious the city had seen – mansions and townhouses furnished like European palaces and filled with priceless art. Since then, the Carnegies, the Fricks and the Astors have moved to greener pastures, but the Upper East Side has never lost its taste for the good life, even the areas east of **Lexington Avenue**, formerly fairly affordable, now put on airs.

An air of wealth

The air of wealth is, not surprisingly, most intoxicating on the stretch of **Fifth Avenue ❶** facing the park, known to old-time New Yorkers as **Millionaires Row**. At the corner of 60th Street is J.P. Morgan's stately **Metropolitan Club ❷**, founded in 1892 after one of the financier's *nouveau riche* buddies was denied membership of the Union Club. The enormous **Temple Emanu-El ❸** cuts a brooding figure at the corner of 65th Street, where 2,500 worshippers can gather under one roof, mak-

ing this cavernous, echoing temple one of the largest reform synagogues in the world.

Up in the East 70s are a number of splendid old mansions. These include the **Harkness House** (1 East 75th Street); the château-style **Duke Mansion** (1 East 78th Street), which houses the New York University Institute of Fine Arts; and Payne Whitney's fabulous Renaissance-style *palazzo*, which now serves as a branch of the **French Embassy** (972 Fifth Avenue).

Map on page 106

LEFT: the Metropolitan Museum.
BELOW: the Upper East Side's romance with wealth began in the late 1800s.

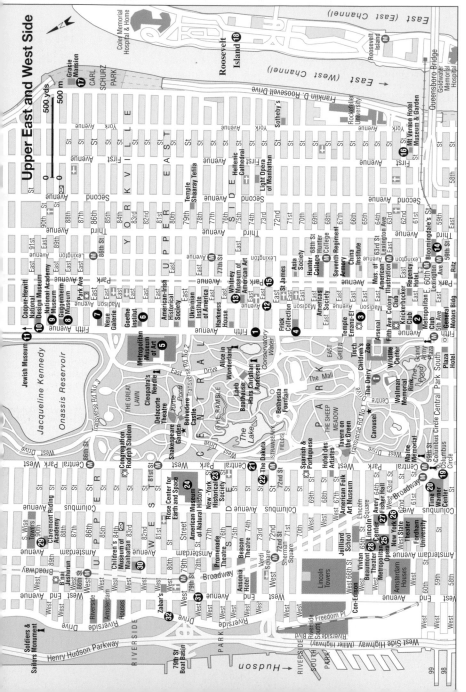

International relations are the order of the day on the Upper East Side: the former Stuyvesant mansion at 79th and Fifth is the **Ukrainian Institute**, with the **American-Irish Historical Society** farther up the street at No. 991. Between 68th and 70th streets, the classic McKim, Mead and White building at 680 Park Avenue is now home to the **Americas Society**, while the Georgian-style house at No. 686 is the **Italian Cultural Institute**.

Frick Collection

At the corner of Fifth Avenue and 70th Street, the **Frick Collection ❹** (1 East 70th Street, tel: 212-288 0700; closed Mon; charge) is showcased in the former home of steel magnate Henry Clay Frick. Frick's passion for art was surpassed only by his ruthlessness in business.

The collection includes mainly European works of the 16th to 19th centuries. The gallery is also one of the city's more successful marriages between art and setting, graced by comfortable appointments like the tranquil courtyard, and providing soft furnishings to luxuriate in when art lovers' feet are tired from standing in front of the paintings.

Museum Mile

Between 82nd and 104th streets are nine cultural treasures so lavish that this stretch of Fifth Avenue has become known as **Museum Mile** *(see photo feature on page 114)*. First is the **Metropolitan Museum of Art ❺** (82nd Street, tel: 212-535 7710; closed Mon; charge). Opened in 1874, the Met is a sprawling Gothic behemoth with displays drawn from the largest art collection in the United States. One block north at 83rd Street is the **Goethe Institut New York ❻** (1014 Fifth Avenue, tel: 212 439-8700; closed Sat, Sun; free). At 86th Street is the **Neue Galerie New York ❼** (1048 Fifth Avenue, tel: 212 628-6200; closed Tues, Wed, Thur; charge).

The **Solomon R. Guggenheim Museum ❽** (1071 Fifth Avenue at 89th Street, tel: 212 423-3500; closed Thur; charge) is worth visiting just for the building and the fantastic exhibition space. Also at 89th

The Guggenheim was one of the youngest buildings in NY (1959) to be granted landmark status.

BELOW: the Guggenheim, designed by Frank Lloyd Wright.

TIP

Leave it to Barneys, the oh-so-cool department store, to pioneer a package for the new "metrosexual" – that's a man who likes shopping, cooking and grooming …and girls instead of boys. For more about this 24-hour transformation that educates, pampers and makes over men – accommodations included – tel: 212-759 4100.

BELOW: boy studies *Girl in Window* by Roy Lichtenstein, the Whitney Museum.

is the **National Academy Museum and School of Fine Arts** ❾ (1083 Fifth Avenue, tel: 212-369 488; closed Mon, Tues; charge) with a collection of over 8,000 19th to 21st century American artworks. Next come the **Cooper-Hewitt National Design Museum** ❿ (2 East 91st Street, tel: 212-849 8300; closed Mon; charge); the **Jewish Museum** ⓫ (at East 92nd Street, tel: 212-423 3200; closed Fri and Sat; charge); the **Museum of the City of New York**, (103rd Street, tel: 212-534 1672; closed Mon; suggested charge); and **El Museo del Barrio** (at 104th Street, tel: 212-831 7272; closed Mon and Tues; suggested charge). *(For the last two, see map on page 126; also see pages 114 and 129).*

Ritz and glitz

Geographically, Fifth Avenue is only one block away from **Madison Avenue** ⓬, but in spirit they're worlds apart. Wave goodbye to the prim and proper salons of the Four Hundred, because Madison Avenue is the land of ritz and glitz – a slick marketplace custom-crafted for the

hyperactive consumer. It's a little bit mellower in the pleasant low-90s neighborhood of **Carnegie Hill** than it is in the 60s, but if you cross over from the top of Museum Mile you'll still find plenty of upscale boutiques and art galleries worth exploring.

At 75th Street is the **Whitney Museum of American Art** ⓭ (945 Madison Avenue, tel: 212-570 3676; closed Mon and Tues; charge except Fri 6–9pm). As well as displaying challenging American art, Marcel Breuer's angular, cantilevered structure is a work of art in its own right, second only to the Guggenheim among the area's most striking and original architectural expressions.

The Whitney collection was founded in 1930 by Gertrude Vanderbilt Whitney, whose tastes were for American realists like Edward Hopper and George Bellows. Since then, the museum's policy has been to acquire pieces that represent the full range of 20th-century American art, including the works of Georgia O'Keeffe, Willem de Kooning, Jackson Pollock and Jasper Johns. Every other year, the museum mounts the

Map on page 106

Whitney Biennial, a survey of the most provocative American art of the previous two years.

Serious shopping

From the Whitney Museum to 59th Street, Madison becomes a bacchanalian feast of conspicuous consumption. The names on the storefronts read like a roster of the fashion elite: Ralph Lauren, Yves Saint Laurent, Kenzo, Giorgio Armani, Prada, Emmanuel Ungaro, Calvin Klein.

Most of these megastar stores are more for browsing than serious and prolonged buying, except for those accompanied by a serious and durable bankroll. One of New York's quintessential shopping scenes is **Barneys New York** on 61st Street, which offers a chic lower-level restaurant to refresh and revive the weary wallet-wielders.

Serious shoppers may want to head straight for one of the city's retail queens: **Bloomingdale's** ⓮ on 59th Street – a minor institution that most dyed-in-the-wool New Yorkers could not live without. Style and quality are the keynotes at Bloomies. The shop is almost always crowded – and oppressively so leading up to holidays and at sale times – but if you only go to one department store in New York, this should be the one. The store is so popular, there's now a Bloomingdale's in Soho *(see page 172)*. As a reward for the kids after shopping, make a stop at Dylan's Candy Bar, a sweet dream come true just behind Bloomie's. It's owned by Ralph Lauren's daughter, Dylan.

Skipping crosstown to **Park Avenue** ⓯, the scene changes dramatically. Compared to the flashy indulgence of Madison Avenue, Park seems like a noisy version of a Parisian boulevard. A highlight is the **Regency Hotel**, a favorite for power breakfasts among big-wheel media-types, and where the library bar serves a jolly decent afternoon tea. Another is the **Colony Club** at 62nd Street, which has a stately red-brick facade, appropriate to the stately demeanor of the society women who make up its members list.

There are two fine cultural sites nearby: the **Museum of American**

Bloomies' perfume department: apparently 500 ounces of scent is sprayed here every day.

BELOW: for fans, this is one-stop shopping.

Illustration (128 East 63rd Street, tel: 212-838 2560; closed Sun, Mon) and the **China Institute** (125 East 65th Street, tel: 212-744 8181; closed Sun; charge). Both are between Park and Lexington and offer, respectively, exhibits covering the history of illustration, and those by contemporary Chinese artists.

Continuing north, it's almost impossible to miss the imposing **Seventh Regiment Armory** at Park and 66th Street. Built to resemble a medieval castle, the Armory was constructed in the 1870s, and serves as an exhibition hall for art shows.

Asian art

A few blocks up at 70th Street, the **Asia Society** (725 Park Avenue, tel: 212-517 ASIA; closed Mon; charge) houses the Rockefellers' fine collection of Asian art. It also has a performance hall, a lecture theater and a movie theater for shows and events relevant to Asian culture.

East of Park Avenue, the Upper East Side slips a few notches in the prestige department, but makes up for it with an ebullient dash of self-indulgence. Once dominated by East European immigrants, much of the area is now thoroughly gentrified, although remnants of the old German, Hungarian and Czechoslovakian quarters survive in the area known as **Yorkville**, which runs between 79th and 98th streets.

Between First and York avenues, the **Mount Vernon Hotel Museum and Garden** ⓰ (421 East 61st Street, tel: 212-838 6878; closed Mon and all of Aug; charge), is one of the few 18th-century buildings still standing proud in Manhattan. It is a marvel of survival, seeing as how it nestles under the busy 59th Street Bridge (also known as the Queensboro Bridge).

The museum has been meticulously furnished with period antiques, reminders of its former incarnation as a hotel, and gives a good indication of what life was like in the early to mid-19th century. **Sotheby's**, the high-stakes auction house frequented by art collectors from all over the world, is about 10 blocks away, near the corner of York Avenue and 72nd Street.

BELOW: the Mount Vernon Hotel Museum nestles under the Queensboro Bridge.

Mayor's house

At 88th Street and East End Avenue is **Gracie Mansion** ⓲, the mayor's official residence and another fortunate survivor from the 18th century. It was built by Scots-born Archibald Gracie as a summer home and in 1942 was first used by Mayor Fiorello LaGuardia. Before that the house served as the Museum of the City of New York. Tours can be arranged by appointment (tel: 212-570 4751 for details).

Gracie Mansion is located in **Carl Schurz Park**, a pleasant patch of green overlooking the treacherous currents of Hell Gate, where the waters of the East River and the Harlem River meet and flow together. If time allows, hitch a ride on the **Roosevelt Island Tramway** at Second Avenue and 60th Street. The riverfront views are spectacular, especially at sunset.

Roosevelt Island

Across the water by monorail tram, **Roosevelt Island** ⓭ is a 147-acre (60-hectare) respite from heavy urban living. Lying only about four minutes by tram from the East Side, this tiny (2-mile/3.2 km), tranquil, cigar-shaped island contains one main street, one church, one supermarket, a few restaurants, and the amenity of one of New York City's more recent subway extensions.

This annexation to the B&Q lines made Roosevelt a desirable residential neighborhood – witness the highly luxurious apartment complex, **Manhattan Park**, which would not look out of place on the other side of the river. As an added bonus, amenities include an indoor swimming pool, several playgrounds and five small parks – plus an active community center congregated in the ecumenical Chapel of the Good Shepherd, a landmark Victorian stone-and-brick structure that dates back to 1899.

From the specially built walkways edging the shoreline, there are panoramic views of the Upper East Side. You can also walk to a small park at the northern end and admire a stone lighthouse built in 1872. From here, Madison Avenue seems a long way away. ❑

The extension of the city subway line made Roosevelt Island a desirable place to live.

BELOW: Upper East Side slumber party.

RESTAURANTS, BARS AND CAFÉS

Restaurants

L'Absinthe
227 E. 67th St (between.
2nd and 3rd aves). Tel: 212-
794 4950. Open: L and D
Tues–Sat, D only Sun, Mon,
closed Sun July, Aug. **$$$**
The etched mirrors, pol-
ished brass and French
waiters in white aprons
are as authentic as the
classic brasserie fare.

Barbaluc
135 E. 65th St (between
Lexington and Park aves).
Tel: 212-774 1999. Open:
L and D Mon–Sat. **$$$**
The minimalist decor
makes it all the easier to
pay attention to the
unusual and satisfying
dishes, nicely compli-
mented by the wine list,
which includes 20 vin-
tages by the glass.

Coco Pazzo
23 E. 74th St (between 5th
and Madison aves). Tel: 212-
794 0205. Open: L & D
Mon–Fri, D Sat–Sun. **$$$$**
Great Tuscan food
inspired by legendary
Pino Luongo. A touch of
Upper East side attitude
sets it apart.

Daniel
60 E. 65th St (between
Madison and Park aves). Tel:
212-288 0033. Open: D only
Mon–Sat. **$$$$**
A great chef, Daniel
Boulud, presides over
this most expensive food
kingdom, but gourmets
will gladly spend for the
unique quality and ser-
vice he delivers.

Demarchelier
50 E. 86th St (at Madison
Ave). Tel: 212-249 6300.
Open: L & D daily. **$$$**

Upper East Side bistro
with a sense of style and
moderately priced all-day
prix-fix.

E.J.'s Luncheonette
1271 3rd Ave (at 73rd St).
Tel: 212-472 0600) Open: B,
L & D daily. **$**
Anybody longing for a
1950's style chrome
interior have found
home. Cash only is
accepted.

Ferrier
29 E. 65th St (between
Madison and Park aves). Tel:
212-772 9000. Open: L & D
daily. **$$$**
The pencil-thin clientele
is distractingly gorgeous,
the noise level distract-
ingly loud, the Gallic wait
staff distractingly charming. Even so, your atten-
tion might not be
so easily diverted once
the food arrives.

Gino's
780 Lexington Ave (between
60th and 61st sts). Tel: 212-
758 4466. Open: L & D daily.
$$$
Eating at this pasta
house is as much an
experience as watching
the regulars for whom
this East Side institution
(since 1945) is like a
club. A block up from
Bloomies.

La Goulue
746 Madison Ave (between
64th and 65th sts). Tel: 212-
988 8169. Open: L & D daily.
$$$
A stylish French bistro

where almost as much
time is spent looking at
who's at the next table
than eating the reason-
ably prepared dishes.

Heidelberg
1648 2nd Ave (between
85th and 86th sts). Tel: 212-
628 2332. Open: L & D daily.
$$
Yorkville's last tribute to
the glory of what was
once Germantown. The
weiner schnitzel and
dumplings are the real
thing for lovers of tradi-
tional German fare.

Jackson Hole
1270 Madison Ave (at 91st
St). Tel: 212-427 2820.
Open: B, L & D daily. **$**
Juicy rare-red, or well-
done burgers – not for
vegetarians. East side,
west side, a NY tradition.

J.G. Melon
1291 3rd Ave (at 74th St).
Tel: 212-744 0585. Open: B,
L & D daily; closes 4am. **$$**
Upper East Side main-
stay for great Bloody
Mary's and delicious
burgers.

JoJo
160 E. 64th St (between
Lexington and 3rd aves). Tel:
212-223 5656. Open: L and
D daily. **$$$$**
The rich, emerald-and-
burgundy color scheme,
luxurious fabrics, and
warm-hued tiles are all
as inviting as the menu.
JoJo's serves up one of
Manhattan's best French
food extravaganzas.

LEFT: smiling staff member, the Boat House, Central Park.

Kai's

822 Madison Ave (between 68th and 69th sts). Tel: 212-988 7277. Open: L & D daily. **$$$$**

Elegant Asian eatery, specializing in the "kaiseki" multi-course Japanese tradition.

King's Carriage House

251 E. 82nd St (between 2nd and 3rd aves). Tel: 212-734 5490. Open: L & D daily. **$$$**

Cozy, two-story colonial carriage house conversion to restaurant with pre-arranged seatings. This is a different kind of dining experience.

Lenox

1278 3rd Ave (at 73rd St). Tel: 212-772 0404. Open: L and D Mon–Sat, D only Sun. **$$$$**

Come well dressed and well groomed and you'll fit right in with the plush, clubby, wood-paneled setting. A predictable array of meat and fish dishes, but always reliable and a blessedly hushed dining room.

Mary Ann's

1503 2nd Ave (between 78th and 79th sts). Tel: 212-249 6165. Open: L & D daily. **$$**

Tasty, reliable, reasonable Mexican (one of four around town).

Paola's

245 E. 84th St (between 2nd and 3rd aves) Tel: 212-794 1890. Open: L and D Tues–Sun. **$$$**

Neighborhood high-rise dwellers love this little hidey-hole, which man-

ages to be comforting and sophisticated at the same time.

Pascalou

1308 Madison Ave (between 92nd and 93rd sts). Tel: 212-534 7522. Open: L & D Mon–Fri, Br & D Sat–Sun. **$$**

Delicious and excellent value for this expensive area, especially the prix-fix early dinner.

Saigon Grill

1700 2nd Ave (at 88th St). Tel: 212-996 4600. Open: L & D daily. **$**

Top of the Thais for taste and price; another on the Upper West Side.

Sarabeth's

1295 Madison Ave (between. 92nd and 93rd sts). Tel: 212-410 7335. Open: B, L, T, and D Mon–Fri, Br and D Sun. **$$**

Waffles, fluffy eggs and other brunch favorites keep the neighborhood lining up, while succulent roasts and other well-prepared dishes come out at dinner time. Child-friendly environs and homey decor.

Sassy's Sliders

1530 3rd Ave (at 86th St). Tel: 212-828 6900. Open: L & D daily. **$**

Famous for 99¢ bite-size burgers that are really very tasty.

Il Vagabondo

351 E. 62nd St (between 1st and 2nd aves). Tel: 212-832 9221. Open: L & D Mon–Fri, D only Sat–Sun. **$$$**

Complete with its own indoor *bocce* court, not to mention more than decent Italian food.

Vivolo

140 E. 74th St (between Park and Lexington aves). Tel: 212-737 3533. Open: L & D Mon–Fri, D only Sat–Sun. **$$$**

Charming Italian that's been serving Upper East Siders for years in a hard-to-please district.

Bars and Cafés

Fred's at Barney's, 660 Madison Ave (at 60th St), is a good coffee re-charge stop before hitting more of Madison's shopping possibilities.

Boat House in Central Park, enter at 5th Ave and 72nd St and walk north to this lively scenic spot overlooking the lake; have coffee or cocktails on a deck.

Café Subursky, Neue Galerie, 1048 5th Ave (at 86th St), is an elegant and hidden treasure

of a Viennese café. Good pastries, too.

Elaine's, 1703 2nd Ave (between 88th and 89th sts), is feted as an old-style celebrity hang-out, best enjoyed with a glass of wine at the bar.

Le Pain Quotidien, 1131 Madison Ave (between 84th and 85th sts), is good value for excellent French pastries.

Sant Ambroeus, 1000 Madison Ave (between 77th and 78th sts). Elegant espressos to marzipan and more – all is heavenly here.

RIGHT: everyone is welcome at Sarabeth's.

MUSEUM MILE

Some of the finest cultural treasures in America, housed in nine stately museums, line the East Side of Central Park

On the second Tuesday in June each year, the Museum Mile Festival closes Fifth Avenue to traffic from 79th Street, at the majestic Metropolitan Museum of Art all the way north to the Museum of the City of New York and El Museo del Barrio at 104th Street. Musicians, street performers, art activities and food stalls line the route, and all nine of the museums are open for free in what is the city's biggest block party.

The Goethe Institut / German Cultural Center, along with the Neue Galerie New York feature German art or cultural exhibits. The Solomon R. Guggenheim Museum, housed in the remarkable spiral Frank Gehry architectural masterpiece, hosts exhibitions on a grand scale. The Guggenheim has spawned an international museum "brand," with branches in Bilbao, Spain and Las Vegas.

Specializing in American art, the National Academy Museum and School of Fine Arts has tutored John Singer Sargent and Thomas Eakins, among many other talents. A branch of the Smithsonian Institute, the Cooper-Hewitt National Design Museum showcases decorative arts in a spectacular beaux-arts mansion.

For opening times and map references to all nine museums, see page 107.

Above: *Pershing Square Bridge,* 1993, Bascove, from the Museum of the City of New York.
Above Left: the Arms and Armor Gallery shows a tiny fraction of the Metropolitan Museum of Art's three million pieces.

Above: *Garden at Sainte-Adresse,* 1867, Claude Monet, is one of the thousands of paintings from the Metropolitan Museum of Art.
Right: the Cooper-Hewitt National Design Museum's textiles and wallpapers are housed in this exquisite mansion on the edge of Central Park.

JOHN D. ROCKEFELLER

Born on a farm in upstate New York, philanthropist John D. Rockefeller (1839–1937) established the Standard Oil Company in 1870 and became the country's first billionaire.

Retiring in 1911, he spent the latter part of his life giving much of his fortune to various worthy causes and created a cultural legacy that was to span three generations. His namesake and son, John D. Rockefeller, Jr (1874–1960), financed The Cloisters to house the Metropolitan Museum's medieval art collection, not only donating the tract of land it sits on but also providing land (and financing) for the Museum of Modern Art, which his wife co-founded.

His grandson, Nelson Rockefeller (1908–79), who served as governor of New York and vice president of the United States, continued the tradition of gift-giving by donating a collection of "primitive art" to the Met; another grandson, John D. Rockefeller III (1906–78), was a key financial supporter of the Lincoln Center and founded the Asia Society, to which he contributed nearly 300 works of art that form the basis of the society's collection.

BELOW: *First Night Game, Yankee Stadium, May 28, 1946*, Paolo Corvino, from the Museum of the City of New York. In addition to exhibits, the museum owns a 1851 double-decker fire engine, and organizes excellent walking tours of the city.

ABOVE: *Goldfish Vendor*, 1928, by Reuven Rubin, from *Culture and Continuity: The Jewish Journey* at the Jewish Museum.

UPPER WEST SIDE

Geographically, the Upper West Side is laid out like a pepper sandwich: it looks tempting on the outside, but it's spicy in the middle

The spicy highlights of the Upper West Side are Broadway, Columbus and Amsterdam avenues, a sort of 24-hour circus squeezed between the dignified calm of Riverside Drive and Central Park West. The entrance to all this is **Columbus Circle** ⓳ with its hustling bustle of cars and pedestrians, and the new Time Warner Center, whose asymmetric glass towers loom over the stately statue of Christopher Columbus.

The area has moved up in the world in recent years. On the south side of Columbus Circle is where the Museum of Contemporary Arts and Design will make its new home, as will the new Hearst Tower, while the gleaming **Trump International Tower and Hotel** is located on the northern end. The hotel is across from the gateway to Central Park, which is usually thronged by people playing music, eating lunch, passing through or just plain hanging out. Vendors crowd the sidewalks and Pedicab drivers troll for passengers.

The **Time Warner Center** ⓴ has made space for dozens of new stores and some very pricey restaurants, including one that is currently New York 's most expensive, Masa, where dinner for one can run to $300. **CNN**'s **studios** are on the third floor, with daily tours of the facilities open to the public (tel: 212-275 8687; large charge). On the north side of the complex at the corner of 60th Street and Broadway is the entrance to the new, eagerly awaited home of **Jazz at Lincoln Center** (tel: 212-258 9800), a world-class concert venue.

Apartment architecture

Central Park West ㉑ branches off Columbus Circle and heads up into the area's most affluent residential section. The apartment houses over-

Map on page 106

LEFT: the American Museum of Natural History.
BELOW: The Dakota.

The Lincoln Center's outdoor fountain (see photo on page 38) *is controlled by an indoor computer to the wind velocity so people don't get splattered by the spray.*

BELOW: the
Time Warner Center
has transformed
Columbus Circle.

looking the park are among the most lavish in the city, and the cross streets, especially 74th, 75th and 76th, are lined with equally splendid brownstones. At the corner of West 67th Street, the **Hotel des Artistes** has numbered Valentino, Isadora Duncan, Noel Coward and Norman Rockwell among its tenants, and is home to the **Café des Artistes**, an exquisite hide-away on the first floor with the perfect ambience for a romantic rendezvous *(see page 122)*.

The most famous apartment building on this stretch is **The Dakota ㉒** (1 West 72nd Street), built in 1884 by Henry Hardenbergh, who also designed the Plaza Hotel. At the time, people joked that it was so far outside the city, "it might as well be in the Dakota Territory," which explains the Indian's head above the main entrance.

Urban streets caught up with it soon enough, and over the years The Dakota has attracted tenants like Boris Karloff, Leonard Bernstein and Lauren Bacall, as well as being the setting for the 1968 movie *Rose-*

mary's Baby. **Strawberry Fields**, a quiet and touching knoll dedicated to the memory of John Lennon, who lived at The Dakota and was shot outside in 1980, is located across the street, a few steps into Central Park *(see page 80)*.

From 72nd Street, it's a short walk uptown, past the somber facades of the Universalist Church and the **New-York Historical Society ㉓** (2 West 77th Street, tel: 212-873 3400; closed Mon; charge), to the 79th Street entrance of the **American Museum of Natural History ㉔** (tel: 212-769 5100; charge), a gentle giant sprawing over four city blocks.

Tallest dinosaur

Guarded by an equestrian statue of Theodore Roosevelt, the museum's main entrance is actually one of many additions built around the original structure. The old facade – a stately Romanesque arcade with two ornate towers – was built in 1892 and can be seen from the 77th Street side.

For children, a visit to the museum is an absolute must, though with 40 exhibition halls housed in 23 buildings, there's plenty for grown-ups to see, too, including a 34-ton (31,000 kg) meteorite, the largest blue sapphire in the world, a full-sized model of a blue whale and a renowned anthropological collection. The world's tallest dinosaur – the 50-ft (15-meter) *Barosaurus* – is in the Theodore Roosevelt Rotunda.

The museum also includes a gigantic screen **Imax Theater**, in addition to the **Rose Center for Earth and Space**, which houses the **Hayden Planetarium**. Don't even think about doing the whole place in one shot, especially if you're on a tight schedule.

Returning to Columbus Circle, Broadway swerves west toward

Columbus Avenue and just nicks the corner of Lincoln Center, flanked on one side by Juilliard and on the other by **Fordham University**. Even to be accepted at the **Juilliard School of Music** is an honor, as the school's highly selective enrollment practice and small classrooms draw some of the most talented students in America. Trumpeter Miles Davis was among the alumni, and for a while lived just a few blocks north on West 77th Street.

Lincoln Center for the Performing Arts (tel: 212-721 6500; guided tours available) began construction in 1959 as part of a massive redevelopment plan to clean up the slums that occupied the site. Now, the Lincoln Center is one of the city's most popular venues, with attendance running at about 5 million people a year.

The black marble fountain in the middle of the plaza is surrounded by the glass-and-white-marble façades of the Lincoln Center's three main structures. The prestigious, well-regarded **Metropolitan Opera** ㉕ is directly in front, with two large

murals by Marc Chagall behind the glass wall – *Le Triomphe de la Musique* to the left, *Les Sources de la Musique* to the right. The Met is home to the Metropolitan Opera Company from September to April and the American Ballet Theater from May to July. Although marvelous, its productions and performers carry a hefty price tag.

To the left of the central fountain, the **New York State Theater** ㉖ is shared by the New York City Opera and the New York City Ballet – both more adventurous than the Met and less expensive. The third side of the main plaza is occupied by **Avery Fisher Hall** ㉗, home of the New York Philharmonic and the Mostly Mozart summer concert series.

Two secondary courtyards flank the Metropolitan Opera. The **Vivian Beaumont Theater** ㉘, on the right, is fronted by a shady plaza and reflecting pool where office workers gather for lunch. The oxidized bronze sculpture in the center of the pool is by Henry Moore. A spindly steel sculpture by Alexander Calder is near the entrance to the **Library**

Map on page 106

Catch a rising star: both the New York City Opera and the New York City Ballet perform at the State Theater.

BELOW: Hayden Planetarium at the American Museum of Natural History.

Upper West Side shopping includes upscale boutiques and a flea market on Sundays between 76 and 77th streets for funky vintage clothes.

BELOW: the Claremont has been in business for more than a century.

of the Performing Arts. The Bandshell in **Damrosch Park** is used for free concerts during the summer. These are usually conducted around lunchtime, although there are occasional performances in the early evenings as well.

After soaking up culture at Lincoln Center, cross Columbus Avenue for the **American Folk Art Museum** (2 Lincoln Square, tel: 212-595 9533; closed Mon; suggested donation). This branch of the museum *(see page 98)* has a great little gift shop.

Head uptown for some high-grade browsing. New to the area is an Uptown branch of **Kiehl's** (150 Columbus Avenue), a generations-old natural cosmetics and perfume apothecary. Hair accessory headquarters, Boyd's of Madison Avenue, has also opened a West Side branch at 309 Columbus.

There are far too many clothes stores to list by name, but those that deserve special mention are north of 68th Street. There's outrageous fashion at Betsey Johnson (248 Columbus), upscale women's wear

at Eileen Fisher (341 Columbus) and equally upscale men's wear at Frank Stella (440 Columbus). A few doors farther up is Penny Whistle Toys, with intriguing old-fashioned amusements to delight not-so-childish hearts. There's also a wide selection of funky vintage wear (and wares) at a flea market held every Sunday between 76th and 77th streets. At 84th Street, look for April Cornell's colorful blockprint fabric and dress designs for women and children alike.

Ride a white horse

For more than a century, the address of the **Claremont Riding Academy** ㉙ has been 175 West 89th Street. When the Claremont was built, there were many stables in this part of town; now it's the only one left on the island. If you want the experience of riding through Central Park with your horse's nostrils flaring and mane flying, the Claremont Academy is the place to come.

Skipping west to Amsterdam Avenue, the scene is dressed down but still trendy: restaurants, boutiques and bars with a twenty-something clientele dominate, although there are a few remaining Latino-flavored groceries and traditional neighborhood shops like West Side Kids at 84th Street, with its unusually intelligent toy inventory.

At 80th and Broadway, **Zabar's** is the gourmet store against which gourmet stores are measured. Even if you're not in the mood for buying, it's worth elbowing your way up to the counter for a free taste of all the cholesterol-soaked goodies. Just visiting the store is worthwhile for the smells alone.

At 212 West 83rd Street, the amusing **Children's Museum of Manhattan** ㉚ (tel: 212-721 1223; closed Mon and Tues; charge) is a multilevel kiddy kingdom with interactive exhibits and special

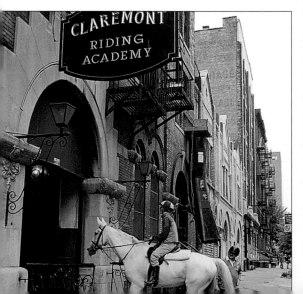

events. The noise level is high, so arrive very calm or come equipped with ear plugs.

In recent years, new meaning has been added to the term "off-Broadway," with a burgeoning Upper West Side theater scene that includes performances and literary readings at **Symphony Space**, on Broadway between 94th and 95th streets, and hits produced at the **Promenade Theatre** between 76th and 77th streets. Meanwhile, the **Beacon Theatre** (2124 Broadway at 74th Street) is a popular music venue where you might catch James Taylor (either one) one night and a gospel group the next.

Occupying the entire block between 73rd and 74th streets is the **Ansonia Hotel**, and while it's a little worn around the edges, this is still the *grande dame* of West Side apartment buildings, with a resident guest list that over the years has included Enrico Caruso, Igor Stravinsky, Arturo Toscanini and Theodore Dreiser. Although retailers now dominate the first floor, the Ansonia's mansard roof, towers and fabulous terracotta detailing still add up to a beaux-arts fantasy that captures the gaze and won't let go.

Down by the Riverside

A tour finishes nicely by taking 72nd Street west to **West End Avenue** ③, then on to Riverside Drive. North of 72nd Street, West End is affluent and strictly residential; a great place to live, but not fascinating to see. Humphrey Bogart lived for a while in Pomander Walk, an English-style mews between 94th and 95th streets, bordered by West End Avenue and Broadway.

Riverside Drive ③ winds along the edge of Frederick Law Olmsted's **Riverside Park**; the 72nd Street entrance is marked by a bronze sculpture of Eleanor Roosevelt, one of only four statues of real-life women gracing New York's parks. This is one of the most picturesque corners of Manhattan, with exceptional architecture and sweeping views of the Hudson River. At the **79th Street Boat Basin**, a few hardy Manhattanites brave the elements all year long. ❏

Map on page 106

The Ansonia Hotel was popular with singers like Caruso in part because of its architecture: thick internal walls allowed vocalists to rehearse without disturbing their neighbors.

BELOW: Riverside Park: eat here and enjoy the views.

RESTAURANTS, BARS AND CAFÉS

Restaurants

AIX
2398 Broadway (at 88th St). Tel: 212-874 7400. Open: D daily, Br Sun. **$$$$**
An outstanding corner on the Upper West Side for ambitious French cuisine. Chef Didier Virot presides over daringly creative dishes and a faithful new following.

Artie's Deli
2290 Broadway (between 82nd and 83rd sts). Tel: 212-579 5959. Open: B, L & D daily. **$$**
Lower East side Jewish deli-food, gentrified and kid-friendly.

Barney Greengrass
541 Amsterdam Ave (between 86th and 87th sts). Tel: 212-724 4707. Open: B & L Tues–Sun. **$$**

For nearly a century, an Upper West Side deli landmark for lox and other Jewish delights.

Boat Basin Café
W. 79th St on the Hudson River. Tel: 212-496 5542. Open: L & D daily May–Oct. **$$**
Hands down, the most popular Upper West Side outdoor eating spot, complete with a boisterous Thursday night bar scene. While the menu is mainly grills, unbeatable Hudson River sunsets more than make up for the food.

Burritoville
166 W. 72 St (between Broadway and Columbus Ave). Tel: 212-580 7700. Open: L & D daily. **$**
Many others try, but this is the best of the budget

Mexicans, with 10 other locations scattered around town. Good, fresh ingredients.

Café des Artistes
1 W. 67 St (between Central Park W. and Columbus Ave). Tel: 212-877 3500. Open: L & D Mon–Fri, Br & D Sat–Sun. **$$$$**
Still tantalizing after all these years, this gorgeous room where Howard Christy Chandler's "naïve nude" murals make for an unforgettable atmosphere. The French food is delicious, too.

Café Frida
368 Columbus Ave (between 77th and 78th sts). Tel: 212-712 2929. Open: L & D daily. **$$$**
Unusually rich-tasting Mexican cuisine located behind the Museum of Natural History.

Café Luxembourg
200 W. 70th St (between Amsterdam and West End aves). Tel: 212-873 7411. Open: B, L & D daily. **$$$**
This classic and consistently good French bistro is within walking distance of the Lincoln Center. Together with a classy art deco room, the Luxembourg is a long-running success.

Calle Ocho
446 Columbus Ave (between 81st and 82nd sts). Tel: 212-873 5025. Open: D Mon–Sat, Br and D Sun. **$$**

Regular young professionals dine well on innovative versions of Latin classics, washed down with what many claim are New York's best mojitos

Cosi
2160 Broadway (at 76th St). Tel: 212-595 5616. Open: B, L & D daily. **$**
A popular chain (there are nearly a dozen in Manhattan) serving flatbread sandwiches with made-to-order fillings.

Dallas BBQ
27 W. 72 St (between Central Park W. and Columbus Ave). Tel: 212-873 2004. Open: L & D daily. **$**
Hard to believe there's a chicken and ribs platter (with two side dishes) for under $10 on this block. That's why this place is so noisy and crowded.

Gray's Papaya
2090 Broadway (at 72nd St). Tel: 212-799 0243. Open: 24/7. **$**
A two hot-dog dinner with a fruit-juice chaser. Stand-up only. Whaddya expect for three bucks?

Isabella's
359 Columbus Ave (between 76th and 77th sts). Tel: 212-724 2100. Open: L & D daily, Br Sun. **$$**
Crowded all the time for all the right reasons: great food and a great location on a Columbus Avenue corner; several outdoor tables when the weather permits.

LEFT: Calle Ocho for great mojitos.

It's A Wrap
2012 Broadway (between 68th and 69th sts). Tel: 212-362 7922. Open: B, L & D daily. **$**
Sweet or savory (from peanut butter and jelly with bananas to a "Basil Wrapbone," this little storefront rolls up a treat of tasty flatbreads.

Jean Georges
1 Central Park W. (between 60th and 61st sts). Tel: 212-299 3900. Open: L & D Mon–Fri, D only Sat. **$$$$**
Chef Jean-Georges Vongerichten's four-star culinary experience in ultra-chic surroundings is an experience well worth the price.

Luzia's
429 Amsterdam Ave (between 80th and 81st sts). Tel: 212-595 2000. Open: L & D Tues–Sun, Br Sun. **$$**
Amsterdam affordable Portuguese, home-style cooking with robust and pungent flavors.

Niko's Mediterranean Grill
2161 Broadway (at 76th St). Tel: 212-873 7000. Open: B, L & D daily. **$$**
Huge menu of fish and meats at excellent value – a neighborhood find.

Ocean Grill
384 Columbus Ave (between 78th and 79th sts). Tel: 212-579 2300. Open: L & D Mon–Sat, Br & D Sun. **$$$**
Excellent West Side fish house, but the volume of noise can detract from the culinary experience – best at lunchtime.

Ollie's Noodle Shop & Grille
1991 Broadway (between 67th and 68th sts). Tel: 212-595 8181. Open: L & D daily. **$$**
Yummy Chinese "comfort-food" and delicious dim-sum. There's another Ollie's about a mile north of here.

Ouest
2315 Broadway (between 83rd and 84th sts). Tel: 212-580 8700. Open: D daily, B Sun. **$$$$**
This Upper West Side eatery is a place to be "scene." The clubby atmosphere says it all, but the food should not be missed or dismissed.

Ruby Foo's
2182 Broadway (at 77th St). Tel: 212-724 6700. Open: L & D daily. **$$$**
Fun, delicious, Asian food extravaganza; this calm restaurant is much more appealing than its sister location in busy Times Square.

Tavern on the Green
Central Park W. (between 66th and 67th sts). Tel: 212-873 3200. Open: L & D daily, Br Sun. **$$$$**
Glitzy, but beautiful, parkland fantasy with rooms decorated in fairytale style. Some consider it a must; others merely touristy.

Zen Palate
2170 Broadway (between 76th and 77th sts). Tel: 212-501 7768. Open: L & D daily. **$$**
One of three Zen vegetarians with loyal followers.

RIGHT: Ouest has stylish food to match its clientele.

Alice's Tea Cup, 102 W. 73rd St (between Columbus and Amsterdam aves), is a whimsicall place for light lunch, tea and intimate chats.
Edgar's Café, 255 W. 84th St (between Broadway and West End Ave). Poe once haunted this neighborhood as a New Yorker. A hideaway in his memory serves light fare, teas and coffees.
French Roast, 2340 Broadway (at 85th St). French Roast is a step above the usual coffee shop for breakfast, lunch and more. Open 27/7.
The Ginger Man is a fixture in the Lincoln Center area for drinks and food; lots of celebrity spotting on the menu too.
Krispy Kreme, 141 W. 72nd St (between Columbus and Amsterdam aves), serves sinful, sweet donuts.
Le Pain Quotidien, 50 W. 72nd St, is one of several Belgian farmhouse-style communal patisseries serving coffee, eggs, breads, spreads and more.
Popover Café, 551 Amsterdam Ave (between 86th and 87th sts), is a great place for a breakfast or lunch meeting.
Stone Rose, 10 Columbus Circle, is a bar located in the soaring Time Warner Center with intoxicating views.

PRICE CATEGORIES
Prices for a three-course dinner per person with half a bottle of wine:
$ = under $20
$$ = $20–$45
$$$ = $45–$60
$$$$ = over $60

AROUND HARLEM

Fidel Castro and The Beatles couldn't wait to visit. Artists and professionals are moving into historic brownstones. The first Harlem Renaissance was in the 1920s, but a new one may be coming up fast

An Alabama-born, African-American professor recalled being an 18-year-old in Europe in the late 1950s. He was asked repeatedly about Harlem, a place he'd never been in his life. His inquisitors didn't want to hear this. The man was black; he lived in the United States; therefore he had to be from Harlem. What they didn't know was that the only thing he "knew," was based on the same stereotypes shared by the Europeans; that Harlem was full of naughty nightlife, devilish dancing, mind-blowing music, dangerous dudes and wicked women.

Harlem heritage

That heritage is palpable up and down the neighborhood's avenues. But there was, and is, much more to Harlem. As well as the area's well-documented attractions, urban pioneers driven out of the rest of Manhattan by rising prices have recently discovered Harlem's handsome buildings – even former president Bill Clinton has an office on 125th Street. These buildings are now being restored to their former elegance, and real-estate prices are climbing. Harlem is recapturing some of its classy heyday.

Geographically there is an **East Harlem** (Madison Avenue to the East River and sometimes called **Spanish Harlem**), **Central Harlem** (Fifth Avenue to St Nicholas Avenue), whose citizens are overwhelmingly African-American, and **West Harlem**, which extends to Riverside Drive. In general, West Harlem has a larger population of white residents and includes **Morningside Heights** and **Hamilton Heights**. Farther up, and close to Manhattan's northern tip, is **Washington Heights**, an ethnically mixed area with fine cultural treasures.

Map on page 126

LEFT: the Apollo still holds its famous Amateur Night.
BELOW: 125th Street, Harlem's main drag.

Originally the home of Native Americans, Harlem was settled by the Dutch in 1658 as Nieuw Haarlem, after the city in the Netherlands. In 1664, it fell to the British.

Basically still farmland in the early 1800s, Harlem became New York City's first upscale suburb when Alexander Hamilton, the country's Secretary of the Treasury, built a country home called Hamilton Grange (it still stands today, although not in its original spot). The exclusivity was punctured in 1837 by the opening of the Harlem River Railroad, followed by the area's 1873 annexation to New York City, the extension of the elevated rapid transit lines in 1880 and, in 1904, by the completion of the IRT Lenox Avenue subway.

All of this made Harlem more accessible, which in turn led to an influx of immigrants. In the early 1900s, black people began moving into homes on 135th Street, west of Lenox Avenue. From then on, Harlem became a place where Americans of African descent made their presence felt. Poet Langston Hughes *(see page 129)* and writer Zora Neale Hurston, along with musicians Duke Ellington, Louis Armstrong and Bessie Smith, all launched their careers here in the 1920s and '30s, during what was termed the Harlem Renaissance.

Meet the Beatles

Later, Harlem, or more precisely, a restaurant called Sherman's Barbeque at 151st Street and Amsterdam Avenue, was where music producer Phil Spector's all-girl singing group, the Ronettes, brought the Beatles in 1964. It was the Fab Four's first American tour, and their Midtown hotel, the Plaza, was surrounded by hysterical fans.

By sneaking out of a side door and escaping up to Sherman's, the Beatles were able to breathe easy,

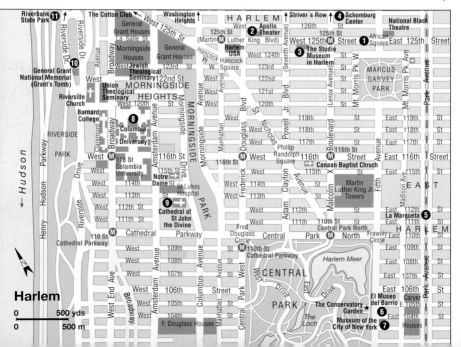

Harlem

play the jukebox, and relax with like-minded musicians. More headlines were made in the mid-1970s when Cuba's Fidel Castro took up residence in Harlem's Hotel Teresa, where he brought in live chickens and made his own food for fear he might be poisoned while attending UN functions in Midtown.

That Harlem no longer exists; neither does the Harlem historically portrayed in the press as a place where every other resident is a drug pusher. What does exist is a diverse community where Irish, Italian, Dominican, Haitian, Puerto Rican, West African and other residents sometimes live side by side, and where ongoing renovations are attracting increasing numbers of middle-class African-American and white professionals and artists.

Nevertheless, there are some areas where inexperienced tourists should go only with a knowledgeable guide. The easiest way to experience this part of the city safely is to take an organized tour, or contact the Greater Harlem Chamber of Commerce (tel: 212-862 7200).

Main drag

A good place to begin is Harlem's famous main drag, **125th Street ❶**. It's Fifth Avenue and Times Square compressed into one river-to-river street, a street where every north–south Manhattan subway stops and several north–south buses cross over. A main shopping area, it's vibrant with throngs of people, street vendors, and music blasting from the nearby record stores. Officially, 125th Street is known as **Martin Luther King Boulevard**.

Several of Harlem's important attractions are here; most notable is the **Apollo Theater ❷**. This is where the presence of singers Billie Holiday, Mahalia Jackson, Dinah Washington and Ella Fitzgerald can still be felt, especially during the Apollo's weekly Amateur Night. (Among other stars whose careers have been launched here are Michael Jackson and Boyz ll Men.)

The experience of seeing rising young talent, while at the same time being a part of the highly responsive, and sometimes harshly critical Apollo audience, is not to be missed.

Map on page 126

The Studio Museum in Harlem has contemporary works as well as extensive archives.

BELOW: Striver's Row, in the St Nicholas Historic District.

*Hoo-ray for
Hollywood,
Harlem-style.*

BELOW: Sunday at
the Abyssinian
Baptist Church.

For information about tours or current shows, call 212-749 5838. For more nightlife, there's **Showman's Café**. And, yes, there is a **Cotton Club**, although it's not the original on 142nd Street; this one is at 565 125th Street, west of the Apollo.

The **Studio Museum in Harlem ❸** (144 West 125th Street, tel: 212-864 4500; closed Mon, Tues and weekend mornings; charge) is where you'll find changing exhibitions as well as a permanent collection of contemporary paintings and sculpture by artists of the African diaspora. It also has extensive archives, including the work of James Van Der Zee, who photographed Harlem's jazzy dancing days of the 1920–40s. The Studio Museum also holds workshops and shows films.

A short distance away, at 2035 Fifth Avenue, the **National Black Theatre** is an innovative performing arts complex.

Name change

From 125th Street in Central Harlem, walk up one of the neighborhood's north–south streets, like **Malcolm X Boulevard** (Lenox Avenue) or **Adam Clayton Powell Jr Boulevard** (Seventh Avenue). Malcolm X Boulevard is probably Central Harlem's best known street after 125th Street.

Several landmarks are located along here, including the **Schomburg Center for Research in Black Culture ❹** at 135th Street (tel: 212-491 2200; closed Sun and Mon). Here lie the ashes of the acclaimed poet Langston Hughes. And what more fitting spot than this library, a gold mine of books, records, films and photos about black Americans in general and Harlem in particular, and where Alex Haley did much of the research for his book, later a TV epic, *Roots*.

From here it's a short distance to the **St Nicholas Historic District**, four rows of 19th-century townhouses between 137th and 139th streets, known as **Striver's Row** in honor of the professionals who moved here in the 1920s. Along the side streets are evidence of the regeneration being achieved by this new era of professionals.

On a Sunday morning in Central Harlem, don't miss the opportunity to attend services at a local church. The fervor of the singing and the response of the congregations is stirring; it's a spiritual experience that is hard to replicate elsewhere.

To judge by the diversity of the congregation who show up at the **Canaan Baptist Church** on 116th Street every Sunday morning, visitors from all over the world have been making this discovery already, as non-New Yorkers are as much in evidence as Harlemites.

Harlem churches have long played a significant role in the political, economic and cultural life of the community. In addition to the Canaan Baptist Church, other establishments like the **Abyssinian Baptist Church**, the **St Philip's Episcopal Church** and the **Mother AME Zion Church** have all been socially and politicaly influential since the early 1900s.

Organized gospel tours are conducted by Harlem Spirituals/New York Visions (tel: 212-391 0900). Sometimes lunch is included.

East Harlem

Traditionally, this is considered **Spanish Harlem**, its residents by and large having close ties with Puerto Rico. But East Harlem also includes a strong Haitian presence, as well as the remnants of an old Italian section along First and Pleasant avenues, above 114th Street. Frank Sinatra enjoyed the pizzas at Patsy's, 2287 First Avenue (between 117th and 118th streets) so much that it's said he used to have stacks of them flown across the country to his mansion in California.

One of the most colorful spots is **La Marqueta ❺**, located under the elevated train lines on Park Avenue, from 111th to 116th streets. Mangos, papayas, cassavas, tamarinds, exotic herbs and other imported tropical staples are displayed here, along with freshly grown regional produce. Fridays and Saturdays are the best time to come and shop – or just to stroll around and browse.

Two other East Harlem attractions are part of the famous "Museum Mile": **El Museo del Barrio ❻** at Fifth Avenue and 104th Street, and

Map on page 126

El Museo del Barrio, at Fifth Avenue and 104th Street, is the only museum in New York devoted to Latin-American art. The Museum of the City of New York, one block south on 103rd Street, has exhibits from more than 300 years of local history, and organizes great walking tours.

BELOW: Columbia University, where numerous Pulitzer Prize winners were educated.

Langston Hughes

Born February 1, 1902, in Joplin, Missouri, jazz poet James Langston Hughes' novels, columns and plays made him a luminary of the Harlem Renaissance of the 1920s and 30s. Hughes' earthy dialect and sketches of black life were often controversial among members of his own race. He said, "I knew only the people I had grown up with, and they weren't people whose shoes were always shined, who had been to Harvard, or who had heard Bach." Hughes published more than 60 books before he died in 1967. His ashes are held in a place of honor in the Schomburg Center on Harlem's 135th Street.

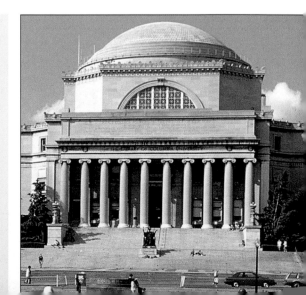

TIP

The Greater Harlem Chamber of Commerce is at 200 West 136th Street, tel: 212-862 7200. There's also a small information bureau with maps and details of attractions on 125th Street, not far from the Apollo Theater. The excellent Harlem Week/Harlem Jazz & Music Festival takes place in August.

BELOW: the medieval Cloisters are worth the trip north to Washington Heights.

one block south at 103rd Street, the **Museum of the City of New York** ❼ (*see pages 108 and 114.*)

West Harlem

West Harlem extends from around Amsterdam Avenue to Riverside Drive, taking in the Convent Avenue and Sugar Hill areas, along with Hamilton and Morningside Heights. Many of Harlem's white residents live in this district, which encompasses **Columbia University** ❽ and **Barnard College** (for women) as well as the Jewish Theological and Union Theological seminaries. All these are located on or near upper Broadway.

At 112th Street and Amsterdam Avenue, the impressive **Cathedral of St John the Divine** ❾ is home to the city's largest Episcopal congregation; it's also said to be the world's second-largest Gothic cathedral. At Riverside Drive and 120th Street, the non-denominational **Riverside Church** has the world's largest bell carillon atop its 22-story tower. Both churches host special religious and cultural events throughout the year.

Grant's Tomb ❿ at 122nd Street is the final resting place of Civil War general and former president Ulysses S. Grant and his wife, Julia; it was dedicated in 1897 as a national park site and is said to be inspired by Les Invalides in Paris, which contains Napoleon's tomb.

Farther north on Riverside Drive, Manhattan's only state park opened in 1993 on the 28-acre (11-hectare) roof of a former sewage treatment plant stretching along the Hudson River between 137th and 145th streets. Today, the swimming pools, skating rink and spectacular views of **Riverbank State Park** ⓫ are enjoyed by an estimated 3 million people every year.

Continuing north, West Harlem has numerous other historical attractions, including the lovely **Morris-Jumel Mansion** (65 Jumel Terrace at 160th Street, east of St Nicholas Avenue, tel: 212-923 8008; closed Mon and Tues; charge).

George Washington's headquarters during the American Revolution, the Palladian-style home was visited by Queen Elizabeth II and

Prince Philip during the American Bicentennial of 1976. Adjacent to the mansion, **Jumel Terrace** is a series of 20 beautifully presented row houses built around the turn of the 19th century; the famous singer and activist Paul Robeson had a home nearby on Sylvan Terrace.

Cultural complex

Audubon Terrace, back on Broadway between West 155th and 156th streets, is lined by stately neoclassical buildings built between 1905 and 1923 as a cultural complex. Among these is the **American Academy and Institute of Arts and Letters** (tel: 212-368 5900), whose members have included luminaries from Mark Twain to Toni Morrison; the **American Numismatic Society** (tel: 212-234 3130; closed Sun am, Mon; free), with exhibits of old money; and the **Hispanic Society of America** (tel: 212-926 2234; closed Sun am, Mon; free), with a collection including El Greco and Goya.

Once mainly Irish, today the far-northern **Washington Heights** area is pleasantly and ethnically mixed,

Map on page 126

as Dominicans, Puerto Ricans, Haitians, Irish and others claim it for their own. (The largest Jewish educational institution in the city, **Yeshiva University**, is located on West 185th Street).

Frederick Law Olmsted designed **Fort Tryon Park** (62 acres/ 25 hectares) on West 192nd Street, which includes a branch of the Metropolitan Museum of Art. Here, too, is an inspiring spot, **The Cloisters** (tel: 212-923 3700; closed Mon; charge), French and Spanish monastic quarters. A 12th-century chapter house, the Fuentaduena Chapel and a Gothic and a Romanesque chapel were shipped from Europe and reassembled here, stone by stone. The prize of the medieval collection is the six handwoven 15th-century Unicorn Tapestries.

Farther north, at 204th Street and Broadway in the area called **Inwood**, is the **Dyckman Farmhouse Museum** (tel: 212-304 9422; closed Mon; charge). The Dyckman is a two-story Dutch colonial dwelling built in 1785 and restored in 1915 *(see page 169).* ❏

GOD'S LOVE WE DELIVER

RESTAURANTS

Amy Ruth's
113 W. 116th St (between Lenox and 7th aves). Tel: 212-280-8779. Open: L and D daily. **$**
The restaurant attracts political, sports and entertainment luminaries, but the big pull is the Southern food.

El Rincón Boricua
158 E. 119th St (between 3rd and Lexington aves). Tel: 212-534 9400. Open: L daily. **$**
Tender barbecued pig dished up with rice,

beans and plaintains. This is Puerto Rican home cooking at its best.

Miss Maude's Spoonbread Too
547 Lenox Ave (between 137th and 138th sts). Tel: 212-690 3100. Open: L and D daily. **$**
Miss Maude's is one of Harlem's most inviting restaurants. Most diners come for the fried chicken, Southern style.

Rao's
455 E. 144th St (at Pleasant Ave). Tel: 212-722 6709.

Open: D only Mon–Sat. **$$$$**
A small, southern Italian that's so hard to get into it might as well be a club; celebrity clientele make headlines here.

Sylvia's
328 Malcolm X Boulevard (Lenox Ave between 126th and 127th sts). Tel: 212-996 0660. Open: D only Mon–Sat. **$$**
Headquarters for Southern soul food, Harlem style. It's a good idea to make a reservation.

Sugar Hill Bistro
458 W. 145th St (between Amsterdam and Convent aves). Tel: 212-491 5505.

Open: D daily. **$$$**
A four-story brownstone serving Harlem-American food, including a Sunday gospel brunch.

Terrace in the Sky
400 W. 119th St (between Amsterdam Ave and Morningside Dr). Tel: 212-666 9490. Open: L Mon–Fri, D Tues–Sat, Br Sun. **$$$$**
The ultimate Uptown romance. Food, views, atmosphere: the sky's the limit.

● ● ● ● ● ● ● ● ● ● ● ● ●

Prices for a three-course dinner per person with half a bottle of wine: **$** *under $20,* **$$** *$20–$45,* **$$$** *$45–$60,* **$$$$** *over $60*

DOWNTOWN

A guide to Lower Manhattan and the
Outer Boroughs, with principal sites
cross-referenced by number to the maps

Downtown and uptown New York are very different places. Uptown, where life can scream with a neon fury and adrenalin is high, passions run hot and furious. Downtown's attitude is cool – if you don't count the frenzy of the Stock Market at closing time. Some of the oldest sites in the city are located here, but some of New York's newest hotspots are here, too.

Downtown, nightclubs spring up as fast as the beats per minute, and close again quicker than you can change your dancing shoes. Restaurants are fashionable, then fade, at a pace which only the *gastroscenti* can follow. Downtown is Alphabet City – Avenues A, B, C and D – NoHo, NoLita and SoFi: a large-scale map of Downtown looks like a kidnapper's ransom note. In a few years these neighborhoods will be so familiar the letters will be all the same size, as are those in the areas previously written as SoHo (South of Houston) and TriBeCa (Triangle Below Canal). The newest acronym skips across the river into Brooklyn: DUMBO, which stands for Down Under Manhattan Bridge Overpass.

Lately, Downtown has attracted the city's new media community, ranging from the Flatiron District above Union Square to Soho and Lower Manhattan (skirting Chinatown and the Village), and known as Silicon Alley. The southern part of Downtown is the center of financial New York, where Wall Street banks keep tabs on the money, before the Meatpacking District soaks it away again in high-class boutiques and restaurants. Battery Park City is a residential complex whose riverside walkways inspired the development of the Hudson River Park, a welcome green space stretching north from the tip of Manhattan all the way up the west side of town.

The Outer Boroughs – Brooklyn, Queens, Staten Island and the Bronx – are included here, too. This is where the hot dog was born and where the newest arts scene has decamped to and developed, as rising prices in Manhattan make "over the river" increasingly attractive. Art galleries, sculpture gardens, museums and wildlife refuges attract increasing numbers of New Yorkers and visitors alike.

"The Bronx? No thonx," said poet Ogden Nash. Be surprised.   ❑

LEFT: icons and ephemera in NoLita.

GRAMERCY PARK TO CHELSEA

Genteel Gramercy, SoFi, in the shadow of the Flatiron Building, wired-for-action Union Square and gallery-hopping Chelsea are some of Downtown's most innovative neighborhoods

The area from Madison Park to Union Square – loosely referred to as the Flatiron District – is home to writers, photographers, ad agencies, publishers, new restaurants and new media firms. Chelsea has a thriving art gallery scene, a thriving gay scene, and a riverside sports and entertainment development that attracts an estimated 8,000 visitors a day. Only Gramercy Park maintains its usual well-heeled reserve.

Gramercy Park

On the East Side between 20th and 21st streets, **Gramercy Park ❶** is a genteel square that punctuates Lexington Avenue and Irving Place with a welcome leafy greenery. This is Manhattan's sole private park, established in the 1830s. Only residents of the surrounding townhouses have keys, although guests at the **Gramercy Park Hotel** (currently being transformed into an ultra-hip hostelry) are allowed in.

On the park's southern perimeter, look at the elaborate 19th-century facades of the **National Arts Club**, home to the Poetry Society of America, and the **Players Club** next door, where members have included leading American theater actors, as well as Mark Twain, Winston Churchill and Frank Sinatra.

Irving Place, which Samuel Ruggles named for his friend Washington Irving, runs south from Gramercy Park to 14th Street, and is lined by pretty brownstones that continue with particular charm along East 19th Street. At 18th Street, **Pete's Tavern** is a dark, historic bar where the atmosphere reeks of speakeasies and spilled beer. Short-story scribe O. Henry is said to have written *The Gift of the Magi* here. Down at 15th Street, **Irving Plaza** is one of the city's best

Map on page 136

LEFT: the Flatiron Building was erected in 1902.
BELOW: the the Greenmarket in Union Square.

The land that makes up the Chelsea Historic District (between Eighth and Tenth avenues from 19th to 23rd streets), was inherited in 1813 by Clement Clarke Moore. He sold the land but imposed restrictions that kept its elegance intact. Moore is better known for writing A Visit from St Nicholas, *which became the modern-day* 'Twas the Night Before Christmas.

small venues for rock music performances. Drifting northward, the often overlooked green space wedged between Madison Avenue and Broadway from 23rd to 26th streets is **Madison Square Park ❷**.

A block south, the **Metropolitan Life Insurance Tower ❸**, completed in 1909, was briefly considered the world's tallest building at 54 stories. Until its recent incarnation as a place to meet and greet like-minded fashion and media types in a number of watering holes, however, the Madison Park area was noted mainly for its proximity to one of Manhattan's favorite architectural whimsies, which rises from the corner where Broadway crosses Fifth Avenue below 23rd Street.

Flatiron District

The triangular Fuller Building raised eyebrows and hopes for a bright future when it was erected in 1902. It soon became known as the

Flatiron Building ❹ because of its distinctive shape. The neighborhood below it has been dubbed **SoFi**, which stands, not surprisingly, for **S**outh o**f** **Fl**atiron.

From here, Broadway follows the old "Ladies Mile," a shopping route that, during the latter part of the 19th century, ranged along Broadway and Sixth Avenue, from 23rd Street down to 9th Street. Lord & Taylor, which began as a small shop Downtown on Catherine Street and opened on the southwest corner of Broadway and 20th Street in 1872, moved Uptown to 38th and Fifth in 1914, where it is still open for business. At 28 East 20th Street is the **Theodore Roosevelt Birthplace ❺** (*see page 169*).

Union Square

Named for the busy convergence of Broadway and Fourth Avenue, **Union Square ❻** sits comfortably between 17th and 14th streets. A

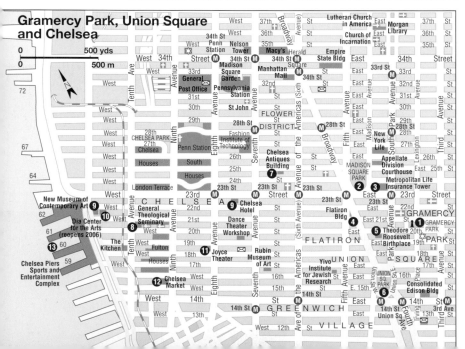

Gramercy Park, Union Square and Chelsea

stylish prospect in the mid-1850s, by the turn of that century it was more or less deserted by genteel residents and became a thriving theater center. Eventually the theaters moved north to Midtown and the square became best known for political meetings – in the years preceding World War I, anarchists and socialists regularly addressed sympathizers here.

Rallies continued to draw crowds throughout the 1930s, but finally even radicalism dwindled, and the area went into a decline that lasted until the 1980s.

Today, Union Square brims with life, a resurgence that might be attributed to the **Greenmarket**, which brings farmers and their produce to the northern edge of the square four days a week. While there are other greenmarkets in other parts of the city, this is the biggest and the best. In a recent move, *Wired* magazine made Union Square fit for Wi-Fi, and Manhattanites with portable computers can be seen leisurely surfing the Net near the market porters.

Food for the soul can be found at the **Union Square Theatre**, 100 East 17th Street (tel: 212-505 0700), an historically appropriate locale in light of Union Square's 19th-century theatrical past.

Chelsea

West of Fifth Avenue to the Hudson River, from 14th up to about 30th Street, Chelsea borders the midtown Garment District and includes the **Flower District**. In the spring and summer, these blocks are crowded with leafy vegetation and bathed in a sweet loamy odor.

Fifth Avenue between 14th and 23rd streets has stores like Emporio Armani and Paul Smith, while Avenue of the Americas (**Sixth Avenue**) is lined by modern chains that have continued the fashion business by moving into the historic Ladies Mile buildings.

One of Chelsea's most popular shopping arenas is the **flea market** on Sixth between 25th and 27th streets. It's only open weekends, so if you have a yen for vintage stuff during the week, then head for the

To visit a Chelsea art gallery on Monday, you need to make a big noise: most of them are closed.

BELOW LEFT:
Chelsea Market.
BELOW RIGHT:
genteel Gramercy.

The lobby of the infamous Chelsea Hotel; artists who have lived here since 1909 include Thomas Wolfe, Arthur Miller, Jack Kerouac and Brendan Behan.

BELOW: shop for vintage va-va-voom at Chelsea's flea market.

Chelsea Antiques Building ❼ at 110 West 25th between Sixth and Seventh avenues.

The **Chelsea Historic District** consists of the blocks between Eighth and Tenth avenues from 19th to 23rd streets. The lovely **General Theological Seminary ❽** was established on Ninth Avenue in the mid-19th century. Among its best buildings are the Chapel of the Good Shepherd and St Mark's Library. The Seminary's tree-lined quadrangle can be visited from noon–3pm every day except Sunday, providing a calm oasis from the urban streets.

A walk west on long, busy 23rd Street (or better yet, a ride on the M23 crosstown bus) takes you past the **Chelsea Hotel ❾** *(see page 219)*. One of the city's most famous residential hotels, this is where Andy Warhol filmed *Chelsea Girls* in 1967 and where punk-rocker Sid Vicious murdered his girlfriend before dying of a drug overdose. A recent renovation has made it a reasonable, if eccentric, place to stay. There's a cool basement bar, too. By

all means have a look at the unusual artwork in the lobby (done by guests and changed at a whim), or stop in for a drink or a meal in the restaurant El Quijote *(see page 140)*.

An abandoned freightline trestle stretching some 20 blocks through Chelsea called the **High Line** is a treasured greenway which will soon be improved parkland.

Chelsea culture

In the early days of moving pictures, the Famous Players Film Studio was located on West 26th Street; today, the **Silver Screen Studios** at Chelsea Piers *(see page 139)* are where such popular TV shows as *Law and Order* have been filmed.

Once Soho became overrun with boutiques and restaurants, gallery owners moved north to Chelsea. Although galleries are scattered throughout the neighborhood, 22nd Street between Tenth and Eleventh avenues is particularly packed, spearheaded by the **Chelsea Art Museum**. Gallery hopping is popular on Thursday nights, when most venues keep later hours, but note that all art galleries tend to be closed on Mondays.

A popular Chelsea arts destination, the **Dia Center for the Arts ❿** is undergoing renovation until 2006. However the **New Museum for Contemporary Art** (tel: 212-219 1222; closed Sun and Mon, open Thur until 8pm), a hotbed of activity with readings, performance art and book signings, has moved to 556 West 22nd Street until its ultra-modern Bowery building is ready in 2006. The **Rubin Museum of Art** at 150 West 17th Street, is Chelsea's newest museum, opened in 2004.

Walking east on 20th and 21st streets from Tenth Avenue brings you to one of the Chelsea Historic District's most scenic stretches of Greek Revival and Anglo-Italianate townhouses. A block farther south,

between Tenth and Eleventh, **The Kitchen** (512 West 19th Street) is a long-standing center where video, dance and performance art are staple fare. The **Joyce Theater ⓫** (175 Eighth Avenue at 19th Street) presents some of the city's most innovative dance performances, from Spanish Gypsy flamenco to Native American troupes. Other work is staged at the always-interesting **Dance Theater Workshop** (219 West 19th Street).

Around here, the neighborhood starts melding into the West Village – or, more accurately, the cool and gritty Meatpacking District that stretches west along 14th Street to the Hudson (*see page 147*).

Before making the scene there, stop by the **Chelsea Market ⓬**, 75 Ninth Avenue between 15th and 16th streets. An ambitious renovation transformed what were 18 buildings erected between 1883 and 1930 into a single indoor food market, with a waterfall, sculpture, and more than 20 stores selling specialty foods and home design items as well as housing tempting places to eat.

Piering into the distance

The last stop for crosstown buses is **Pier 62**, the start of the **Chelsea Piers ⓭** Sports and Entertainment Complex (tel: 212-336 6500) that sprawls south along the Hudson River from 23rd to 17th Street.

A Fitness Club is open to members only, but there are several other facilities the public can use for a fee. In addition to Pier 62, which has two outdoor roller rinks and a public "pier park," the development includes **Pier 61**, with two 24-hour ice skating rinks and a riverside restaurant; and **Pier 59**, which offers a four-story golf driving range and a brewery pub/restaurant with views across the river.

The transformation of these dilapidated piers – which served the Cunard Line until 1930 – has given new access to the Hudson River. Passenger boats (World Yacht, tel: 212-630 8100, or Spirit Lines, tel: 866-399 8439) offer day and evening cruises. The walkway weaves around the piers for more than a mile, providing riverside views and good sunsets. ❑

The Rubin Museum of Art on West 17th Street is dedicated to the art of the Himalayas.

BELOW: all-night ice skating at the Sky Rink is just one of the activites offered at Chelsea Piers.

RESTAURANTS, BARS AND CAFÉS

Restaurants

L'Acajou
53 W. 19th St (between 5th and 6th aves). Tel: 212-645 1706. Open: L and D Mon–Fri, D only Sat. **$$**
When the craving for French brasserie food hits, try this neighborhood institution.

Bar Jamon
125 E. 17th St (at Irving Pl). Tel: 212-253 2773. Open: L & D daily. **$$$**
Lusty Spanish *tapas* and snacks served up by Mario Batali.

Blue Smoke
116 E. 27 St (between Park and Lexington aves). Tel: 212-447 7733. Open: L & D daily, Br Sun. **$$**
Great BBQ (Jazz Standard club downstairs), plus a kids' jazz brunch.

Blue Water Grill
31 Union Sq W. (at 16th St). Tel: 212-675 9500. Open: L & D daily. **$$$**
Big beautiful fish house; excellent seafood in a converted bank building.

Bright Food Shop
216 8th Ave (at 21st St). Tel: 212-243 4433. Open: B, L & D daily. **$**
Quirky little Asian/ Mexican combo joint.

Chat 'n Chew
10 E. 16th St (between 5th Ave and Union Sq). Tel: 212-243 1616. Open: L & D daily. Br Sat–Sun. **$**
American comfort food and prices to match in a funky retro-decor room.

Chelsea Bistro
358 W. 23rd St (between 8th and 9th aves). Tel: 212-727 2026. Open: D daily. **$$$**

Romantic and French. with a garden in summer and a fireplace in winter. What could be sweeter?

Chop't Creative Salad
24 E. 17th St (between 5th Ave and Broadway). Tel: 646-336 5523. Open: L & D daily. **$**
It's fun to watch as selected salad bar ingredients are minced and tossed into big bowls for eat-in or take-out.

Craft
43 E. 19th St (between. Broadway and Park Ave S.) Tel: 212-780 0880. Open: L & D Mon–Fri, D only Sat–Sun. **$$$$**
The menu is split into sections (vegetable, sides, meat, and fish) and you concoct your own meal – a nightmare for the indecisive, but wildly popular otherwise.

El Quijote
226 W. 23rd St (between 7th and 8th aves). Tel: 212-929 1855. Open: L & D daily. **$$**
Old-time Spanish mainstay beneath the Chelsea Hotel, with a great bargain: the lobster dinner. Be patient.

Empire Diner
210 10th Ave (at 22nd St). Tel: 212-243 2736. Open 24/7.
Chrome/retro decor and a decent menu makes this a great place while doing the Chelsea art gallery or club scene.

Fleur de Sel
5 E. 20th St (between 5th Ave and Broadway). Tel: 212-460 9100. Open: L Mon–Sat, D daily. **$$$$**
Elegant Flatiron French bistro with unique atmosphere and heavenly food.

Friend of a Farmer
77 Irving Pl (between 18th and 19th sts). Tel: 212-477 2188. Open: B, L & D Mon–Fri, Br & D Sat–Sun. **$$**
It feels like a Vermont bed-and-breakfast in this cozy and casual restaurant serving hearty portions of American fare. Great for families.

Gramercy Tavern
42 E. 20th St (between Broadway and Park Ave). Tel: 212-477 0777. Open: L Mon–Fri, D daily. **$$$$**
The Gramercy Tavern is on everyone's Top Ten list for everything: food, service, great New American cuisine and the handsome high-ceilinged dining room.

Les Halles
411 Park Ave S. (between. 28th and 29th sts). Tel: 212-679 4111. Open: L and D daily. **$$$**
This steakhouse packs in the crowds who come to soak up the French atmosphere and deliberate over the expansive menu of classics.

Le Madri
168 W. 18th St (at 7th Ave). Tel: 212-727 8022.

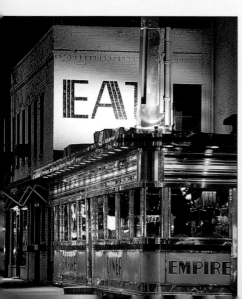

LEFT: the Empire Diner is open 24/7.

Open: L Mon–Fri, D daily.
$$$$
The Tuscan haute cuisine of Pino Luongo fame is worth the tab.

Mandler's
26 E. 17th St (between 5th Ave and Broadway). Tel: 212-255 8999. Open: B, L & D daily. **$$**
Calling all sausage lovers – this is the place.

Mary Ann's
116 8th Ave (at 16th St). Tel: 212-633 0877. Open: L & D daily. **$$**
Bueno Mexican; other locations around town.

Mesa Grill
102 5th Ave (between 15th and 16th sts). Tel: 212-807 7400. Open: L Mon–Fri, D daily, Br Sat–Sun. **$$$**
Sophisticated Southwestern fare that put energetic Bobby Flay on the culinary map. Still hot after all these years.

Novità
102 E. 22nd St (between. Park Ave S. and Lexington) Tel: 212-677 2222. Open: L and D daily. **$$$**
This northern Italian restaurant remains an undiscovered gem. Delicious, freshly prepared dishes, gracious service and reasonable prices.

Patria
250 Park Ave S. (20th St). Tel: 212-777 6211. Open: L & D Mon–Fri, D only Sat–Sun. **$$$**
Considered one of the city's top Latin American restaurants, hip, multi-leveled Patria serves inventive and tasty Nuevo Latino dishes.

Pongal
110 Lexington Ave (between 26th and 27th sts). Tel: 212-696 9458. Open: L and D daily. **$$**
This Kosher vegetarian restaurant specializing in the food of Gujarat, Punjab and southern India, is a very good choice on a block filled with many Indian eateries.

Pure Food and Wine
54 Irving Pl (between 17th and 18th sts). Tel: 212-477 1010. Open: D daily. **$$$**
There's nothin' cookin' at this all-raw food restaurant – healthy and unusual for sure.

Red Cat
227 10th Ave (between 23rd and 24th sts). Tel: 212-242 1122. Open: D daily. **$$$**
Hep cats love the Red Cat. Great room, excellent food, cool clientele – a stylish place before or after gallery hopping.

Republic
37 Union Sq W. (between 16th and 17th sts). Tel: 212-627 7172. Open: L & D daily. **$$**
There are oodles of tasty noodles at this noisy, Asian eatery. Communal tables are fun.

Tabla
11 Madison Ave (at 25th St). Tel: 212-889 0667. Open: L Mon–Fri, D daily. **$$$$**
Unique Indian/New American fusion food ; there's a great *prix fix* lunch at the downstairs Bread Bar.

Union Square Café
21 E. 16th St (between 5th Ave and Union Sq). Tel: 212-243 4020. Open: L & D daily. **$$$$**
A winning formula of four-star food, wine and service. Year after year, this is voted the best restaurant in NYC.

Bars and Cafés

City Bakery, 3 W. 18th St (between 5th and 6th aves), is a popular Flatiron hang-out with pastries, soups, sandwiches and more.

Heartland Brewery, 35 Union Sq W. (between 16th and 17th sts), is a terrific stopping-off place for a mug and pub grub.

Lady Mendl's, Inn at Irving Place, 56 Irving Pl (between 17th and 18th sts), is an elegant tea salon in a Gramercy Park townhouse.

Mayrose, 920 Broadway (at 21st St), has large diner windows – great for people-watching.

Old Town Bar and Restaurant, 45 E. 18th St (between Broadway and Park Ave S.), has a wonderful long bar and great hamburgers.

Pete's Tavern, 129 E. 18th St (at Irving Pl), is better for drinks than dinner, but there's loads of atmosphere.

'wichcraft, 47 E. 19th St (at Park Ave S.), is a relative of fancier spots, Craft and Craft Bar. Come here for imaginative sandwiches.

PRICE CATEGORIES

Prices for a three-course dinner per person with half a bottle of wine:
$ = under $20
$$ = $20–$45
$$$ = $45–$60
$$$$ = over $60

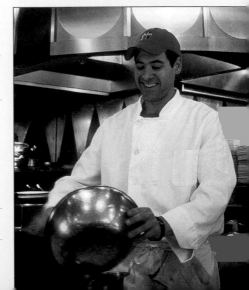

RIGHT: Tabla serves Indian/New American fusion food.

GREENWICH VILLAGE

Greenwich Village was the country's first true bohemian neighborhood, a place where Dylan Thomas and Bob Dylan found inspiration. Now, Stella McCartney and Alexander McQueen are doing the same in the Meatpacking District

Writers and poets, artists and radicals, runaway socialites and others seeking freedom from conventional lifestyles have long flocked to Greenwich Village, spotlit in recent history by poets and musicians of the 1950s and '60s.

Today, as other neighborhoods set the trends, New Yorkers often think of "the Village" as one big tourist attraction. Untrue. Though a commercial element exists, serviced by red double-decker tour buses, many of the streets are as quietly residential as they were in the late 18th and early 19th centuries, when the village of Greenwich was first settled by pioneers fleeing illness and epidemics at the tip of the island.

Success and the city

Spiraling real-estate prices have forced out all but the most successful, but the Village (both Greenwich and the West Village) is still where many people would choose to live, witness the "Gold Coast" buildings facing the Hudson River, home to stars like Meryl Streep and Nicole Kidman. Around here, it's easy to find cobblestone alleys, Italian bakeries, a neighborhood atmosphere, theaters, cinemas and the oldest gay community in New York. Not to mention restaurants, bars, clubs and the Meatpacking District.

Bordered by 14th Street to the north, the Hudson River to the west and Broadway to the east (where the East Village begins), this is where the offbeat and the fashionable mingle with ease, and where the annual Halloween Parade is a riotous spectacle attended by both.

Walking south on Fifth Avenue, **Washington Arch** rises in the distance. Designed in wood by Stanford White to commemorate the 1889 centennial of the first president's inauguration, the imposing marble

Map on page 144

LEFT:
lovers love
Washington Arch.
BELOW:
the *Village Voice*
started in the 1950s.

arch from 1918 is the entrance to **Washington Square ❶**, the symbolic heart of Greenwich Village.

Booksellers Row

Walking east to Broadway leads to the **Strand** bookstore (open until 10:30pm every night), one of the last survivors of what was once known as "Booksellers' Row." Occupying a townhouse on the corner of 12th Street, the Strand offers "eighteen miles" of used books, and the stalwart searcher may just be able to unearth that rare first edition they have been hunting for.

Grace Church ❷, just down the street, is one of the city's loveliest ecclesiastical structures. Built in 1846, its exterior white marble, now a muted gray, was mined by convicts from the infamous Sing Sing prison in upstate New York.

Turn right at 10th, walk toward Fifth Avenue crossing **University Place**, which runs parallel to Fifth

from 14th to 8th Street, to West 12th Street, where the **New School for Social Research** offers classes in everything from Arabic to screen-writing. Around the corner, the **Forbes Magazine Galleries ❸** (62 Fifth Avenue, tel: 212-206 5548; closed Sun, Mon; free) hold the late Malcolm Forbes's groupings of tin soldiers and art; alas, the famed Fabergé collection is no longer here.

The nearby **Salmagundi Club**, at 47 Fifth Avenue, is the country's oldest artists' club, and was founded in 1870. Then, take a stroll along 9th and 10th streets, two of the most picturesque in the city. Lined by stately brick and brownstone houses, these have been home to numerous artists and writers (Mark Twain lived at 14 West 10th). The **Church of the Ascension ❹** on the corner of Fifth and 10th Street, was designed by Richard Upjohn in 1840 and features a marble altar relief by sculptor Augustus St-Gaudens.

TIP

Just can't finish it? A new law in New York permits taking that expensive, half-empty bottle of wine home from restaurants. The law requires the bottle be "securely sealed" before being bagged.

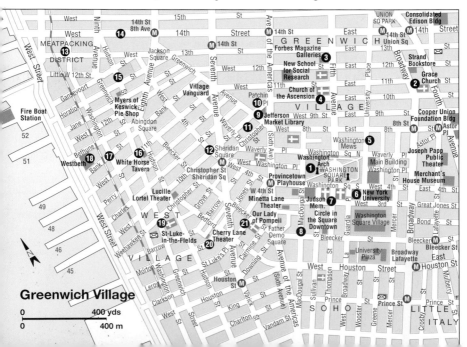

Greenwich Village

0   400 yds
0   400 m

Hopper and Henry James

Tucked away just above Washington Arch are two tiny dead-end streets that look just like stage sets.

Washington Mews ❺ is located between Fifth and Washington Square North, an extension of Waverly Place. Originally built as stables for the townhouses along Washington Square North (where the artist Edward Hopper lived), the pretty rowhouses here and along nearby **MacDougal Alley** are now highly sought-after.

All of this eventually leads to **Washington Square** itself. Originally a potter's field, where the poor and unknown were buried, it later became a parade ground, and still later a residential park. Although it's lost the cachet it gained in the days of Henry James – who was inspired to write his novel of the same name while living nearby – on weekend afternoons the park is filled with musicians and other street performers playing to appreciative crowds of Japanese camera crews, out-of-town students, tourists, chess hustlers and pot dealers.

With two blocks of Greek Revival townhouses, **Washington Square North** retains a 19th-century elegance at odds with the monolithic **New York University ❻** buildings that adjoin the park. Past NYU's new Kimmel Student Center, Bobst Library and Catholic Center (all situated on Washington Square South), is **Judson Memorial Church ❼**. Designed in 1890 by Stanford White in Romanesque Revival-style, the church has been a cultural and religious center for decades.

The Beatnik beat

Turn off Washington Square South onto **MacDougal Street ❽**, into the heart of what was once a beatnik haven, where world-weary poets wore black, sipped coffee and discoursed on the meaning of life late into the night. These days, the area is a magnet for out-of-towners, drawn by ersatz craft shops and "authentic" ethnic restaurants. Nevertheless, a stroll around these streets offers the pleasure of a pilgrimage down passageways of past grooviness; cloisters of cool.

Map on page 144

Chess has been a Washington Square pastime for decades.

BELOW: Washington Square was once a potter's field.

The modern gay liberation movement got a spontaneous start on June 27 1969 – the day Judy Garland was buried – at the Stonewall Inn, 53 Christopher Street. The Stonewall was a gay bar whose habitués got tired of being rousted by police. When they protested, riots broke out. Today, there's a bar with the same name next door.

BELOW LEFT: the Jefferson Market Library building dates from 1877.
BELOW RIGHT: the West Village's Christopher Street, symbolic center of the gay community.

Some nights echoes of the young Bob Dylan or Jimi Hendrix seem to drift around the intersection of Bleecker and MacDougal streets. Nearby entertainment opportunities include performances by the world's jazz greats at the **Blue Note** *(see page 224)*; and excellent contemporary drama at the **Minetta Lane Theater** (tel: 212-420 8000).

Besides a profusion of juice bars, shoe stores and souvenir shops, every other door seems to lead to a restaurant, and the aromas of Indian, Spanish, Japanese and Italian cuisines mingle across the sidewalk in a mist of olfactory overkill.

The West Village

The area west of the Avenue of the Americas (Sixth Avenue) and a few blocks north is where the Village hosts the annual Halloween Parade; witnessed the gay-rights riots at the Stonewall Inn in the late 1960s; and where attractive knots of streets wind around confusingly between the major avenues.

A good place to start is the striking **Jefferson Market Library 9**

at 10th Street and the Avenue of the Americas. Originally part of a complex that included the old Women's House of Detention, it was built as a courthouse in 1877 and is where Harry Thaw went on trial for shooting Stanford White, in 1906. Next door is a pretty community garden open to the public; signs somewhat aggressively urge us to buy potted plants as this supports the park, staffed by volunteers.

Walk west on 10th Street to **Patchin Place 10** – a mews where Eugene O'Neill, the journalist John Reed and the poet e. e. cummings lived. From here, continue west on **Christopher Street 11**, symbolic center of the gay community and a main cross-street that slants across the heart of the West Village to a renovated pier, walkway and bike path that, on a sunny day, make New York seem like a brand-new city. (At night, however, it's still the haunt of hustlers, so be alert.)

There is a wide selection of books with gay themes at the Oscar Wilde Memorial Bookshop (15 Christopher Street), beyond a series of

stores called Amalgamated, which offer unusual decorative items.

Just past **Waverly Place**, with its curved row of small Federal-style houses, is the **Northern Dispensary**. A non-profit health clinic from 1831 until fairly recently, it's one of the oldest public buildings in the city. A few doors up and some three decades ago, the modern gay rights movement got its spontaneous start one night in 1969 at the Stonewall Inn (53 Christopher Street), a gay bar whose habitués got tired of being rousted by police.

Today, there's a bar with the same name operating next door. Just across the street, tiny fenced-in **Christopher Park** has a statue of the Civil War general Philip Sheridan. **Sheridan Square ⑫** – in the traditional spirit of Village confusion – is actually at the triangular junction where Grove, Christopher and West 4th streets meet, a tangled example of city non-planning.

Shopping opportunities await on the other side of Seventh Avenue South – including McNulty's Tea and Coffee Company at 109 Christo-

pher. At 121 Christopher Street is the **Lucille Lortel Theater** (tel: 212-239 6200), the playwright's friend. If it's music that gives a cultural *frisson*, this is the neighborhood for you: the tiny **Village Vanguard** (178 Seventh Avenue South, *see page 224*) has been in business for more than half a century, and helped to launch the careers of Miles Davis and John Coltrane.

Meatpacking District

Improbably, even for New York, a district where the streets are lined with hanging animal carcasses and trucks unloading meat, has transformed itself into the hottest place in town. But in the watering holes of the **Meatpacking District ⑬**, the part of the West Village that runs from 14th Street south and Ninth Avenue west toward the river, restaurateurs, club owners and shopowners are laughing.

This formerly earthy neighborhood of prostitutes and cobble-stone pavements, centered mainly around **Gansevoort Street**, has taken its own place in the Manhattan firma-

Map on page 144

Detail from the Blue Note club logo.

BELOW LEFT: Dylan Thomas drank here.
BELOW RIGHT: some Village jazz clubs have been around for over half a century.

Shop for couture on West 14th Street; for cow carcasses on West 13th Street.

BELOW: the world of butchers and beautiful people collide on Little West 12th Street.

ment with a constellation of stellar eating spots, clandestine clubs, galleries and fashion houses. It's difficult to get dinner reservations unless you happen to be Stella McCartney or Alexander McQueen, both of whom have boutiques on the area's increasingly classy thoroughfare, **West 14th Street** ⑭. As things change quickly here, there's little point in picking out highlights: much better to throw on fabulous gladrags, check the scene, be seen, and be glad you experienced it before all the butcher shops were replaced by fashionista fantasies.

Some of the Chelsea gallery scene has spilled south into the district. A stalwart is **White Columns**, a gallery founded in 1969, and located at 320 West 13th Street, between West 4th and Hudson streets. **Hudson Street** ⑮ runs south from 14th. What it lacks in the glitz of the Meatpacking District is made up for in low-key neighborliness; one favorite is **Myers of Keswick** (No. 634), a British specialty shop where Keith Richards, Elton John and the late Princess Margaret have stocked up

on homemade pork pies. The **White Horse Tavern** ⑯ has been serving drinks from the corner of 11th Street since 1880. This was the haunt of Dylan Thomas, where he had one too many before repairing to expire at nearby St Vincent's Hospital.

Above the White Horse, cute little **Abingdon Square** leads to the start of **Bleecker Street**, which at this end is lined by pleasant stores and bisected by some of the Village's prettiest thoroughfares.

Bank Street ⑰ is particularly scenic, with its cobblestones and pastel houses, and lies in the center of the **Greenwich Village Historic District**'s finest 19th-century architecture. Toward the end of Bank Street, **Westbeth** ⑱ is a sprawling, government-funded artists' enclave that looks out over the Hudson River. It contains galleries and performance spaces, as well as rehearsal studios that are often used for Broadway and off-Broadway productions, and is one of Downtown's most interesting and off-the-beaten-track event venues.

It's only a short walk from here to

St-Luke-in-the-Fields ⓳, the city's third oldest church, built in 1821 when this area was still pretty much open countryside. You can arrive here by walking west on **Grove Street** from Seventh Avenue South, a route which meanders through a rabbit-warren of lanes and byways that cross themselves and sometimes change name without warning.

Byways and speakeasies

Number **17 Grove Street**, built in 1822, is a wooden home that brims with character, as does **Grove Court**, an alleyway with a cluster of white-brick houses. Grove Street intersects **Bedford Street**, one of the oldest Village byways, named after the street of the same name in London's Covent Garden. If you turn right here, you'll discover the original "Twin Peaks" (102 Bedford Street), which was built in 1830 as an artists' residence with two peaks in the gabled roof.

A left turn leads to Chumley's *(see page 151)*, a former speakeasy turned bar and restaurant, where novelist John Steinbeck and play-wright Eugene O'Neill were regulars. Leftover from Prohibition, there's an unmarked entrance around the corner on quaint **Barrow Street**.

Tiny poet Edna St Vincent Millay was a tenant at **75 Bedford Street**, Manhattan's narrowest house at just over 9 ft (2.7 meters) wide. A bigger tenant of the same premises was larger-than-life John Barrymore, of the theatrical Barrymore family. More recently, before her break into stardom, Barbra Streisand worked as an usher at the **Cherry Lane Theatre ⓴** (38 Commerce Street, tel: 212-727 3673). The building was originally a farm silo, and later a box factory.

St Luke's Place is lined by gracious Italianate rowhouses. New York's Jazz-Age mayor, Jimmy Walker *(see page 28)*, lived at No. 6, and two lamps – a sign of mayoral honor – are at the foot of the steps. At Seventh Avenue South, St Luke's turns into Leroy Street before coming to a stop at Bleecker, where **Our Lady of Pompeii Church ㉑** is a signal you've reached the South Village, an old Italian neighborhood. ❑

Map on page 144

The Meatpacking District's Hog Pit attracts meat-lovers and movie stars.

BELOW: Pastis, one of the most popular of the bright and beautiful watering holes.

RESTAURANTS, BARS AND CAFÉS

Restaurants

AOC z
314 Bleecker St (at Grove St). Tel: 212-675 9463. Open: L & D daily. **$$**
The dishes are served as simply and perfectly as in a Paris bistro. Unlike other hurried New York spots, here *le savoir vivre* reigns, and you can linger and chat all night if no one needs your table.

Babbo
110 Waverly Pl (between MacDougal St and 6th Ave). Tel: 212-777 0303. Open: D only daily. **$$$$**
Make a reservation well in advance for Mario Batali's top-of-the-line Italian gem. Some say it's now the best, most elegant Italian cuisine in New York City.

Barbuto
775 Washington St (at W. 12th St). Tel: 212-924 9700. Open: L Mon–Fri, D daily. **$$**
Another wonderful restaurateur, Jonathan Waxman, forges into the Meatpacking District at – what's this? – reasonable prices. Waxman presents Imaginative American cuisine using first-class, seasonal ingredients.

Blue Hill
75 Washington Pl. (between 6th Ave and Washington Sq W.) Tel: 212-539 1776. Open: D only daily. **$$$$**
A mellow, sophisticated spot that gets rave reviews for its beautifully conceived American dishes created from fresh food from the Blue Hill family's farm.

Caliente Cab Company
61 7th Ave S. Tel: 212-243 8517 Open: L & D daily. **$$**
A friendly Mexican with bright tiled tables and music adding to its warm atmosphere. Does great guacamole.

Chow Bar
230 W. 4th St (at W. 10th St). Tel: 212-633 2212. Open: L & D daily. **$$$**
Pan Asian, trendy and utterly delicious.

Café Asean
117 W. 10th St (between Greenwich and 6th aves). Open: L & D daily. Tel: 212-633 0348. **$**
Cash only, but worth it when the priciest item on the Southeast Asian menu is around $20. A local secret.

CamaJe
85 MacDougal St (between Bleecker and Houston sts). Tel: 212-673 8184. Open: L & D daily. **$–$$**
Chef Abigail Hitchcock prepares top-notch French bistro dishes with imagination and heart. The casual atmosphere and reasonable prices make this a real find.

Da Silvano
260 6th Ave (between Bleecker and Houston sts). Tel: 212-982 2343. Open: L & D daily. **$$$**
A guaranteed celebrity sighting at this Tuscan hotspot that's always in the gossip columns.

Florent
69 Gansevoort St (near Washington St). Tel: 212-989 5779. Open: 24/7. **$$**
The first restaurant to open in the Meatpacking District long before it became a style scene. Florent's clientele and the fact that it's open all night make a great people-watching spot.

Gavroche
212 W. 14th St (between 7th and 8th aves). Tel: 212-647 8553. Open: L Mon–Sat, D daily. **$$$**
Excellent straightforward French bistro on the fringes of the Meatpacking District and to its credit lacking a high-fashion attitude.

Il Mulino
86 W. 3rd St (between Sullivan and Thompson sts). Tel: 212-673 3783. Open: L & D Mon–Fri, D only Sat. **$$$$**
A loyal clientele has made this Italian Village classic almost like a club. Endless courses justify the expensive tab, and after decades of excellent service, no one complains.

Lemongrass Grill
80 University Pl (at 11th St and other locations). Tel: 212-604 9870. Open: L & D daily. **$$**
Savory Thai cuisine, dependable and delicious every time, at every location.

LEFT: hitch a ride to the Caliente Cab Company.

Macelleria
48 Gansevoort St (at 9th Ave). Tel: 212-741 2555. Open: L & D Mon–Fri, Br & D Sat–Sun. **$$$**
The name is Italian for '"butcher shop,"as befits this simple but chic dining room in a former meat warehouse. Reservations are essential at the weekend.

Meet
71–3 Gansevoort St (between Greenwich and Washington sts). Tel: 212-242 0990. Open: D only Mon–Fri, Br and D Sat–Sun. **$–$$$**
The playfulness of this meeting place in the Meatpacking District extends from the name to a water trough in which you can wash prior to dining. Creative fish, meat and pasta dishes.

Minetta Tavern
113 MacDougal St (between Bleecker and W. 3rd sts). Tel: 212-475 3850. Open: L & D daily. **$$$**
Old-time, comfy, red-sauce Italian landmark whose walls are line with great photographs.

Old Homestead
56 9th Ave, (between 14th and 15th sts). Tel: 212-242 9040. Open: L & D daily. **$$$$**
A steakhouse since 1868 that keeps up with the times, serving, among other choices, a breathtakingly expensive Kobe beef burger.

Pastis
9 9th Ave (at Little W. 12th St). Tel: 212-929 4844. Open: B, L & D daily. **$$$**

There's food for most tastes most hours at this ultra-fashionable Meat-packing French brasserie – from onion soup to frites – all as tempting as the pretty people who come here.

Paradou
8 Little W. 12th St (between 9th Ave and Washington St). Tel: 212-463 8345. Open: D only Mon–Fri; L & D Sat–Sun. **$–$$**
What might seem like just another Meatpack-ing District bistro is a real gem – what a shame the small, bright room and lovely garden are no longer a secret.

Risotteria
270 Bleecker St (at Morton St). Tel: 212-924-6664. Open: L & D daily. **$**
Nestled in the Italian heart of Bleecker Street, this casual restaurant knows its arborio from its canaroli; this is the place to come for risotto.

Peanut Butter and Co.
240 Sullivan St (between Bleecker and W. 3rd sts). Tel: 212-677 3995. Open: L & D daily. **$**
Anything and everything ever imagined with this staple of the American diet, from peanut butter milkshakes to peanut butter/fluffernutter sandwiches and much, much more.

Pearl Oyster Bar
18 Cornelia St (between Bleecker and W. 4th sts). Tel: 212-691 8211. Open: L & D Mon–Fri, D only Sat. **$$**
Raw-bar discovery

tucked into a Village side-street populated with other tiny little restaurants. Chowder is served, in addition to what some call "perfec-tion on the half-shell."

Ye Waverly Inn
16 Bank St (at Waverly Pl). Tel: 212-929 4377. Open: D daily, br Sun. **$$**
A Village landmark established in 1844. Although this more recent location isn't that old, it feels like it, with low-ceilinged rooms and fireplaces. The atmosphere is far better than the decent, but not great, food.

Bars and Cafés

Caffe Reggio, 119 Mac-Dougal St (between Bleecker and W. 3rd sts), is the best of the Village Italian coffeehouses.

Cedar Tavern, 82 University Pl (at East 11th St), is a funky old hangout with great bar prices.

Chocolate Bar, 48 8th Ave (between Jane and Horatio sts), exists for all your chocolate needs.

Chumley's, 86 Bedford St (at Commerce St), has an unmarked door from the Prohibition era.

White Horse Tavern, 567 Hudson St (at W. 11th St), is legendary; no bar tour of the West Village is complete with-out visiting Dylan Thomas's last pub stop before he expired.

PRICE CATEGORIES

Prices for a three-course dinner per person with half a bottle of wine:
$ = under $20
$$ = $20–$45
$$$ = $45–$60
$$$$ = over $60

RIGHT: Florent, Meatpacking old-timer.

THE EAST VILLAGE TO CHINATOWN

From historic synagogues on the Lower East Side to the newest style shops in NoLita; from garlicky food in Littly Italy to cutting-edge clubs in Alphabet City – this is Manhattan's melting pot

Bordered by 14th Street to the north and Houston Street to the south, and roughly centered between Third Avenue and Avenue B, the **East Village** is a place that stays up late, where fashion and politics have always been more radical than elsewhere in the city, and whose residents have included Beat icons like Allen Ginsberg and William Burroughs, as well as Yippies and Hell's Angels.

Beneath its scruffy avant-garde surface, the East Village is also a neighborhood of immigrants, with Ukrainian and Puerto Rican social clubs next to cutting-edge boutiques, and free health clinics not far from expensive co-op buildings. Like other Downtown neighborhoods, old and new are juxtaposed here in an ever-changing mosaic.

NoHo

At the beginning of the 20th century, lower Broadway around 9th Street was part of the "Ladies Mile" of fashionable retailing that extended north to 23rd Street. Later it was just a dingy pause away from Soho (when it was still known as SoHo), but all that changed when Tower Records and other meccas for the young consumer moved in. Unofficially known as **NoHo ❶** (**No**rth of **Ho**uston), this stretch of the East

Village includes Broadway from Astor Place down to Houston Street, a neighborhood crowded with fashion, art, antiques and furniture stores.

Interesting home furnishing emporia also tempt along Lafayette Street, where the **Time Café** (380 Lafayette, at Great Jones Street) has a nice outdoor terrace, as well as Fez, a basement jazz club with a loyal following. At the corner of Astor Place and Broadway, a large, busy Kmart reflects the changing times, but just a few steps away is

Map on page 154

LEFT: East Village attitude.
BELOW: celebrating Hanukkah *and* Christmas in Chinatown.

East Village, Chinatown, Soho and Tribeca

Astor Place Hair Designers, a Downtown institution where the latest "do" is yours for the asking – cutting time: 10 minutes.

Velvet Underground

St Mark's Place ❷, a continuation of 8th Street between Third Avenue and Avenue A, is the East Village version of main street. In the 1960s, this was the East Coast's counterculture center, where Andy Warhol presented Velvet Underground "happenings" and, later, barefoot freaks tripped out at the Electric Circus. It's now a gentrified condo/retail center of stores and residences.

The Fillmore East, which presented rock concerts around the corner on Second Avenue, is also long gone, but St Mark's Place is still one of the city's liveliest thoroughfares. Sidewalk cafés and restaurants heave with customers, and the bazaar-like atmosphere is augmented by street vendors selling T-shirts, leatherwear, jewelry and bootleg CDs and DVDs.

Shop for retro, punk or retro-punk gear here, then pause for refreshment around the corner – down Third Avenue to East 7th Street – at a true drinking man's pub.

McSorley's Old Ale House has been in business since the 1850s, although women weren't allowed inside until more than a century later. This was one of New York City's favorite hangouts for the Irish writer Brendan Behan.

Continuing on St Mark's, the block between Second and Third is lined by a motley array of record stores, tattoo parlors and places to get piercings in a variety of body parts; it's also home to the Pearl Theater Company, who are in residence at **Theatre 80** (80 St Mark's Place, tel: 212-598 9802).

In fact, the East Village has been a center for live performances since Second Avenue was lined by Yiddish theaters at the end of the 19th century. Today only a few are still used as theaters (the **Orpheum Theatre** on Second Avenue is one).

But there's also **La Mama etc**, just west of Second Avenue at East 4th Street, a pioneer of the avant-garde, with three popular performance

Map on page 154

The cast-iron kiosk of Astor Place subway station; the station interior is worth seeing, too.

BELOW: McSorley's Old Ale House has been in business since 1850, but only opened to women in 1970.

St Mark's-in-the-Bowery, at 10th Street and Second Avenue, is the second-oldest church in Manhattan. It was built in 1799 on land belonging to Peter Stuyvesant.

BELOW:
East Village ambiance
in a store window.

spaces, and **P.S. 122** (First Avenue at 9th Street), where an annual benefit offers a lively taster of what's happening on the cutting edge of music, dance and performance poetry.

Clubs in the East Village spring up with regularity, and often close just as quickly. One old-timer is the **Pyramid Club**, which opened on Avenue A back when it was still frontier territory and before it became an enclave for young professionals. **CBGB-OMFUG** on the Bowery, the place where American punk and New Wave exploded in the 1970s, is still going and has its own souvenir shop next door, but has been eclipsed by cooler venues.

St Mark's-in-the-Bowery ❸, at Second Avenue and 10th Street, is the second-oldest church building in Manhattan – and a good place to start exploring. Built in 1799 on a *bouwerie* (farm) belonging to Dutch governor Peter Stuyvesant, St Mark's has a long history of liberal religious thought, a reflection of the neighborhood that manifests itself in such long-standing community programs as the Poetry Project.

Historic Fish

The red-brick Anglo-Italianate houses across from the church on East 10th Street and on Stuyvesant Street, which veers off at an angle from Second Avenue, form the heart of the **St Mark's Historic District**. The handsome home at No. 21 is known as the **Stuyvesant-Fish House**, a national historic landmark built by Stuyvesant's great-grandson by marriage, Hamilton Fish.

Keep walking on Stuyvesant Street to Third Avenue, where **St Mark's Bookshop** is well-stocked with obscure new fiction and political tomes. It's a short walk from here to **Astor Place** ❹, named for John Jacob Astor, who arrived in New York in 1784 as a penniless immigrant, and was the richest man in New York by the time he died 36 years later.

Today the area's most notable landmark, besides the **Astor Place subway kiosk** nearby, is the giant rotating black cube by Tony Rosenthal called *The Alamo*. One of the first abstract sculptures installed on city property, it stands at the inter-

section of Astor Place, St Mark's Place and Lafayette Street.

The brown Italianate **Cooper Union Foundation Building** ❺, between Third and Fourth avenues, opened in 1859 as one of the country's earliest centers of free education. Famous as an art school, this is also where Abraham Lincoln gave the speech said to have launched his presidential campaign.

A statue of founder-philanthropist Peter Cooper, by Augustus St-Gaudens, who was a student here, stands behind Cooper Union at **Cooper Square**, where Third and Fourth Avenues converge at the top of the Bowery.

Colonnade Row on Lafayette Street, which runs south from Astor Place, was originally a group of nine columned homes built in 1833, when this was one of the city's most elegant neighborhoods. Only four of the houses still stand, with current occupants including the perennially stylish Indochine restaurant at No. 430 *(see page 166)*, and the **Astor Place Theatre** (No. 434). Across the street is the five-theater complex, the **Joseph Papp Public Theater** ❻ (tel: 212-539 8500), originally the Astor Library.

The library was John Jacob Astor's only public legacy, which he envisioned as a center of learning for the common man – the fact that it was only open during working hours didn't strike him as a problem. Since 1967, this has been the home of the city's Shakespeare Festival, as well as almost contemporary productions (from *Hair* and *A Chorus Line* to *Bring in 'Da Noise, Bring in 'Da Funk*), that have gone on to be produced on Broadway.

A block farther down, drop in and see the city as it used to be at the **Merchant's House Museum** ❼ (29 East 4th Street, tel: 212-777 1089; closed Tues and Wed; charge), a small Greek Revival-style brick townhouse built in 1832. The same family lived here for generations, and their furnishings and personal effects are on display. Guided tours Saturday and Sunday; self guiding on weekdays.

Little India

As befits a neighborhood that's a typical melting pot, you can find just about any cuisine here, from trendy to traditional. If cheap and exotic is your preference, you can't do much better than "**Little India**" ❽ on 6th Street between First and Second Avenues. All the restaurants here are inexpensive, most stay open pretty late, and some have live Indian music on weekend evenings.

Walk north up Second Avenue to the corner of 7th Street, past the **Middle Collegiate Church** (a Reformed Protestant Dutch church built in 1891), and you'll find the Kiev restaurant. Eastern-European style meals are served here, and it stays open late. Kosher meals are the staple at the Second Avenue Kosher Delicatessen and Restaurant on the corner of 10th Street. If you're hun-

Map on page 154

TIP

For great music, head to Joe's Pub, 425 Lafayette Street, tel: 212-539 8770, the innovative small venue and satellite of the Joseph Papp Public Theater. You can have dinner here, too.

BELOW:
blue hair and ready to boogie.

BELOW:
Orchard Street is a favorite Sunday bazaar.

gry for something sweet, there's espresso and pastries at Veniero's on 11th Street near First Avenue, testimony to an Italian enclave that flourished here in the early 1900's.

The **Theater for the New City** (tel: 212-254 1109) on First Avenue was founded in 1971 as another venue for experimental off-Broadway productions. Not far away, the lovely **St Nicholas** Carpatho-Russian Orthodox Greek Catholic Church is a reminder of this ethnic and religious melting pot. Originally built for a predominantly Anglican parish as St Mark's Chapel, the interior tiled walls and beamed ceiling date back to 1894.

At 10th Street and Avenue A is the top of **Tompkins Square Park** ❿, a patch of reclaimed swamp that was used as a drill ground and recruiting camp during the Civil War. It was later the center of the *Kleine Deutschland* (Little Germany) community that thrived here more than 100 years ago.

A gathering place for hippies and runaways in the late 1960s, the park was a focal point for conflicts between homeless activists and police in the 1980s. Today, however, it's a generally peaceful place, frequented by young mothers with kids and neighborhood folk exercising their pets in the specially enclosed dog-friendly area.

Many of the homes have been renovated (the 19th-century row houses on 10th Street at the park's northern border are a good example), fueling a hike in rents like other "reclaimed" parts of the city.

Alphabet City

Nowhere is this urban reclamation more evident than in the area known as **Alphabet City** ⓫, (Avenues A, B, C and D). For decades the very name was synonymous with crime and little punishment, but now slums and graffiti-covered walls have been supplanted by bars and restaurants with a predominately young, hip clientele. Tiny community parks have been divested of drug dealers and twinkle at night with fairy lights, while former *bodegas* have metamorphosed into fashion boutiques.

Like other cutting-edge neighborhoods, however, it's wise to exercise a certain degree of caution, and here it's easy – just follow the alphabet. Avenues A and B are fine anytime, Avenue C is fairly safe until midnight, but for now it's best to avoid Avenue D altogether.

Dining possibilities are seemingly limitless, but a stand-out is Odessa (119 Avenue A at 7th Street), a surviving reflection of the neighborhood's Eastern European heritage, where specialties include home-cooked *pirogi*, *blintzes* and *borscht*.

The Lower East Side

Technically, this area starts east of Tompkins Square Park, where Avenue C becomes Losaida Avenue (*Losaida* is Puerto Rican "Spanish" for "Lower East Side"). But the traditional **Lower East Side**, with its

immigrant roots firmly in place, is south of East Houston Street, bordered by the Bowery and the East River. This is where bargain hunters flock for wholesale deals in everything from bridal gowns to bathroom fixtures, and where the narrow streets are lined by tenements that date back 150 years.

Starting in the mid-19th century, successive waves of immigrants arrived here in pursuit of a new life: first free Africans, followed by Irish and Germans, and later by Eastern European Jews, mainly from Russia and Poland.

These days you'll see stores with Jewish names and Chinese or Hispanic owners, a reminder that this neighborhood still attracts new arrivals to New York – even new arrivals from the rest of New York. This is evidenced by the bohemian-minded bars, clubs and boutiques thriving along Ludlow and other streets, a trend that was kicked off in 1993 when **Mercury Lounge** – one of the city's best small music venues – kicked open its doors at 217 East Houston Street.

Walk along East Houston to the top of **Orchard Street** ⑫ and you've reached a favorite Sunday shopping bazaar (stores close Friday afternoons and all day Saturday for the Jewish sabbath).

Once crowded with peddlers selling old clothes and cracked eggs, today you can find designer fashions, fabrics, linens and shoes at prices often half as much as Uptown. The scene is frenetic (bargaining encouraged), so you may want to stop in first at **Katz's Delicatessen** (205 East Houston, near Ludlow Street). for a little sustenance. The menu here has hardly changed since opening day in 1898 – and their pastrami sandwich has long been a New York culinary landmark.

Along with Katz's, there are several traditional Lower East Side food and beverage options. These include the Schapiro Wine Company (126 Rivington Street, between Essex and Norfolk streets), a kosher winery with tastings. The great city pickle debate rages between **Guss' Lower East Side Pickles** on Orchard Street, and a former employee's store on

Map on page 154

A sign of the times: the Lower East Side's Jewish heritage dates back to the mid-1800s.

BELOW: the menu at Katz's Deli has hardly changed since 1898.

The Lower East Side Tenement Museum offer excellent walking tours of the neighborhood.

BELOW:
car crazy
in NoLita.

Essex called **The Pickle Guys**. For *blintzes* and onion rolls, stop in at **Ratner's** (138 Delancey, near Suffolk Street) or sit down at 175 Chrystie Street, just north of Delancey, to a memorable feast at **Sammy's Roumanian Steak House**, where a traditional pitcher of chicken fat comes with every meal. There's also nightlife in places like the **Bowery Ballroom**, a rock venue opened by the owners of Mercury Lounge on Delancey between Chrystie and the Bowery.

Living history

Grand Street's Seward Park High School counts Tony Curtis and Walter Matthau among its graduates; Sam Jaffe, another actor, was born in an 1863 tenement at 97 Orchard Street, between Delancey and Broome streets. Since 1988, the building and its cramped apartments have been part of the **Lower East Side Tenement Museum** ⓭ (90 Orchard Street, tel: 212-431 0233; closed Mon; charge; guided tours only), which is dedicated to the story of what life was like for poor urban immigrants. In addition to changing exhibits, the museum offers tours of the building and the neighborhood.

In the 19th century, the area's substandard working and living conditions (ably chronicled by journalist-reformer Jacob Riis, *see photo on page 26*) were instrumental in spawning anarchist and socialist movements. Emma Goldman preached her gentle anarchism here, radical newspapers, such as the *Jewish Daily Forward*, flourished, and settlement houses offering immigrants health and education assistance were formed.

In a sign of the times, the faces of Karl Marx and Friedrich Engels peer from a frieze over the entrance to the landmark building at **173 East Broadway** where the old *Daily Forward* was published, now converted to condos. But some of the settlement houses are still in operation, including the **University Settlement House** on Eldridge Street, and the **Henry Street Settlement** (265 Henry Street), which was founded in 1893 as the country's first volunteer nursing and social service center.

Religion played an important role in the lives of immigrants. Although many of the synagogues in the area are no longer used, the **Eldridge Street Synagogue**, a 1887 Moorish-style landmark close to Division Street, has been restored as a cultural center, and still has a small congregation. For information on tours and exhibits, tel: 212-219 0888.

NoLita

Dubbed **NoLita** , for **N**orth of **Li**ttle **Ita**ly, the retail heart of this tiny area, with its good-looking, arty residents and one-off fashion boutiques – think polka dots – is Mulberry Street, particularly between Houston and Kenmore. The best way to enjoy NoLita is simply to stroll around and drink in its exuberant atmosphere – a laid-back mix of the traditional and the trendy – before stopping off for a drink and a tasty tid-bit in one of the watering holes on Elizabeth or Mott streets.

Old St Patrick's Cathedral ⑮, on the corner of Mott and Prince streets, was the seat of New York's Catholic archdiocese until 1879,

when the "new" St Patrick's Cathedral on Fifth Avenue was completed. Construction on the cathedral began in 1809, was interrupted by the War of 1812, and was eventually finished three years later. It was rebuilt in 1868 after being destroyed by fire, and remains a unique landmark.

Across Mott Street from the cathedral's graveyard, a plaque on the wall of a red-brick Victorian building explains that this was the School of the Children's Aid Society, created for the care and education of neighborhood immigrant children. Designed in 1888 by Calvert Vaux, the architect who also helped to create Central Park, it's now one of NoLita's most coveted apartment blocks. The beaux-arts **Police Building** farther south on Centre Street, is another. It served as a police headquarters until 1973.

Little Italy

Crowds – drawn along by tantalizing food stands and raucous games of chance – are an integral part of the festivals that draw visitors to the streets of **Little Italy** ⑯. The Feast

Map on page 154

![TIP]

Here we go 'round Mulberry Street... if you head for Little Italy and walk north, looking for NoLita (**No**rth of **Li**ttle **Ita**ly), you'll end up in NoHo. NoLita is a misnomer: the neighborhood is really "NoSLita", the **No**rthern **S**ection of **Li**ttle **Ita**ly, but this doesn't sound as cool.

BELOW: Littly Italy's Feast of San Gennaro in September lasts for 10 days.

Chinatown has spread from a three-block area to one that sprawls more than 40 blocks, growing larger each decade.

BELOW: Chinatown's heart lies south of Canal Street near Chatham Square.

of St Anthony takes place on Mott Street between Grand and Canal streets in late May, and there's also the 10-day Feast of San Gennaro, in September, when Mulberry Street from Canal to East Houston becomes a lively pedestrian mall.

Now squeezed between Chinatown and Soho, this area has been an Italian neighborhood since the late 1800s, when large numbers of immigrants arrived in New York from Southern Italy. The most pleasant part is along **Mulberry Street**, north of Canal, where the atmosphere abruptly changes from boisterous to almost mellow, and the sidewalks are lined by cafés and social clubs.

Most people come here to eat, and for good reason. **Luna's**, on Mulberry, is an established favorite, a reasonably priced restaurant that's been run by the same family since 1878. **Umberto's Clam House**, now on Broome near the corner of Mulberry Street, is another favorite. The restaurant's previous Mulberry Street location was where gangster Joey Gallo met an abrupt and bloody end over dinner in 1972.

Walking north on Mulberry past the headquarters of the Society of San Gennaro, you come to one of the oldest houses in Little Italy, **Paolucci's Restaurant** – where strolling violinists entertain diners – in a small white Federal-style building. It was erected in 1816 for Stephen Van Renssellaer, who was a well-to-do New Yorker. Originally located at 153 Mulberry Street, the entire house was moved to its present site at No. 149 in 1841.

At the corner of Mulberry and Grand, **E. Rossi and Co** has gifts, novelties and religious relics to browse, before sampling some delicacies at **Ferrara**, a pastry shop and café famous since 1892.

Chinatown

One of the largest Chinese-American settlements in America, as well as one of Manhattan's most vibrant neighborhoods, **Chinatown** got its start in the 1870s, when Chinese railroad workers drifted east from California in the wake of anti-Asian sentiment. Once squeezed into a three-block area bordered by Mott,

Pell and the Bowery, today's Chinatown encompasses around 40 blocks, swinging around Little Italy to Houston Street. Chinatown's heart lies south of Canal, not far from the city's Civic Center, where Worth Street, East Broadway and the Bowery meet at **Chatham Square ⓱**.

Though the square is named after William Pitt – the Earl of Chatham – the **Kim Lau Memorial Arch** here was built in honor of a Chinese-American pilot who died a hero in World War II. Nearby high-rise **Confucius Plaza ⓲** is a complex with apartments, stores, an elementary school and an interior tree-shaded park. A bronze statue of the philosopher Confucius stands in front, facing Chatham Square.

Tucked away among the Chinese banks lining the Bowery is a remnant of Old New York: built in 1785, **No. 18 Bowery** is a Federal-style house and the oldest surviving row house in Manhattan. Another striking local landmark on the Bowery is the elegant, pagoda-style **HSBC Bank Building**.

Walk west to **Columbus Park** to reach the top of **Mulberry Street**, one of Chinatown's two main thoroughfares, the other being **Mott Street**. In the early 19th century this was part of the notorious Five Points slum region, evoked at considerable length in Martin Scorsese's 2002 epic *Gangs of New York*, where street gangs ran rampant and squatters' huts formed an equally notorious shanty town, later cleared to make way for the park.

The best place to learn about the neighborhood is at the old (1900s) school building on the corner of Mulberry and Bayard streets, housing the **Museum of Chinese in the Americas ⓳** (70 Mulberry Street, tel: 212-619 4785; closed Mon; free for children under 12).

Founded in 1970, when the area's population began to explode, the museum features a permanent exhibit on the Chinese-American experience, has a research library and a small gift shop, and organizes regular walking tours and lectures.

From here, pass along sidewalks thick with stands selling fruit, vegetables, fish and leaf-wrapped pack-

Map on page 154

Columbus Park in Chinatown has been the recipient of federal funding to renovate its Grand Pavilion, which stands on the northern edge of the park. The pavilion was built in 1897.

BELOW: the air is thick with incense at Chinatown's temples.

Chinese New Year in Chinatown is threatened by the fact that fireworks, its traditional kick-off, have recently been banned by the City of New York. The community is contesting this new, undesirable ruling.

ets of sticky rice, and turn right on **Canal Street**. Crowded with vendors hawking Taiwanese tapes and stores stocked to the brim with designer "knock-offs," this is a scene that feels far removed from the rest of Manhattan. Turn right down Mott Street to find shiny Singapore-style restaurants with marble facades and plastic signs. Some are excellent, and astonishingly cheap, these are part of the "new" Chinatown built by recent, wealthier immigrants from Hong Kong and Shanghai.

Multi-armed goddess

Signs of the "old" Chinatown are still visible, however, especially at the **Chinese Community Center** run by the Chinese Consolidated Benevolent Association, which first opened on Mott Street in 1883. Next door, inside the **Eastern States Buddhist Temple ⓴**, there's a multi-armed statue of the Goddess Kuan-Yui. The air is thick with the scent of sickly sweet incense.

Farther along, the **Church of the Transfiguration** was constructed for an English Lutheran congrega-

tion in 1801, became the Zion Protestant Episcopal Church in 1810, and was sold to the Roman Catholic Church in 1853. Today, it offers services in Cantonese and runs a school for local children.

Turn right down **Pell Street** and you'll see the **Sun Wui District Association** across the street from the **First Chinese Baptist Church**. This type of organization afforded Chinese immigrants another means of coping with the new world in which they found themselves. Unlike some of the other associations, this group chose an edifice more traditionally Chinese in style, maybe to combat homesickness, or maybe to establish home here.

The pagoda roof is topped by two "good luck" ceramic fish. Nearby is the headquarters of the Hip Sing Association, one of Chinatown's many *tongs*, or fraternal organizations. From the 1870s until the 1930s, these groups were involved in often-violent disputes that were sensationalized as "*tong* wars," mainly by the non-Chinese press.

The narrow lane off to the right is

the most crooked street in Manhattan; in the 1600s it was a cart path leading to Hendrik Doyer's brewery. Later, **Doyers Street** became an important communications center, where men gathered to get the latest news from China and to drop off letters and money for home with the small shopkeepers who served as combination banks and post offices.

In keeping with this tradition, the current Chinatown post office was built on the site of the old brewery.

Dim sum

Just before the post office is the **Nom Wah Tea House**, the oldest restaurant in the neighborhood. Unlike many places in the area, this one generally closes early (around 8pm), but has some of the best *dim sum* in Chinatown. The interior is much as it was in 1921, when it opened, with sagging red-leather banquettes, linoleum floor and ceiling fans. The prices are as old-fashioned as the decor.

Food is one of the main attractions of Chinatown and, with hundreds of restaurants to choose from, the hardest part is making a choice of where to eat. Options range from the tiny five-table Malaysia Restaurant in the **Chinatown Arcade** to the New Silver Palace, which seats 800. There's also the Golden Unicorn on East Broadway, where house specialties are served in rather luxurious surroundings, and the Peking Duck House on Mott Street, which was a favorite of the former New York mayor Ed Koch. *(See page 166 for more options.)*

For a deeper taste and sense of Chinese culture, drop in at one of the movie theaters that show films from Taiwan and China, or visit the **Asian-American Arts Center** (26 Bowery), across from the Confucius Plaza complex, which features ongoing exhibits. Upstairs, the **Asian-American Dance Theater** presents both traditional and contemporary dance productions.

Chinese New Year combines feasts, dance and music, beginning with parades and fireworks. The festivities start around the end of January, and go on for several days, usually into February. ❏

Map on page 154

Finding food is never more than a few steps away in Chinatown.

BELOW:
death in Chinatown.

RESTAURANTS, BARS AND CAFÉS

Restaurants

Angelica Kitchen
300 E. 12th St (between 1st and 2nd aves). Tel: 212-228 2909. Open: L & D daily. **$$**
Veg-out on excellent veggie-cuisine, run by people with a retro mind-set.

Da Nico
164 Mulberry St (between Broome and Grand sts). Tel: 212-343 1212. Open: L & D daily. **$$**
Old-style Little Italy, where former mayor Rudy Giuliani can be seen eating, so it must be good.

Dojo
24–26 St Mark's Pl (between 2nd and 3rd aves). Tel: 212-674 9821. Open: L & D daily. **$**
Inexpensive, popular

with the NYU and Cooper Union student set. Amer-Asian health food featuring tofu-burgers, salads and all the other nutritious works.

Excellent Dumpling House
111 Lafayette St (between Canal and Walker sts). Tel: 212-219 0212. Open: L & D daily. **$**
Chinatown standard, spotlessly clean and well run. The name says it all.

Freeman's
Freeman Alley (off Rivington St between Bowery and Chrystie St). Tel: 212-420 0012. Open: D daily, Br Sat–Sun. **$$$**
Devils on horseback anyone? All is done with American character at this fashionable spot; great bar drinks.

Le Gamin
536 E. 5th St (between aves A and B). Tel: 212-254 8409. Open: B, L & D daily. **$$**
One of several around town, all serving affordable French bistro food in comfortable settings.

Grilled Cheese
168 Ludlow St (between Houston and Stanton sts). Tel: 212-982 6600. Open: L & D daily. **$**
This is a small spot dedicated to numerous, unimaginable variations on the standard cheese on toast.

H.S.F.
46 Bowery (between Bayard and Canal sts). Tel: 212-374 1319. Open: L & D daily. **$$**
Originators of *dim-sum* dining in NYC. Rolling tables of tiny Chinese delectables make the rounds of the dining room 'til meal's end.

I Coppi
432 E. 9th St (between 1st Ave and Ave A). Tel: 212-254 2263. Open: D only Mon–Fri, Br & D Sat–Sun. **$$$**
This Tuscan restaurant oozes authenticity thanks to its brick walls, terracotta floors, wood-burning oven and pretty back garden. The dishes are rustic but sophisticated. It's pricey for the casual neighborhood, but highly romantic and very tasty.

Indochine
430 Lafayette St (between Astor Pl and 4th St). Tel: 212-505 5111. Open: D daily. **$$$**
Trendy, tropical decor, French-Vietnamese, still sexy after all these years. It's located across from the Public Theater, with a decently priced pre-theater deal.

industry (food)
509 E. 6th St (between aves A and B). Tel: 212-777 5920. Open: D daily. **$$$**
Expensive tab, but the demand to get a table at this clubby East Villager pays off for delicious "market-driven" New American cuisine.

Jewel Bako
239 E. 5th St (between 2nd and 3rd aves). Tel: 212-979 1012. Open: D Mon–Sat. **$$$$**
Downtown's tiny "Tiffany" of sushi. And you don't need to cash in the diamonds to eat.

Katz's Delicatessen
205 E.. Houston St (at Ludlow St). Tel: 212-254 2246. Open: B, L & D daily. **$$**
This old-style Jewish deli is a New York institution. The huge space is often filled to capacity, especially on Sunday mornings The portions are huge and the service is friendly. Katz's is a must for any first-time visitor to the city.

LEFT: WD-50, the foodie's favorite.

Maia
98 Avenue B (at 6th St). Tel: 212-358 1166. Open: D onlyTues–Sun. **$$**
Lower East side Turkish Delight – open 'til 4am Friday and Saturday.

Mermaid Inn
96 2nd Ave (between 5th and 6th sts). Tel: 212-674 5870. Open: D daily. **$$$**
Winning formula of kitsch and great seafood makes this a popular and fun place.

Miracle Grill
112 1st Ave (between 6th and 7th sts). Tel: 212-254 2353. Open: D daily, Br Sat–Sun. **$$**
One of the first East Village trend-setters; great Southwestern menu, lovely back garden.

Nom Wah Tea House
13 Doyers St (at Chatham Sq). Tel: 212-962 6047. Open: L daily. **$$**
Oldest of its kind serving *dim sum* in a tiny space.

Pho Bang
157 Mott St (between Broome and Grand sts). Tel: 212-966 3797. Open: L & D daily. **$**
Vietnamese noodle shop (several locations) that can't be beaten for value.

Prune
54 E. 1st St (between 1st and 2nd aves). Tel: 212-677 6221. Open: D daily, Br Sat–Sun. **$$$**
Uptowners venture here for a foodie's dream. Chef Gabrielle Hamilton is always making cuisine news in addition to consistently imaginative and innovative menus.

Puglia
189 Hester St (at Mulberry St). Tel: 212-966 6006. Open: L & D daily. **$$**
The Little Italy of old survives since 1919. Things get "pretty crazy" at night according to manager Joey; but group tables, a singer called "The Fat Lady," plus lots of red sauce and red wine make a party every night here.

71 Clinton Fresh Food
71 Clinton St (at Rivington St). Tel: 212-614 6960. Open: D daily. **$$$$**
Like several other places in this neighborhood, this eatery is the size of a shoebox, but on the strength of its culinary reputation always manages to command a faithful following.

Time Café
380 Lafayette St (at Great Jones St). Tel: 212-533 7000. Open: B, L & D Mon–Fri, Br & D Sat–Sun. **$$**
A NoHo American cuisine mainstay with a good bar and a cousin on the Upper West Side.

Suba
109 Ludlow St (between Delancey and Rivington sts). Tel: 212-982 5714. Open: D daily. **$$$**
Unsurpassed for atmosphere, this expensive Spanish spot has a dining room whimsically surrounded by water.

WD-50
50 Clinton St (between Rivington and Stanton). Tel: 212-477 2900. Open: D daily. **$$$$**

WD, which (in the words of Lemony Snicket) here stands for Wally Dufresne, holds court over a brilliant American-eclectic menu. This is a place (and prices) appreciated by foodies from around the city.

Bars and Cafés

Acme Bar and Grill, 9 Great Jones St (between Broadway and Lafayette St), looks like a truck stop, but is worth closer examination.

ChickaLicious, 203 E. 10th St (between 1st and 2nd aves), is a tiny dessert bar serving yummy sweets with sweet wines.

De Robertis, 176 1st Ave (between 10th and 11th sts), is an Italian pasticceria and café established over a century ago – a must.

Earthmatters, 177 Ludlow St (between E. Houston and Stanton sts), is Vegan, a café, a reading library and a grocery store that's open 'til midnight.

Lucky Cheng's, 24 1st Ave (between 1st and 2nd sts), has a late-night scene with the main attraction being the colorful, cross-dressing wait-staff.

Max Fish, 178 Ludlow St (between E. Houston and Stanton sts), is a rowdy rocker-art bar with its own gang of hipsters.

PRICE CATEGORIES

Prices for a three-course dinner per person with half a bottle of wine:
$ = under $20
$$ = $20–$45
$$$ = $45–$60
$$$$ = over $60

RIGHT: I Coppi – rustic, Tuscan and romantic.

NEW YORK'S LESSER-KNOWN MUSEUMS

Done the Met and MoMA? Feel like some wider culture-hopping? Many of New York City's lesser-known museums are undiscovered delights

It seems that New York City has a museum or cultural society dedicated to just about every interest, every art form, and every corner of the globe, from the Kurds to the Chinese to the Swiss to the Puerto Ricans. There is a museum of the American piano and a museum of skyscrapers; a museum for African art, one for folk art, one for illustration and several for photography; a museum of the American Indian, and one for mathematics. There can be few topics New Yorkers haven't been at pains to curate.

Lovers of the traditional life should visit Historic Richmond Town *(see photograph above)*; followers of fashion should be in touch with Chelsea's Fashion Institute of Technology for exhibitions curated by specialists. Children can choose from three museums specially designed to engage little eyes and minds.

ABOVE: Fire! Fire! Soho's New York City Fire Museum is housed in a renovated 1904 firehouse and has a huge collection of exhibits from the mid-18th century.

ABOVE: Jacques Marchais: this Staten Island museum houses one of the largest collections of Tibetan art in the West. Founded in 1945, the grounds have serene terraced meditation gardens, in addition to tranquil fish and lotus ponds.

Dyckman Farmhouse Museum (4881 Broadway at 204th St, tel: 212-304 9422); Tues–Sun 10am–4pm. Charge.
George Gustav Heye Center of the National Museum of the American Indian (1 Bowling Green, tel: 212-668 6624); daily 10am–5pm, Thur until 8pm. Donations.
Historic Richmond Town (441 Clarke Ave, Staten Island, tel: 718-351 1611); Wed–Sun 1–5pm, extended hours July, Aug. Charge.
Jacques Marchais Museum of Tibetan Art (338 Lighthouse Ave, Staten Island, tel: 718-987 3500); Wed–Sun 1–5pm in summer; call for hours Dec–March. Charge.
New York City Fire Museum (278 Spring St, tel: 212-691 1303); Tues–Sat 10am–4pm, Sun 10am–4pm. Charge.
Theodore Roosevelt's Birthplace (28 East 20th St, tel: 212-260 1616); Tues–Sat 9am–5pm. Charge.
Skyscraper Museum (39 Battery Place, tel: 212-968 1961); Wed–Sun, 12-6 pm. Charge.

SKYCRAPER MUSEUM

RIGHT: The National Museum of the American Indian at the George Gustav Heye Center has an excellent library, as well as kids' events throughout the summer months.

ABOVE: The small Skyscraper Museum uses polished stainless-steel floors and ceilings to give a sense of towering canyons. A large-scale "light box" by artist of light and space, James Turrell, is scheduled to form the entrance. Worth visiting for the physical space alone, it features exhibits on the work of pioneers like Frank Lloyd Wright, as well as the original model for the World Trade Center.

BELOW: The Dyckman Farmhouse Museum is Manhattan's only surviving 18th-century farmhouse. Featuring photographs and well-maintained decorations and furnishings from the period, the house offers a unique glimpse into New York City's simpler, rural colonial days.

ABOVE: Theodore (Teddy) Roosevelt's birthplace features personal mementos of the former president, plus house tours on the hour and occasional recitals of chamber music.

SOHO AND TRIBECA

Great food, streetlife and the chance to carouse in
the heart of Manhattan's hippest movie arena –
Soho and Tribeca reflect cool New York
at its positively picturesque

Soho, an acronym for **So**uth of **Ho**uston, is bordered by Canal Street to the south, Lafayette Street to the east, and the Avenue of the Americas (Sixth Avenue) to the west. When Abraham Lincoln made his first campaign speech at nearby Cooper Union, the area was the center of the city's most fashionable shopping and hotel district. By the end of the 19th century, however, the narrow streets were filled by factories, their imaginative cast-iron facades masking sweatshop conditions so horrific that the city fire department dubbed the entire region "Hell's Hundred Acres."

Temples of industry

The neighborhood could well have been razed to the ground in the 1960s if local artists hadn't started moving into the old lofts, and the city hadn't changed zoning laws to allow them to do so legitimately.

Around the same time, conservationists established the **Soho Cast Iron Historic District** to protect the appearance of these elaborate "temples of industry." Apartments now are too expensive for all but the most successful (or those who got in when prices were low), and many of Soho's art galleries have relocated above street level to avoid the exorbitant rents. Other galleries have

absconded completely – to Chelsea, Fifth Avenue or 57th Street. If Soho is no longer the artists' neighborhood of old, it does maintain a uniquely New York combination of grit and blatant commercialism, where burly men unload trucks right by the outrageous window displays, and double-decker tour buses lumber and wind slowly through the cobble-stoned streets.

The main drag is **West Broadway** ㉑, lined by stores offering everything from jewelry to quirky house-

Map on page 154

LEFT: in this neighborhood, it's all in the jeans.
BELOW: Soho cast-iron "temple of industry."

All New Yorkers rate Dean & Deluca, which sells stylish food fit for any occasion.

hold wares. On Saturdays, in particular, it's packed with crowds of tourists loaded down with shopping bags. From Houston to Canal, you'll find a clutch of boutiques hawking European fashions (René Lezard at 417) and fashionable footwear (Fortuna Valentino at 422), along with a bracing spray of imported Continental attitude. The selection of wares also includes the delicate lingerie at Joovay (436) and the neon cosmetics and clothing of Hotel Venus (382), all interspersed with tempting restaurants, bars and cafés.

Prince Street ㉒, has all but forsaken galleries and turned into prime shopping territory, but a permanent art installation still lingers on the Greene Street side of **114 Prince Street**, where the building's cast-iron facade was reproduced as a *trompe l'oeil* mural by artist Richard Haas. Next door, you can stop and shop for French ready-to-wear at agnès b, or take a coffee break at any one of a number of espresso bars.

Station A (103 Prince) is the hectic new computer retail temple to iPods and everything Apple. The

Romanesque Revival-style building on the opposite corner dates from the same period, but a century or so later has been transformed into the small, luxurious hotel **The Mercer** *(see page 220)*. Beneath the hotel is the highly acclaimed basement-level restaurant, the Mercer Kitchen.

Broadway and beyond

Once home to the city's most elegant stores, and later to textile outlets, discount stores and delis, the stately cast-iron buildings on Broadway below Canal Street reacquired cachet in the 1980s, first as museums, then as galleries, and then as stores like Pottery Barn and Eddie Bauer. A new downtown **Bloomingdale's** (504 Broadway) has added more shopper traffic to the busy sidewalks. And Chinatown "chic" has moved into Soho at Pearl River (477 Broadway), an Asian emporium choc-full of stylish clothes and accessories.

A 1904 cast-iron confection called the **Little Singer Building**, designed by Ernest Flagg, stands across Broadway from the now-famous **Dean & Deluca ㉓** (560 Broad-

way), at the opposite corner of Prince Street. Dean & Deluca has been described by the *Washington Post* as "a combination of Paris' Fauchon, London's Harrod's Food Halls and Milan's Peck all rolled into one," and presents food-as-art: a cornucopia of fruits, vegetables and imported gourmet grocery specialities. This has proved to be so successful a formula that Dean & Deluca stores have branched out. The stand-up coffee bar is stocked with delectable pastries, and is a perfect place for a quick snack.

Several galleries are located on the upper floors of buildings along this part of Broadway. If the Harry Potter novels made J.K. Rowling a millionaire, evidence that it did even more for her publisher **Scholastic Books** is their huge new bookstore at 555 Broadway. Aisles of kids' books and reading events make this a good family stop.

A walk east on Prince Street leads to Lafayette Street, where bits of old New York, literally, can be purchased on the premises of Lost City Arts (275 Lafayette).

In the opposite direction, the **Children's Museum of the Arts** ㉔ (182 Lafayette Street between Broome and Grand streets, tel: 212-941 9198; charge) has great interactive exhibits for kids; it's open every day but Monday and Tuesday.

Back to Broadway, the **Haughwout Building** ㉕ is the Palazzo-style structure near Broome Street. The Haughwout is one of Soho's oldest – and most striking – cast-iron edifices. Designed by John Gaynor, it was constructed in 1857 as one of the country's first retail stores, complete with the country's first elevator. A left on Mercer leads to The Enchanted Forest, a whimsically decorated store between Spring and Broome that's a fantasy world of toys and children's games.

Flora and Miss Lizzie

Named after a Revolutionary War general, **Greene Street** ㉖, like Mercer and Wooster streets, runs parallel to West Broadway and Broadway. In the late 19th century it was the center of New York's most notorious red-light district, where

Map on page 154

So Carrie went off with Big, and Miranda and Steve moved to the suburbs, but what happened to Patricia Field, the designer of Sex and the City*'s fab frocks? Check out her store, Hotel Venus, at 382 West Broadway between Spring and Broome streets.*

BELOW: animal magic in Soho.

Light up your life at Lighting Plus, just a few blocks up Broadway at Number 676

BELOW: making the style scene in Soho.

brothels with names like Flora's and Miss Lizzie's flourished behind shuttered windows.

As befits one of the Soho Cast Iron Historic District's prime thoroughfares, Greene Street also offers a rich concentration of this uniquely American architecture at its best, including (at the Canal Street end) the city's longest continuous row of cast-iron buildings.

At the corner of Broome Street, the 1872 **Gunther Building** is particularly worthy of notice. Before continuing, stop and admire the cream-colored architectural "king" of cast-iron splendor at **72–76 Greene Street** just opposite. This impressively ornate structure was designed and built by Isaac Duckworth in 1873.

More Soho shopping

Soho shopping continues at Louis Vuitton (116 Greene Street) and at Back Pages Antiques (125 Greene Street), where the specialty is classic jukeboxes. At the corner of Spring and Wooster, the white clapboard and brick house built in 1818

is home to Tennessee Mountain, a popular rib joint. The entrance is around the corner on Wooster Street and there's a nice view of Soho's weekend action from the second-floor windows.

Turn onto stone-cobbled **Wooster Street ㉗** for the **Tony Shafrazi Gallery** (119 Wooster) and the **Howard Greenberg Gallery** (upstairs at 120 Wooster), which, like many galleries, seems to hop from street to street. A few have managed to anchor themselves at the same spot for years, however, including the **Dia Center for the Arts'** second-floor space at 141 Wooster Street, where *New York Earth Room* by Walter De Maria is on display (closed in summer).

The Dia Center has another exhibition space on the second floor of a building on West Broadway and a major gallery in Chelsea. Two more examples of New York longevity can be found toward Broome Street, where Printed Matter (77 Wooster Street) specializes in books by artists, and near the corner of Grand Street, where the ever-popular and

Leo Castelli

Leo Castelli's art gallery at 420 West Broadway gave a shop window to the 1960s and 1970s Pop Art movement, and a massive boost to the Soho arts scene. Leo and his wife Ileana first had a gallery in Paris in 1935, showing Surrealist and neo-Romantic works, but when World War II broke out they decamped for New York. It wasn't until 1954, when Leo saw some of Robert Rauschenberg's work, that he felt moved to re-enter the art world, wanting only to work with art that inspired him with "pure enthusiasm."

In the early 1960s, Roy Lichtenstein's children asked him, "Daddy, why can't you paint as good as these comics?" and he took up the challenge by painting Mickey Mouse and Donald Duck pictures for them. Then – WHAM! It hit him; the idea of popular, commercial objects as artistic symbols. This was the same insight that underlay Andy Warhol's Campbell's soup cans and Brillo boxes.

The Pop Art movement exploded, and Castelli led the way in exhibiting these groundbreaking expressions, as well as championing other little-known artists such as Bruce Nauman, Jasper Johns, Claes Oldenburg and James Rosenquist. Leo Castelli died in New York City on August 22, 1999.

experimental **Performing Garage** (33 Wooster, tel: 212-966 3651) has presented theater, dance and performance art since 1967. A great shopping stop on Wooster is No. 136 where Ad Hoc stocks stacks of color-coordinated housewares, china, soaps and linens.

Cast-iron stomachs

John Broome was a successful merchant who imported tea and silk from China at the end of the Revolutionary War, so he might have appreciated the fresh produce and other goods sold at the Gourmet Garage (453 Broome, at Mercer Street) if not the pots, pans and garlic peelers stocked in abundance at Broadway Panhandler (477).

In general, Broome Street is one of Soho's least jazzed-up thoroughfares, unless you count the ornate Calvert Vaux-designed edifice at No. 448, built in 1872. A lunch treat awaits a little farther on at the corner of West Broadway in the **Broome Street Bar**, located in a pretty, 18th-century house.

Crossing West Broadway, you're on the fringe of the South Village, where chic little shoe salons and boutiques nestle among places like the **Vesuvio Bakery** on Prince between West Broadway and Thompson Street, which, until very recently, had been run by the same family since the 1920s. **Milady's**, another nearby neighborhood bar (162 Prince) and restaurant has been around for close to half a century.

One of those refreshment stops should provide the stamina for a detour down Thompson to Spring Street, then west across Sixth Avenue to the **New York City Fire Museum** ㉘ (tel: 212-691 1303; closed Mon; charge), located at 278 Spring Street, between Varick and Hudson streets. It's worth the four-block hike to Engine Company No. 30's former headquarters to see the antique hand- and horse-pulled wagons *(see also page 168)*.

Spiritual refueling awaits at The Sufi Bookstore (225 West Broadway). Stop in to find out about lectures and meditation sessions.

Back on West Broadway, Soho comes to a halt at **Canal Street** ㉙,

Map on page 154

TIP

With a nod to Soho's gallery-dominated past, some consider the Soho branch of Bloomingdale's to be a work of art in itself: check out the chandelier by the atrium.

BELOW: the late Leo Castelli, the influential art dealer who championed Warhol and Lichtenstein.

TIP

Need to recharge?
Slope into Bliss day
spa at its flagship
Soho location, 568
Broadway at Prince
Street, tel: 212-219
8970, for premium
pampering. Other loca-
tions around town, too.

BELOW:
Vesuvio at 160 Prince
Street has been in the
bakery business since
the 1920s.

where stores sell plastic odds and
ends, rubber tubing, neon signs,
household appliances and barrels of
peculiar industrial leftovers. It's all
mixed together in a bedlam of hot-
dog carts and street vendors displaying old books, new CDs and DVDs
and from time to time, some *bona-
fide* treasures.

To end the tour of Soho in grander
fashion, stop in at the **Soho Grand
Hotel** (310 West Broadway, between
Grand and Canal streets, *see page
220*). When it opened, this was the
first new hotel in this part of the city
since the mid-1800s, when the fashionable American House Hotel stood
at the corner of Spring Street, and the
white-marble St Nicholas Hotel on
Broadway and Broome held gala
polka parties.

Rising 15 stories above the rest of
the neighborhood, the Soho Grand
manages to fit in with the "temples
of industry," thanks to its industrial-
chic decor and cozy lobby bar and
lounge, which has become a popular
meeting place for fashion and enter-
tainment-industry types.

It's also the only hotel in town

where pets are not only welcome but
are as pampered as their owners. If
you arrive without an animal companion, you can request a complimentary bowl of goldfish.

Tribeca

In the late 1970s, artists in search of
lower rents migrated south from
Soho to **Tribeca** – the **Tri**angle
Below **Ca**nal – which lies south of
Canal Street to Chambers Street, and
west from Broadway to the Hudson
River. Called Washington Market in
the days when the city's major produce businesses operated here
(before they moved to Hunt's Point
in the Bronx), this part of the Lower
West Side is one of Manhattan's
most pleasant neighborhoods.

An eclectic blend of renovated
commercial warehouses, the area
sports Corinthian columns, condo-
minium towers and celebrity restaurants. Tribeca was where artists like
David Salle and Laurie Anderson
showed their early works at the
Alternative Museum and Franklin
Furnace (both now closed).

Today's Tribeca scene has more to
show from the culinary arts than fine
arts, but its largely residential atmosphere makes a pleasant change of
pace from Soho's congested and
tourist-packed streets.

A block south of Canal, the
Tribeca Grand Hotel, rising from
the triangle bordered by Sixth
Avenue, Walker and White streets,
looms over one of the area's oldest
survivors: an 1809 brick house at **2
White Street**, just off West Broadway, which dates back to an earlier
era when this was the city's original
residential enclave.

The Tribeca Grand, a younger sister to the seriously cool Soho Grand,
keeps the residential tradition alive
with its hip and trendy style of hos-
pitality. Features for glamorous
guests include an atrium lounge and
203 ergonomically designed rooms

with extra-large windows and high-speed internet access.

Walk east on Leonard Street (the next street after Franklin) past some of Tribeca's finest cast-iron architecture, to the **Knitting Factory ③** (74 Leonard Street, tel: 212-219 3006), one of the city's largest music venues. The building, topped by an ornate clock tower that looms ahead, is the former New York Life Insurance Building, which was remodeled by Stanford White in 1898.

The building has belonged to the city since the late 1960s and now houses various offices as well as the top-floor **Clocktower Gallery** (108 Leonard Street, tel: 212-233 1096), occupied by artists' studios and affiliated with the excellent P.S.1 Museum in Queens. It's only occasionally open to the public for special exhibits or events, but try to be there if possible, because the views of downtown New York from here are spectacular.

On the corner of Thomas Street and West Broadway, two blocks below Leonard Street, a red neon sign spells out "Cafeteria," but don't be fooled. This 1930s mock-stone building has housed **Odeon**, one of Downtown's hippest restaurants since it opened in 1980. Unlike many trendy spots, it shows no signs of fading away and is still a favorite with the *cognoscenti*, especially late into the night.

Across the way is Duane Street. Named for New York's first post-Revolution mayor, this byway meets Hudson Street at tiny triangular **Duane Park ③** – all that's left of a farm the city bought for $5 in 1795. **Staple Street**, a narrow strip of cobblestone where "staple" produce was once unloaded, connects the park with the brick, ornate **Mercantile Exchange Building ③**, on the corner of Harrison and Hudson streets. Built in 1884 as the trading center for the egg and butter business (but

now housing offices), the ground-level are the premises of the decidedly upscale Chanterelle, another Tribeca temple of Gallic cuisine.

The neighboring **Western Union Building ③** at 60 Hudson Street soars 24 storys above the rest of the neighborhood like a layered missile, and is made of 19 different shades of brick. Its interior lobby, where even the letterboxes are marvels of art deco artistry, is also quite breathtaking – and provides for a very diverting short cut on the route back to West Broadway.

Old and new

Greenwich Street is where much of Tribeca's new development is centered, although you can still find some authentic early remnants – like the 19th-century lantern factory between Laight and Vestry streets that now houses million-dollar lofts. In the new non-smoking New York, the wine and cigar club provides a growing niche.

The corner of Greenwich and Franklin streets is the place where actor Robert de Niro transformed the

The Taste of Tribeca Food Festival in early summer attracts foodies from all over the city.

BELOW: acclaimed chef David Bouley hard at work; Bouley has two Tribeca restaurants.

Map on page 154

Is the glass half empty or half full?

BELOW: sh-h-h: no smoking allowed anymore.

old Martinson Coffee Factory into the **Tribeca Film Center** ❹. On the first floor is **Tribeca Grill**. Many come here in the hope of seeing de Niro or film biz luminaries from the upstairs offices. Chances are, the closest you'll get to a sighting is one of de Niro's dad's paintings on the walls, and while you do occasionally see people talking "back-end" and reading scripts, most of the clientele are regular business types and star-struck tourists. The food, however, rarely disappoints. **Layla** is another de Niro restaurant *(see page 179)*.

The late 18th- and early 19th-century brick houses on **Harrison Street** look incongrous, like a stage set in the shadow of **Independence Plaza**'s gargantuan 1970s apartment towers, but like the house on White Street, they're survivors of Tribeca's residential beginnings.

A block farther down, **Bazzini's** at 339 Greenwich Street, is a hardy remnant of the area's old commercial incarnation; it has been a fruit and nut wholesaler since 1886, and it's still possible to buy huge bags of pistachios and other delicacies here.

Grass and a gazebo

Opposite the big line of condo dwellings stretching between Duane and Chambers streets, **Washington Market Park** ❺ has a thick grassy meadow to stretch out on, and even a fanciful gazebo to daydream in. Public School 234 – its wrought-iron fence embossed with Spanish galleons in full sail – is across from the park and worth noting.

A right turn here takes you to the Borough of Manhattan Community College, in a southern extension of Independence Plaza. This is where the well-established and attended **Tribeca Performing Arts Center** (tel: 212-220 1406) specializes in multicultural performances.

From Chambers and West Street, you can reach **Hudson River Park** via a **pedestrian bridge** that stretches across the West Side Highway. Landscaped walkways and bike paths extend north along the river beyond Pier 25, and south to connect to Battery Park City. If you continue south, there's a scenic riverside walk, complete with views of the Statue of Liberty. ❑

RESTAURANTS, BARS AND CAFÉS

Restaurants

Balthazar
80 Spring St (between Broadway and Crosby sts). Tel: 212-965 1414. Open: B, L & D daily. **$$$** Parisian-style brasserie; hard to imagine Soho without it.

Bar Tonno
17 Cleveland Pl (at Lafayette and Spring sts). Tel: 212-966 7334 Open: D only Mon–Sat. **$$$** Innovative, indeed: come here for Italian sushi

Bouley
120 W. Broadway (at Duane St). Tel: 212-964 2525. Open: L & D daily. **$$$$** Fans claim that David Bouley's "new French" food experience transcends price, but the fact remains that this is one of New York's Top Ten. Bouley's Viennese waltz is Danube, on Hudson, dishing up Austrian food.

Bubby's
120 Hudson St (at N. Moore St). Tel: 212-219 0666. Open: B, L & D daily. **$$** Funky joint, kid-friendly but also a celeb-spot from time to time. Comfort food comes top of the menu.

Ecco
124 Chambers St (between Church St and W. Broadway). Tel: 212-227 7074. Open: L & D, Mon–Fri, D only Sat. **$$$** Longtime Italian favorite way Downtown.

Jerry's
101 Prince St (between Greene and Mercer sts). Tel: 212-966 9464. Open: B, L & D daily. **$$** Bustling red, white and black chrome and vinyl Soho mainstay serving a more sophisticated form of diner food.

Layla
211 W. Broadway (at Franklin St). Tel: 212-431 0700. Open:D only, Tues–Sat. **$$$** Co-owner Robert de Niro brings star quality to the Mid-Eastern inspired menu. There are even belly dancers.

Lucky Strike
59 Grand St (between W. Broadway and Wooster St). Tel: 212-941 0479. Open: L & D daily. **$$** Hip and seasoned bistro fare, always a good bet. Easily affordable and stays up late.

Montrachet
239 W. Broadway (between Walker and White sts). Tel: 212-219 2777. Open: D Mon–Sat, L Fri only. **$$$$** Still serving four-star French foods with excellent wines; check out the Friday (only) prix-fix lunch – it's a real steal for the neighborhood.

Megu
62 Thomas St (at W. Broadway). Tel: 212-964 7777. Open: D daily. Extravagant Downtown Japanese. Megu's menu is overwhelming, and

perhaps over-priced but much talked about around town.

Nobu
105 Hudson St (between Franklin and No. Moore sts). Tel: 212-219 0500. Open: D daily, L Mon–Fri. **$$$$** Tribeca celeb-spot, unique for its Japanese-Peruvian cuisine and near impossibility of getting a booking. Nobu Next Door is a second-best and does not allow reservations.

Odeon
145 W. Broadway (between Duane and Thomas sts). Tel: 212-233 0507. Open: L & D daily. **$$$** Great bar atmosphere, plus excellent French-American menu, still going hip and strong on the Tribeca scene.

Provence
38 MacDougal St (at Prince St). Tel: 212-475 7500. Open: D daily, L Tues-Fri, Br Sat–Sun. **$$$** Romantic old timer that feels much more like France than Soho.

Raoul's
180 Prince St (between Sullivan and Thompson). Tel: 212-966 3518. Open: D daily. **$$$** French bistro still doing roaring trade after 25 years of serving the international chic set.

Savoy
70 Prince St (at Crosby St). Tel: 212-219 8570. Open: D daily, L Mon–Sat. **$$$** Stylish, but comfy corner

"house" serving highly creative food that employs only the freshest of local farmers' market products.

Zoe
90 Prince St (between Broadway and Mercer sts). Tel: 212-966 6722. Open: L daily, D Tues-Sun. **$$$** One of Soho's first trendy restaurants, still dispensing smart New American food.

Bars and Cafés

Café Borgia II, 161 Prince St at Mercer St, is where espresso and a canola can really perk up a Soho shopping spree.

Cupping Room Café, 359 W. Broadway (between Broome and Grand sts), is a cozy place for brunch .

Fanelli's, 94 Prince St at Mercer, is where trendy Soho grew up, around this down-to-earth corner hang-out.

Puffy's Tavern at 81 Hudson St (between Harrison and Jay sts), stays open 'til 4am for Tribeca's best.

PRICE CATEGORIES

Prices for a three-course dinner per person with half a bottle of wine:

$ = under $20
$$ = $20–$45
$$$ = $45–$60
$$$$ = over $60

LOWER MANHATTAN

Lower Manhattan is where New York began. Now it's
an area of high finance and poignant memories,
WiFi parks and South Street Seaport.
Plus the Staten Island ferry, of course

Below Chambers Street to the west and the Brooklyn Bridge to the east is the original New York, where the Dutch and the English first settled; the country's first hotel was built; the first president was sworn in; and the city's first theatrical opening night took place. Clipper ships bound for the California Gold Rush sailed from Lower Manhattan's piers in the 1850s, and by 1895, the first skyscraper stood 20 stories above lower Broadway.

Over a century later, the city's financial powerhouses and city government areas are bracketed by outdoor recreations like the South Street Seaport and Battery Park. Some of the landmark office buildings on or near Wall Street have been converted to high-tech business use and residential apartments. But Manhattan's oldest neighborhood also has some of its most moving history, being the site of two memorials to modern tragedies. Just as events in the 20th century shifted the area from a maritime economy to one of financial commerce, so, too, have events early in the 21st century changed the face of Lower Manhattan once again.

The changes have been absorbed with typical New York energy, adapting and reconstructing, moving on, without missing a beat.

Moving memorials

The first memorial to the past lies on the southwestern tip of Manhattan. In a prime position overlooking the Hudson River is the **Museum of Jewish Heritage ❶** – A Living Memorial to the Holocaust (18 First Place, tel: 212-968 1800; closed Sat; charge). With more than 2,000 photographs, artifacts and 24 original documentaries, the museum was extended by a new wing in 2003, offering a digitally-equipped performance center. Steven Spielberg con-

Map on page 182

LEFT: South Street Seaport.
BELOW: the Museum of Jewish Heritage.

As the grounds of the former World Trade Center are now a construction site, some visitors feel bereft of a place to reflect on the tragedy. St Paul's Chapel has a permanent exhibit, Unwavering Spirit: Hope and Healing at Ground Zero.

tributed videotaped testimonies from victims of the Holocaust after he directed *Schindler's List*.

Beyond the museum, pathways wind through **Robert F. Wagner Jr Park**, which has beautifully landscaped gardens, a pair of deck-topped brick pavilions, and places to sit with fine views of New York Harbor. Here are opportunities to meditate on the Jewish Museum's stated aim, which is to provide a thoughtful and moving chronicle of history, keeping the memory of the past alive and offering hope for the future.

Site of the Twin Towers

More space for contemplation is provided along the green and leafy esplanade in front of **Battery Park City ➋**, the huge, 92-acre (37-hectare) development stretching along the **Hudson River** – and about which more is written later. These reflections might include more recent events than the Holocaust, however, for between West Street and Trinity Place is the site of the **former World Trade Center ➌**.

Rising an impressive 110 stories into the sky, the World Trade Center was a major New York tourist attrac-

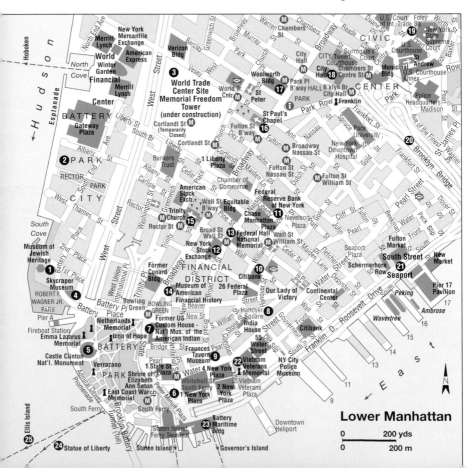

Lower Manhattan

tion. The Twin Towers were the most prominent structures in a 16-acre (6.5-hectare), seven-building complex that took 17 years to complete. It was a classic piece of 1970s architecture, and the view from the South Tower's 107th-floor Observation Deck was one of the best in the city. On September 11, 2001, a day no New Yorker will forget, and witnessed on TV screens around the globe, nearly 3,000 people died as the result of suicide terrorist attacks.

Places of pilgrimage

The grounds of the World Trade Center are now a construction site, as work continues on **Freedom Tower**, a 1,776ft (541-meter) skyscraper to open around 2008. Visitors who would like a moment to reflect on the tragedy away from the sound of bulldozers are encouraged to go to St Paul's Chapel. (For more on the historic significance of St Paul's, *see page 187*.)

Alternatively, there's Battery Park. Fritz Koenig's huge bronze sculpture *The Sphere* had stood for more than 30 years in the World Trade Center Plaza, and withstood the tons of metal and concrete crashing down upon it. In March 2002, the battered globe was moved to Battery Park and re-titled *An Icon of Hope*, at the foot of a bed of roses called *Hope Garden*. An eternal flame burns in memory.

The **World Financial Center**, with its towers and elegant **Winter Garden**, was repaired after structural damage during the attacks, and high-profile occupants such as Dow Jones and the *Wall Street Journal* were soon eager to move back in. Battery Park City, built on river-reclaimed land that included acres of earth from the construction of the World Trade Center, saw a shift in population.

Many residents had moved out to the suburbs, but in that regenerative way of a world-class city, other people moved in, bringing with them energy and a fresh new outlook. A third of the area around Battery Park City is public space, and linked to Manhattan's riverfront expansion by scenic walkways, meandering north to Tribeca and beyond.

Map on page 182

St Paul's Chapel (211 Broadway between Fulton and Vestry streets), offered aid during the World Trade Center tragedy. The photo above shows a memorial service.

BELOW:
the World Financial Center's elegant Winter Garden.

BELOW:
*An Icon of Hope, in
Battery Park, is a
memorial to the
victims of the World
Trade Center tragedy.*

In the direction of the Jewish
Museum is the **Esplanade**, stretching for more than a mile. There are
also benches that offer relaxing van-
tage points for enjoying the splendid views across the Hudson River
and the Statue of Liberty. Those
with an interest in modern architecture may particularly enjoy the interior of the **Skyscraper Museum ❹**
at 39 Battery Place, tel: 212-968
1961, open noon–6pm Wed–Sun
(see page 168).

Earliest New York

At the island's tip, **Battery Park** is
where New Amsterdam was first settled by Europeans, and New York's
history began. Named for the battery
of protective cannons that once
stood here, the area includes **Castle
Clinton ❺**, a reddish-stone former
fort that was built as a defense
against the British in the War of
1812. It originally stood about 200 ft
(60 meters) offshore.

In 1824, as Castle Garden, this
was the city's premier place of
amusement, where Samuel Morse
gave his first public telegraph

demonstration and Swedish singer
Jenny Lind made her American
debut in a tumultuously acclaimed
concert in 1850 (for which some
wealthy New Yorkers paid a then-
unheard-of $30 a ticket). Not long
after, the area was joined to the
mainland by landfill and served as
the New York State Immigration
Station, where more than 8 million
immigrants were processed between
1855 and 1890.

For two years, potential settlers
were processed on a barge moored
in the Hudson River, but when the
new headquarters opened on Ellis
Island in 1892, the tide of immigration shifted. The site of the New
York Aquarium until 1941, Castle
Clinton was declared a national
monument in 1950 and opened to
the public in 1975. Today it is run by
the National Park Service.

New York Unearthed

Peter Minuit Plaza ❻, east of Battery Park, is named for the first governor (director general) of New
Amsterdam. In a tiny park nearby, a
plaque commemorates some of the
city's lesser-known arrivals: 23
Sephardic Jews, dropped off by a
French ship in 1654, who founded
New Amsterdam's first Jewish congregation, Shearith Israel.

Turn left on State Street, once
lined by wealthy merchants' houses,
and you come to the **Rectory of the
Shrine of the Blessed Elizabeth
Ann Seton** (7 State Street), in the
only 18th-century mansion still
standing here. The chapel next door
contains a statue of this American-
born saint, who founded the Sisters
of Charity in 1809 and was canon-
ized in 1975 by Pope Paul VI.

Herman Melville, author of *Moby
Dick,* was born in a house near 17
State Street, where today, **New York
Unearthed** (tel: 212-748 8628)
offers a glimpse of what actually lies
beneath the city streets. Open by

appointment only, tours can be arranged through the South Street Seaport Museum. It includes relics gleaned from ongoing digs in the historic Lower Manhattan area, as well an archeological lab.

On the other side of State Street from Battery Park (and across from Bowling Green subway station), the former **US Custom House** ❼ was designed by Cass Gilbert and built in 1907. A magnificent example of beaux-arts architecture, with a facade embellished by ornate limestone sculpture that represents four of the world's continents and "eight races" of mankind, this grand edifice also has striking Reginald Marsh murals on the rotunda ceiling inside.

Indians at the Smithsonian

In what could seem an ironic twist, standing opposite pretty **Bowling Green Park**, the spot where Peter Minuit is believed to have given goods to the value of $24 to the local Indians for the purchase of Manhattan Island, the Custom House is now the **George Gustav Heye Center of the National Museum of the American Indian** (One Bowling Green, tel: 212-514 3700; free). Operated by the Smithsonian Institution, the exhibits seem dwarfed by the grand surroundings of the Custom House, but the museum is a worthy achievement nevertheless.

From Bowling Green, New York's first public park, you can wander up narrow Stone Street (the city's first paved byway) to Broad Street, or take a quick detour back to State Street before following Pearl Street to **Hanover Square** ❽.

The square burned to ashes in the Great Fire of 1835, one of many fires that destroyed virtually all remnants of Dutch New Amsterdam. According to one eyewitness who was watching from Brooklyn, "the sparks from that fire came over the river so thick that the neighbors...

were obliged to keep their roofs wet all night." The square recovered to become a thriving commercial center and includes **India House** (1 Hanover Square), an 1850s Italianate brownstone that's been home to a private club (at lunchtime) for maritime movers and shakers since 1914. You don't have to be a member, however, to drop in for a drink or dinner at the bar and restaurant, Bayard's, upstairs.

Farther south, at the corner of Pearl and Broad streets, **Fraunces Tavern** is a 1907 reconstruction of the old Queens Head Tavern run by Samuel Fraunces in the late 18th century. The New York Chamber of Commerce got its start over a few mugs of ale here, and George Washington gave an emotional farewell address to his troops in 1783 in the Long Room.

Still a restaurant, the premises also house the **Fraunces Tavern Museum** ❾ (54 Pearl Street, tel: 212-425 1778; closed Sun and Mon; charge), where exhibits include a lock of Washington's hair, the Long Room complete with period furni-

Map on page 182

Detail on an exterior wall of the Museum of the American Indian.

BELOW: sculpture outside the US Custom House.

BELOW: the New York Stock Exchange building dates from 1903.

ture; a fragment of one of Washington's teeth (not, contrary to legend, wooden), and a shoe that belonged to his wife, Martha. The Flag Gallery exhibits more than 200 flags from the Revolutionary War era.

Wall Street

Captains of industry have dined at **Delmonico's**, at the corner of Beaver and William streets, since the mid 1800s, when two Swiss brothers established the city's first formal French restaurant. Stop and admire the impressive marble columns at the entrance, reputedly shipped over from Pompeii *(see page 193)*.

Then walk north on William Street (its twists and turns a reminder of when it was known as Horse and Cart Street) to **Wall Street** ❿, the traditional center of city commerce, where the narrow stone canyons are lined by towering banks, brokerage houses and law offices.

Remembered for many traumatic scenes during the 1929 Stock Market crash, the street took its name from the 17th-century wall – or, more accurately, a wooden stockade

built by the Dutch as protection against the threat of Indian and English attacks. The country's first stock exchange began just in front of **60 Wall Street** in 1792, when 24 brokers gathered beneath a buttonwood tree. The building at **55 Wall Street** is a massive columned landmark that dates to 1841 and served as the original Merchants' Exchange, later as headquarters for the influential First National City Bank. Now it houses the opulent Regent Hotel.

Following William Street to Maiden Lane will lead to **Nevelson Plaza**, with seven tall **abstract sculptures** by the late Louise Nevelson, a long-time New York resident. Money may not be art, but there's a lot of it at the **Federal Reserve Bank** ⓫ (33 Liberty Street), west of Nevelson Plaza.

Constructed in 1924, as well as wheelbarrows-full of old and counterfeit cash, this imposing edifice is said to house a quarter of the world's gold reserves. Guided tours are by reservation only, tel: 212-720 6130).

Easy Street

Double back to Wall Street and the corner of Broad Street, where the **New York Stock Exchange** ⓬ building was constructed at the corner of Broad Street in 1903, and is fronted by an impressive facade of Corinthian columns. The well-known Visitors' Gallery is, alas, no longer open to casual visitors.

The Greek temple-style **Federal Hall National Memorial** ⓭ (26 Wall Street, tel: 212-825 6888) is, however, open to the public, but on weekdays only. It's on the site of the original Federal Hall, where on April 30, 1789, George Washington was sworn in as the first President of the United States (there's an impressive statue of him on the steps); it later became a branch of the US Treasury Department. Today it's run by the National Park

Service and includes exhibits of historical memorabilia, including the suit that George Washington wore at his historic inauguration.

Financial history

A couple of blocks south, at the corner of Beaver Street, the intriguing **Museum of American Financial History** ⓮ (28 Broadway, tel: 212-908 4110; closed Sun and Mon; small charge) is appropriately located inside a landmark skyscraper built in 1922 by Standard Oil, the company that made John D. Rockefeller rich and famous. While the museum is dedicated to the celebration of the trading and financial industries, it includes a collection of antique stocks and bonds, as well as memorabilia from the era of the robber barons, a group that included Messrs Carnegie and Frick, as well as canny John D. himself.

At the very top of Wall Street, where it meets Broadway, the pretty, neo-Gothic **Trinity Church** ⓯ is a serene survivor of early New York. First established in 1698, the present 1846 church is the third one built on the same site. **Trinity Church graveyard** contains some of the oldest graves in the city – including that of Alexander Hamilton, the US's first Secretary of the Treasury, who owned a house at 33 Wall Street and was killed in a duel with Aaron Burr. A small **museum** (tel: 212-602 0800; open except when services are being conducted) offers a look at the original charter, among other historic artifacts. Behind the church is a bookstore that sells books with theological and religious themes.

Five blocks north on Broadway, between Fulton and Vesey streets, George Washington's personal church pew is preserved at **St Paul's Chapel** ⓰, part of the Trinity Church Parish, and Manhattan's oldest public building in continuous use. Built in 1766, this Georgian-style landmark is the only church left from the colonial era, when luminaries like Prince William (later William IV) and Lord Cornwallis worshipped here.

Although it is located one block east of the World Trade Center, remarkably, it was not damaged and

Map on page 182

Wall Street: named for the barrier erected by the Dutch against the English in the 1600s.

BELOW: stockbrokers trading stock.

The Woolworth Building was known as the "cathedral of commerce."

BELOW: City Hall Park.

is now the site of a permanent 9/11 exhibit (*see page 182*).

Though not exactly spiritual, the gargoyle-topped **Woolworth Building** ⑰ (233 Broadway) was known in its heyday as the "cathedral of commerce." Designed by architect Cass Gilbert, from 1913 until 1929, when the Chrysler Building was completed, its 60 stories and soaring height of almost 800 ft (245 meters) made it the tallest building in the world. The Gothic-Revival tower cost five-and-dime baron Frank W. Woolworth $13 million, and was officially opened by President Woodrow Wilson, who pushed a button in Washington that successfully lit up all of the floors.

Power complex

Since 1910, New York has honored everyone from Teddy Roosevelt to Nelson Mandela (and, of course, the New York Yankees) with ticker-tape parades that conclude at handsome **City Hall** ⑱. At the junction of Broadway and Park Row, this French Renaissance/Federal-style edifice has been the seat of city government since DeWitt Clinton was mayor in 1812, and was co-designed by French architect Joseph François Mangin, responsible for the Place de la Concorde in Paris.

City Hall Park, a triangular, tree-shaded former common in front of City Hall, has played an important role throughout the city's history: as the site of public executions, almshouses for the poor and a British prison for captured Revolutionary soldiers. It's also where Alexander Hamilton led a protest against the tea tax in 1774, and where, two years later, George Washington and his troops heard the Declaration of Independence for the first time. Behind City Hall stands the former New York County Courthouse, dubbed on its completion in 1878 the **Tweed Courthouse**.

This was after the revelation that "Boss" Tweed and his Tammany Hall cronies had pocketed some $9 million of the final $14 million construction costs. After extensive refurbishment, the courthouse is the new home of the New York City Department of Education.

The Brooklyn Bridge

The Brooklyn Bridge was the inspiration of engineer John Augustus Roebling, the inventor of wire cable, and the span between its two towers of almost 1,600 ft (488 meters) was the longest in the world. The bridge spans the East River from City Hall to Brooklyn's Cadman Plaza. The unprecedented use of steel cable in a suspension bridge was to provide unmatched stability and strength, as well as present a striking image to the public.

Construction, which began in 1867 and took 16 years to complete *(see photo on page 27)*, was marred by tragedy. Two years into the project, Roebeling was killed by a ferry boat. His son, Washington Roebling, took over his role and fell victim to the bends while working on the riverbed excavation. An invalid for the rest of his life, Roebling Jr carried on, monitoring the works through a telescope, relaying messages via his wife. When the bridge opened in 1883, 12 people were trampled to death in a panic, fearing that the span was about to collapse. Despite its tortuous beginnings, the Brooklyn Bridge was seen as the "new eighth wonder of the world," and has inspired artists and accolades ever since.

Past the sumptuous **Surrogate's Court** (31 Chambers Street), with its eight Corinthian columns, **Foley Square** ⑲ is named for another Tammany Hall politician. It's also the site of such worthy civic structures as the 1936 Cass Gilbert-designed **United States Courthouse** (1 Foley Square), and the **New York State Supreme Court** (60 Centre Street), built in 1913, where New Yorkers are summoned for jury duty selection. When workers were excavating the foundations of a new Federal courthouse building, the skeletons of African slaves were discovered. Now a city, state and Federal landmark, the **African Burial Ground** is commemorated by a memorial at the corner of Duane and Elk streets.

The **Municipal Building** (1 Centre Street), slightly to the south, is an enormous, ornate 1914 McKim, Mead and White confection. In the second-floor civil wedding chapel you can tie the knot in about five minutes (after the proper preliminaries have been completed, of course). **City Books** in the lobby is a terrific bookstore for information on the city and its memorabilia.

For one of the best views of the **East River** and Lower Manhattan, walk down Frankfort Street or along Park Row. Both lead to the pedestrian walkway of the **Brooklyn Bridge** ⑳, one of the world's first suspension bridges *(see box on left)*.

South Street Seaport

Walk along **Fulton Street** toward the East River where, until the Brooklyn Bridge was built, ferries carried New Yorkers to Brooklyn from the Fulton Street pier. In the 1800s, this part of town was the center of New York's maritime commerce, where spices from China, rum from the West Indies and whale oil from the Atlantic were bought and sold, where ships were built, and where sailors thronged to enjoy a seedy red-light district. All that ended after the American Civil War, when the old port fell into a decline, and ships no longer sailed here.

The **South Street Museum** (founded in 1967) joined forces with the Rouse Corporation, which had previously revived historic areas in Boston and Baltimore, to create **South Street Seaport** ㉑, a 12-block "museum without walls." For more than 100 years, the Fulton Fish Market kept things bustling as fishmongers haggled over sales to retailers and restaurants, but the market has now moved uptown to Hunt's Point in the Bronx.

Near the **Titanic Memorial Lighthouse**, at the corner of Fulton and Water streets, **Schermerhorn Row** is lined by the last surviving Federal-style commercial buildings in the city, and part of a block of early 19th-century warehouses. The **Museum Visitors' Center** (12 Fulton Street, tel: 212-748 8600) is halfway down the block and sells tickets for tours, cruises around the harbor and exhibitions at nearby gal-

Map on page 182

South Street Seaport is just one of dozens of stops on the free, seven-day-a-week bus service in Lower Manhattan. Buses run from 10am to 8pm at roughly 10-minute intervals.

BELOW:
South Street Seaport calls itself a "museum without walls."

Map
on page
182

*The New York City
Police Museum is at
100 Old Slip, the site
of the First Precinct
stationhouse.*

BELOW: the Vietnam
Veterans Memorial.

leries. Next door, the South Street
Museum Shop sells books and gifts
with nautical themes. **Cannon's
Walk** is another block of restored
buildings, between Fulton and Beekman streets. Stores on the Front
Street side include a retail outlet of
the J. Crew catalog clothing company. Around the corner on Water
Street, the **Herman Melville
Gallery** and the **Whitman Gallery**
are on either side of **Bowne and Co.**
(211 Water Street), a 19th-century
printing shop.

Pier 17 is a three-story pavilion
that juts over the East River at the
end of Fulton Street. In addition to
the third-floor food court's various
ethnic delicacies, there are dozens of
stores. In summer, free evening concerts are presented on **Pier 16**. The
adjacent booth sells tickets for one-
hour **Seaport Liberty Cruises** and
two-hour music cruises, operated by
Circle Line (tel: 212-630 8888).

The sloop *Pioneer*, along with the
Peking, a four-masted sailing bar-
que, and the *Ambrose*, last of the
city's lightships, are part of the Seaport Museum's collection of **historic
vessels**, graceful ships that occasionally cast off to conduct elegant
cruises around the island.

Back to Battery Park

Several blocks south – past Pier 11,
and just beyond Old Slip, a land-
filled 18th-century inlet where ships
berthed to unload their cargo – is a
park where stranded sailors used to
congregate. Today the **Vietnam Veterans Memorial** ㉒, a 14-ft (4-
meter) monument erected by the
city in 1985 stands at the foot of a
brick amphitheater near the corner
of Coenties Slip and Water Street.
Made of green glass etched with
excerpts of letters written to and
from soldiers serving in Vietnam, it
is movingly illuminated at night.
Nearby is the **New York City Police
Museum** (100 Old Slip, tel: 212-
480 3100; closed Sun, Mon; free.)

A few blocks away, the rusting
Battery Maritime Building ㉓ (11
South Street), a steel landmark
beaux-arts structure built in White-
hall Street in 1909, was the boarding
point for ferries to **Governor's
Island**, a Coast Guard facility until

Statue of Liberty

Like millions of other immigrants, Italian-born writer Edward Corsi's first glimpse of America was the heroic figure of the Statue of Liberty standing on tiny Liberty Island, her "beacon-hand" thrust skyward bearing a torch to light the way, the shackles of despotism broken at her feet. He wrote, "I looked at that statue with a sense of bewilderment, half doubting its reality. Looming shadowy through the mist, it brought silence to the decks of the *Florida*. This symbol of America – this enormous expression of what we had all been taught was the inner meaning of this new country we were coming to – inspired awe in the hopeful immigrants."

Of course, the Statue of Liberty is herself a French immigrant. In 1865, Edouard-René Lefèvre de Laboulaye, a French intellectual, politician and admirer of America, made an off-hand suggestion to a young sculptor by the name of Auguste Bartholdi for a monument honoring French and American brotherhood, symbolizing the spirit of successful revolutions in both countries.

Bartholdi seized the idea, seeing in it the perfect opportunity to indulge a longstanding interest in colossal statuary. It took more than eight years for the project to crystallize, but by 1874 enough money had been raised by the people of France through subscriptions, lotteries and entertainments for the construction of their gift to the people of New York. Funding for the pedestal was slower to materialize in the United States, and it took a concerted campaign from Joseph Pulitzer through his newspaper *The World* to raise the neccessary finance.

Gustave Eiffel, who later built the Eiffel Tower, designed the ingenious framework that supports the thin copper skin, hammered to less than an eighth of an inch thick but still weighing over 90 tons (81,650 kg). In 1885, Bartholdi's statue, called *Liberty Enlightening the World*, was shipped to the United States. It was formally dedicated in a moving ceremony on October 28, 1886.

RIGHT: Lady Liberty was dedicated in 1886.

The statue, when not closed by security alerts, attracts well over a million tourists a year. In this age of high-tech wizardry, it's still a stirring and uncanny sight, made almost unreal by its enormous size. The big attraction had previously been the arduous climb to the top by the narrow spriral staircase, all the way up to the viewing gallery in the crown.

Now, in the new spirit of security, visitors are allowed only as far as the top of the pedestal, where a glass ceiling allows for a view up the inside of the bronze structure, but the observation platform does additionally offers views out over New York Harbor. As well as the views from the pedestal, there are exhibits worth visiting at the base of the statue.

To minimize lines, timed passes are issued for access to the inside of the monument, available for a small fee by calling 1-866 782-8834. Tickets for the Circle Line ferry to Liberty Island are sold at Castle Clinton in Battery Park. Depending on the time of year, the ferry departs every 45 minutes or every hour. Round-trip ferry fare is about $10 and includes a visit to Ellis Island.

There are now strict security controls on visits to Liberty Island, so be prepared for bag checks and fingerprinting. ❑

Map on page 182

In 2005, Staten Island ferries commemorate 100 years of service. On July 4, 1997, fares were abolished.

BELOW: Ellis Island, the "Island of Tears."

1998. Now the island is the site of fancy corporate parties and occasional tours as the city figures out what to do with it.

On the next pier down is the massive **Staten Island Ferry Terminal**. The 25-minute cruise to Staten Island not only offers close-up views of the Statue of Liberty but is also free, making it the best bargain in town. There's a short wait at the other end before reboarding for the trip back to Manhattan. Ferries depart for the **Statue of Liberty ㉔** and Ellis Island (call 1-866-STATUE4 for departure time and prices), a few steps from the **East Coast War Memorial** in Battery Park.

Romantics should check out **Shearwater Sailing**, tel: 212-619 0885, which offers trips on a 1929 double-masted schooner that cruises close to the Statue of Liberty and Ellis Island. There's a cash bar on board, or you can book for the excellent brunch cruise.

Ellis Island ㉕, (tel: 212-363 3200) was known as the "Island of Tears" because of the medical, mental and literacy tests that applicants

had to undergo during the 32-year period that it served as gateway to the United States. Today, it is a national monument and one of the city's most popular tourist destinations, although actual ownership has been oddly divided between New York and New Jersey.

Ellis Island ancestors

The original immigration station, which was transformed into a museum-of-the-melting pot in 1990, tells the often wrenching stories of the millions who passed through here on their way to new lives in the New World. Many arrivals were turned away, but an estimated 40 percent of the American population has at least one ancestor who entered the country via Ellis Island between 1892 and 1924 (1,285,349 immigrants arrived in 1907 alone).

Outside the museum, a promenade offers wonderful views of the Statue of Liberty and the Lower Manhattan skyline – and includes the **American Immigrant Wall of Honor**, which is inscribed with more than 500,000 names.   ❑

RESTAURANTS, BARS AND CAFÉS

Restaurants

Au Mandarin
World Financial Center, 200-50 Vesey St. Tel: 212-385 0313. Open: L & D daily. **$$**
Upscale Chinese, one of many reasonable restaurants in the WFC.

Battery Gardens
Battery Park (opposite 17 State St). Tel: 212-809 5508. Open: L & D Mon–Sat, L only Sun. **$$$**
Multileveled dining rooms facing the Statue of Liberty. It serves lots of tourists, but it's well worth the trip.

Bayard's
1 Hanover Square (at Pearl St). Tel: 212-514 9454. Open: Mon–Sat, D only. **$$$$**
Handsome, clubby French-American eatery situated in the historic *circa* 1850 India House.

Bridge Café
279 Water St (at Dover St). Tel: 212-227 3344. Open: L & D daily. **$$$**
Located "under" the Brooklyn Bridge, this hideaway has been here since the late 1700s. When Ed Koch was mayor, he brought the place back to life.

Delmonico's
56 Beaver St (at William St). Tel: 212-509 1144. Open: L & D Mon–Fri. **$$$$**
The place for power lunches; a club-like steakhouse that closes at weekends.

Fraunces Tavern
54 Pearl St (at Broad St). Tel: 212-968 1776. Open: L & D Mon–Sat. **$$$**
Historic, welcoming dining rooms just below the museum. Great place to meet for lunch or a drink.

Gigino at Wagner Park
20 Battery Place (at West St). Tel: 212-528 2228. Open: L & D daily. **$$**
Gorgeous sunsets with a view of Lady Liberty at this moderately priced Italian spot – ideal during summer months for the terrace dining.

Harbour Lights
South St Seaport, Pier 17, 3rd Flr (between Fulton and South sts). Tel: 212-227 2800. Open: L & D daily. **$$$**
Spectacular view of the East River and the Brooklyn Bridge while enjoying pleasing seafood.

Lili's Noodle Shop & Grill
102 North End Ave (at Vesey St). Tel: 212-786 1300. Open: L & D daily. **$**
A huge menu and quick service make this yum on the run.

Quartino
21–23 Peck Slip (at Water St). Tel: 212-349 4433. Open: L & D daily. **$$**
Good, affordable Italian in a quiet setting for this neighborhood.

Roy's NY
130 Washington St (between Albany and Carlisle sts). Tel: 212-266 6262. Open: L & D Mon–Sat. **$$$**
The best fusion fare out of Hawaii – it's either this or head for Maui; uniquely flavorful.

Steamer's Landing
1 Esplanade Plaza (between Albany and Liberty sts). Tel: 212-432 1451. Open: L & D daily. **$$**
Tables facing the Hudson River watch the cruise ships set out to sea.

Bars and Cafés

Paris Bar, 119 South St (at Peck Slip), is a long-time seaport hang-out with a great polished wood bar.

Rise, 2 West St, is on the 14th floor of the Ritz-Carlton Battery Park – it's expensive, but the drinks with a sunset view are worth it.

SouthWest NY at 2 World Financial Center, has good terrace food in warm weather, but is great all the year round for cocktails.

St Maggie's Café, 120 Wall St (between Front and South sts), has a fine Victorian feeling and serves food too.

Ulysses, 95 Pearl St (off Hanover Square), is a gathering spot for young Wall Street tycoons.

PRICE CATEGORIES

Prices for a three-course dinner per person with half a bottle of wine:
$ = under $20
$$ = $20–$45
$$$ = $45–$60
$$$$ = over $60

RIGHT: Delmonico's is the place for power lunches.

THE OUTER BOROUGHS

Today's pioneers in art and real estate
are beating a path to the Outer Boroughs,
attracted by green fields, watery vistas, excellent
museums and 18th- and 19th-century enclaves

Staten Island, Queens, Brooklyn, the Bronx: these are places visitors to Manhattan simply don't go, except maybe to the zoo, a ballgame or to take the ferry.

They're missing out. The Outer Boroughs offer parks, cafés and gourmet restaurants, museums and history. Cool bars buzz around Williamsburg in Brooklyn; woodlands and the Verrazano-Narrows Bridge beckon on Staten Island; the heart of New York's oldest – and thriving – movie studios are in Queens; and the home of Edgar Allen Poe engages the mind in the Bronx. There are architectural sites of old New York. As well as the zoo and Yankee Stadium, of course.

Being so overlooked, these tourist treasures – all less than an hour's journey from Broadway, and all accessible by public transportation – have the added advantage of being almost complely uncluttered by other out-of-towners.

Neighborhoods

The key word in the boroughs is "neighborhood." Neighborhoods change. They overlap. They can also be a bazaar of ethnic delight. Stroll through Middle Eastern stores that stock frankincense and myrrh, order pasta in Italian, and have *kasha* served in Yiddish.

Some of these new neighbors are artists and young professionals in search of affordable rents. As the popularity and the prices of Manhattan soar, a new generation has turned to former industrial zones, like **Long Island City** in Queens and **Willamsburg** in Brooklyn, to live. Now, co-ops flourish where warehouses once thrived. Burnedout buildings become galleries or restaurants. And immediately, realestate values skyrocket, and the artists turn their sights elsewhere.

Map
on page
196

LEFT: leaving
Manhattan; entering
the Outer Boroughs.
BELOW: the late artist
Isamu Noguchi; visit
his tranquil sculpture
garden in Queens.

Amid the new is the older side of the boroughs: the avenues, parks and palazzos built as grand civic projects at the end of the 19th century. Architects like Frederick Law Olmsted and Calvert Vaux found open space in the Outer Boroughs that was unavailable in Midtown. With sweeping gestures, they decked the boroughs with buildings inspired by the domes and gables of Parisian boulevards.

Despite this grandeur, however, one thing that "the boroughs" do lack is Manhattan's easy grid system. Heading up the Moshulu Park-

way or Flatbush Avenue, they are a maze of streets and expressways. With the aid of a little attention, though, a good map will quickly uncover neighborhoods that can be explored at a comfortable pace on foot – places where the boroughs really breathe.

Brooklyn

The 70 sq miles (180 sq km) on the southeast tip of Long Island encompass the second most populous borough of New York City, **Brooklyn ❶**. More than 2.4 million people live here, which would make

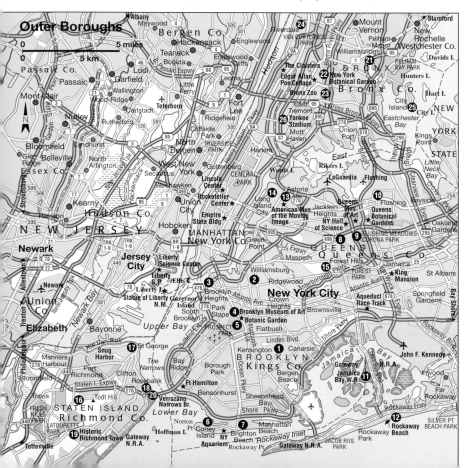

it the fouth largest metropolis in the United States if it weren't a part of New York City. Just a 20-minute ride on the subway from the heart of Manhattan will reach Williamsburg or Prospect Park.

Another scenic way to escape from Manhattan is via the **Brooklyn Bridge**. A stroll across the walkway leads to **Fulton Ferry Landing**, where cobblestone streets are coming back to life after lying dormant for decades. It was here that the borough inaugurated its first mass transit to Wall Street. In 1814 Robert Fulton's steam ferry, the *Nassau*, replaced the East River rowboats, sailboats and vessels powered by horses on treadmills until the Brooklyn Bridge was opened in 1883.

East River waterfront

The modern-day renaissance of Brooklyn began in the now-classic New York style – by following the trail of Manhattan's artists. When Soho became too expensive, they moved over the water to lofts in DUMBO (which stands for **D**own **U**nder **M**anhattan **B**ridge **O**verpass), now a thriving neighborhood that includes the innovative cultural hub **Arts at St Ann's** (58 Water Street, tel: 718-834 8794).

Young families followed – so many that nearby **Brooklyn Bridge Park**, now completing its first phase of regeneration, incorporated into its designs a children's playground, open grass fields and a rock beach on the East River. When DUMBO became too expensive, the artists moved to Williamsburg, and now that they are priced out of Williamsburg, they are beginning to colonize Red Hook.

Wherever artists went, they left behind when they moved a series of neighborhood revivals. For instance, you can listen to chamber music and innovative rock at **Bargemusic** (tel: 718-624 4061), a converted coffee

barge moored at the end of Old Fulton Street. It's on the other side of the Fulton Ferry Landing from the **River Café** (1 Water Street, at the Brooklyn Bridge), considered not only the city's most romantic restaurant but also one of the best. Around the bend to the east is the old **Brooklyn Navy Yard**, where ships like the *USS Missouri* were built during World War II.

Continue south along the water to **Red Hook**, one of the latest communities to break out of the old industrial mold, with art studios and performance spaces everywhere. Creative businesses as well as high-end store complexes are already putting down roots among the restaurants and galleries, although the advent of a large IKEA store has been greeted with mixed feelings by residents. On the one hand is the growth in local employment; on the other are worries about the sudden increase in traffic.

Up the East River from the Brooklyn and Manhattan bridges, the Williamsburg Bridge is another connection to Manhattan, and the

Map on page 196

TIP

Over the next few years, Brooklyn's East River waterfront is set to undergo the same upscale transition as has the Hudson River in Manhattan. See it all before it changes. Oh-so-cool Red Hook is difficult to reach by subway or bus, but it's easy if you hop on a water taxi in Manhattan *(see page 184)*.

BELOW: Manhattan Bridge, with its elevated streets, inspired the acronym DUMBO.

The Miss Williamsburg Diner on Kent Avenue is a restored greasy spoon that's become a very good Italian eatery.

entry to **Williamsburg ❷**. At the foot of the bridge is the **Peter Luger Steakhouse** *(see page 211)*. Across Broadway, the lovely, Renaissance-style Williamsburg Savings Bank building was constructed in 1875, while much further east, on Driggs Avenue, the onion-domed **Russian Orthodox Cathedral of the Transfiguration**, dating to 1921, displays the area's traditional ties to Eastern Europe.

Williamsburg has a vibrant arts community, and some of the outdoor murals and graffiti are of near-museum quality. This part of Brooklyn is hopping right now with weekend visitors, but during the week the streets are as quiet as a country village. **Bedford Avenue** is the main drag "of the moment," with clothing stores and funky cafés neighboring happily.

One block west is **Berry Street**, another place with hip restaurants, cafés for people watching, and an intriguing corner at North 9th occupied by the eclectic Sacred Gallery of Art and Craft – part clothing shop, part antiques store.

Brooklyn Heights

On the other side of the Fulton Ferry district, the property has always been hot. **Brooklyn Heights ❸**, where streets are lined with narrow rowhouses, brownstones change hands for sums in the million dollars. Along the river edge of the Heights is the **Promenade**, a walkway that overlooks the East River and the Brooklyn Bridge, and offers a movie-star view of the Manhattan skyline. A stroll along here and through the Heights can be extremely pleasant. Each block is iced with wrought-iron flourishes, stained-glass windows, stone busts and trims. On the corner of **Willow Street** and **Middagh** is the oldest wooden house in the district, dating to 1824.

During the Civil War **Plymouth Church**, on **Orange Street** between Henry and Hicks, served as a stop on the Underground Railroad, while Henry Ward Beecher (Harriet Beecher Stowe's brother) preached abolitionism to the congregation.

Many streets in the Heights, like Middagh and Hicks, take their

names from the neighborhood's early gentry. Five, however, are named after the flora of the period – **Pineapple**, **Cranberry**, **Orange**, **Poplar** and **Willow streets**.

The **Brooklyn Historical Society** (128 Pierrepont Street, tel: 718-222 4111; closed Mon and Tues; charge) is in a landmark Heights building. Browse around and enjoy its rich mix of "Old Ebbett's Field" Dodgers baseball memorabilia, maritime artifacts and Coney Island exhibitionism. A block away is St Ann and the Holy Trinity church, on the corner of Montague and Clinton streets. Dating to the 1840s, it includes the oldest stained-glass windows made in America.

At the foot of Brooklyn Heights is the **Civic Center**, with its Greek Revival **Borough Hall** (209 Joralemon Street; free tours every Tues). From here, it's a short walk down Boerum Place to reach the fun **New York Transit Museum** (Boerum Place and Schermerhorn Street, tel: 718-694 1600; closed Mon; charge). In a classic 1930s-era subway station, the museum includes exhibits about the city's transportation systems, along with vintage subway cars and buses.

Keep walking past State Street and turn right on **Atlantic Avenue**. Between Court and Henry Street, shops are bulging with imported spices, dried fruits, olives and *halvah*. Some bakeries cook their filo pastries in coal-burning ovens. This Middle-Eastern bazaar shares the sidewalk with a number of antiques shops. The stores have plenty of interesting stock (Victorian, art deco, 1930s, 1940s), and are usually open on weekends if not every day of the week.

Flatbush

To the east, where Atlantic meets **Flatbush Avenue**, look for the monumental **Williamsburg Savings Bank**, the tallest building in Brooklyn. Nearby on Lafayette Avenue at Ashland Place, is the innovative **Brooklyn Academy of Music (BAM)**, where the performance spectrum has included multimedia maestro Laurie Anderson, Martha Clarke's performance art and the

Map on page 196

Brooklyn is known for its brownstone houses. Brownstone is iron oxide, and was used extensively in the 1840s. Skinny walk-ups built wall-to-wall with the houses next door, the design was meant to conserve heat and retard fire.

BELOW: Brooklyn Heights' Promenade has movie-star views of Manhattan.

music of the minimalist composer Philip Glass. Home to the experimental Next Wave Festival since 1982, it includes the beautifully restored **Majestic Theatre**, as well as a café and four screening rooms known as the BAM Rose Cinemas. (For information, call 718-636 4100.) Just around the corner is the massive new shopping mall, **Atlantic Terminal**.

In neighboring **Crown Heights**, Hasidic Jews and immigrants from the West Indies are building communities that are worlds apart, but only a few doorsteps away. Even farther east is **Brownsville**. Before World War II, this was a mainly Jewish slum, where local legend locates the headquarters for Murder Inc. – the notorious 1930s gangster ring – in a candy store on **Livonia Avenue**. (For a Brownsville classic, check out *A Walker in the City* by Alfred Kazin.)

The Brooklyn Children's Museum, dating from 1899, was the first kids' museum to be founded in America.

Brooklyn museums

The thoroughfare of eastern Brooklyn is **Eastern Parkway**. It runs through Bedford-Stuyvesant and Crown Heights to Prospect Park, along the way passing the **Brooklyn Children's Museum** (145 Brooklyn Avenue, tel: 718-735 4440; closed Mon and Tues; charge). Founded in 1899, this is the oldest children's museum in America and is very much a hands-on learning experience, with thousands of interesting artifacts to gaze and wonder at – and almost as many buttons and knobs to twiddle.

The marvelous **Brooklyn Museum of Art ❹** (200 Eastern Parkway, tel: 718-638 5000; closed Mon and Tues; charge) includes an Egyptian collection considered by many the best outside of Cairo and London. The museum displays a changing array of world-class exhibits, 28 period rooms and an unusual outdoor sculpture garden of New York building ornaments.

Next door, at the 50-acre (20-hectare) **Brooklyn Botanic Garden** (tel: 718-623 7200; closed Mon; charge), the Japanese gardens alone are worth a visit, especially when the cherry trees bloom in the spring. But it's a pleasant visit any month.

BELOW: the Japanese Garden at the Brooklyn Botanic Garden.

The neighborhood of **Park Slope** runs along Prospect Park's western border and is filled with Victorian rowhouses, many of which have been divided up into apartments. It has become quite the popular neighborhood for Manhattan defectors and young families. **Seventh Avenue**, wall to wall with shops and restaurants, is two blocks down from the park.

The huge trafic circle at the western end of the Parkway is **Grand Army Plaza**, while the **Soldiers' and Sailors' Memorial Arch** provides a formal entrance to the 526 acres (213 hectares) that make up **Prospect Park ❺**. The park, plaza and boulevards were all designed by Frederick Law Olmsted and Calvert Vaux and are considered to be their best work, even better, perhaps, than Central Park.

The Plaza is their most literal tribute to Paris – an Arc de Triomphe placed at the focal point of the borough. Roam dreamily through the romantic park: the Long Meadow, the Vale of Cashmere and the **Rose Garden**, or ride the antique carousel. Information is available by calling the park at 718-965 8999. In an eastern corner of the park, the **Lefferts Homestead Children's Museum** (tel: 718-789 2822; closed Mon and Wed; free) is a two-story, eight-room Dutch farmhouse, built between 1777 and 1783. There are interactive exhibits designed for children, portraying African, European and Native American life in 19-century Flatbush.

Coney Island

On the coast to the south lies **Coney Island ❻**, which is not actually an island, but a peninsula. The **New York Aquarium for Wildlife Conservation** (tel: 718-265 3474; charge), is located in-between, at West 8th Street and Surf Avenue. With an outdoor theater where frisky and lovable sea lions perform, this metropolitan home for ocean life is one of the borough's most popular attractions.

The famous name of Coney Island really belongs to what was once Brooklyn's premier vacation center. New Yorkers have been

Map on page 196

11th-century exhibit from the Brooklyn Museum of Art: Seated Buddha Sakyamuni.

BELOW: *An Out-of-Doors Study*, an oil painting by John Singer Sargent, on display at the Brooklyn Museum of Art.

TIP

In honor of jazz legend Louis "Satchmo" Armstrong, who lived in Corona and whose home is now a museum, Jazz Trail tours can be booked through the Flushing Town Hall, tel: 718-463 7700.

BELOW: New Yorkers have been escaping the city heat by going to Coney Island for over 150 years.

escaping to Coney Island ever since the summers of the 1840s. Get a **Nathan's Famous** hot dog at the stand on Surf and Stillwell, where fans insist the mass-produced sausages were invented in 1916. The grills sizzle up to 1,500 dogs an hour on a hot summer's day.

Tempt fate aboard **The Cyclone,** the grand-daddy of roller coasters, with 3,000 ft (914 meters) of wooden track and cars speeding at 68 mph (109 kph). It's the centerpiece of **Astroland Amusement Park** (tel: 718-372 0275. Then, take a calming stroll along the boardwalk, and watch the seagulls swooping over the ocean.

Farther east on the boardwalk is **Brighton Beach** ❼, which for many years was the enclave of elderly Jews and made famous by playwright Neil Simon. But in the mid-1970s, a new wave of immigrants, mostly Russians and Ukrainians, began moving into Brighton Beach, which soon became known as "**Little Odessa**." Today, Russian restaurants, bookstores, markets and other businesses have infused the neighborhood with

vitality. Dance the night away at one of the exuberant nightspots on **Brighton Beach Avenue**.

Queens

Visitors taking taxis from JFK International Airport into Manhattan pass as swiftly as traffic allows through **Queens** ❽, but the borough is more than just a point of arrival. Named for Queen Catherine of Braganza, wife of Charles II of England, it is a diverse community, with one of the largest Greek neighborhoods outside of Athens, and immigrants from India, Pakistan, Thailand, South America and Europe.

The area between **Northern Boulevard** and **Grand Central Parkway**, which was once a swamp and later the "Corona Garbage Dump," ended up as the glamorous grounds of the 1939 and 1964 World's Fairs.

Flushing Meadows-Corona Park ❾, as it is now known, is an expanse of over 1200 acres (485 hectares) that includes museums, sports facilities and botanical gardens. On display in what was the

1964 Fair's New York City Building – now the **Queens Museum of Art** (tel: 718-592 9700; closed Mon and Tues; charge) – is the **Panorama of the City of New York**, a scale replica of the city as it was then, reconstructed in meticulous detail.

The **New York Hall of Science** (tel: 718-699 0005; closed Mon; charge), near the park's 111th Street entrance, is famous for its interactive high-tech exhibits. Other reminders of the fairs, like the great steel **Unisphere** in the park's heart, are close to attractions like the **USTA National Tennis Center**, the site of the annual US Open.

Right next door is **Shea Stadium**, the home of the Mets, just beyond the subway station (take the Flushing line No. 7 train), with the capacity to seat 57,000 cheering baseball fans. The park also has paths for cycling and strolling, plus an indoor **skating rink** (in the same building as the **Museum of Art**), and an antique carousel.

Close by, the 38-acre (15-hectare) **Queens Botanical Garden** (43-50 Main Street, tel: 718-886 3800;

closed Mon; free) has the largest rose garden in the Northeast and is a good spot for outdoor weddings.

Jazz legend, Louis "Satchmo" Armstrong lived in Corona, and his former home has been turned into a museum. The **Louis Armstrong House and Archives** (34–56 107th Street, tel: 718-478 8274; closed Mon; charge) is a popular destination for jazz pilgrims.

Little Asia

Bordering the park, **Flushing ⑩** is packed with history, and perked up by its "**Little Asia**," home to one of the biggest Hindu temples in North America, on **Bowne Street**. The **Quaker Meeting House**, built in 1696, is the oldest house of worship in New York City. An excellent place to learn about the local history is at the **Queens Historical Society** (143–35 37th Avenue, tel: 718-939 0647). Around the back is a weeping beech tree more than 150 years old – and one of only two "living landmarks" in the city (the other is a magnolia tree in Brooklyn).

Most people assume the largest-

The Unisphere in Flushing Meadows-Corona Park, a relic from the World's Fair, is the largest globe in the world.

BELOW: standing cheek-to-cheek at Coney Island.

Long Island City in QNS (as residents of this part of Queens like to define themselves), promotes itself as the eastern counterpoint to Chelsea, with more light, more space and less glamour. Nearly a quarter of Queens is parkland, and glamour does come its way; both The Sopranos *and* Sex and the City *were made at LIC's Silvercup Studios.*

BELOW: an interior from the Museum of the Moving Image.

stretches of land in Queens belong to **JFK** and **LaGuardia airports**. These sprawling terminals with their long runways *are* huge, but even more impressive acreage remains undeveloped – nearly a quarter of the borough is kept as parkland under preservation orders.

South of the JFK runways, the **Jamaica Bay Wildlife Refuge** ⑪ (tel: 718-318 4340) gives a home to more than 300 species of birds, as well as scores of small creatures like raccoons, chipmunks and turtles. Trail maps, available from National Park Rangers at the visitor center, guide some beautiful hiking routes through the groves of red cedar and Japanese pine trees. Birding workshops are also available here year round. The birds avoid tangling with passing jet-powered flyers, thanks to an innovative program using falcons to encourage them away from the danger areas.

The Rockaways

Along the southernmost strip of Queens, **The Rockaways** ⑫ form the biggest municipal beach in the country, easy to reach by subway from midtown Manhattan. To the east is **Far Rockaway**; to the west is **Neponsit**, where old mansions echo the bygone splendor of Rockaway days when wealthy New Yorkers vacationed here. Sadly, **Belle Harbor** was the site of the tragic incident on November 13, 2001, when an American Airlines jet crashed into four buildings shortly after take-off from JFK, killing 260 people, including some residents *(see page 35)*.

Facing Manhattan from the other side of the East River, **Astoria** ⑬ is a modest section of small apartment buildings and semi-detached homes that has regained its former status as a center for New York's film industry. The motion picture business here dates back to the 1920s, when the Marx Brothers and Gloria Swanson were among those working under contract to what was then the Famous Players-Lasky Studios.

Kaufman Astoria Studios now occupies the old site and surrounding blocks. Films and commercials are rolling again, both here and at

American Museum of the Moving Image

The American Museum of the Moving Image was the first institute in the US devoted to exploring the art, history, technique and technology of motion pictures, television and video. Although nowhere near as glamorous as LA's Hollywood History Museum, AMMI is well worth visiting. The three-story building at 35th Avenue and 36th Street is part of the Kaufman Astoria Studios complex – Paramount Pictures' East Coast facility in the 1920s. The complex, along with nearby Silvercup Studios, is the largest and busiest production facility between London and Hollywood, favored by Woody Allen and Martin Scorsese.

The museum has a pleasing, archival feel, with many examples of early film and TV equipment. Modern exhibits include interactive workstations where you can select the sound effects for famous movies, or insert your own dialogue into classic scenes.

Film retrospectives are held most Friday evenings and weekend afternoons in the 200-seat Riklis Theater; other viewing theaters include a 1920s-style living room, complete with shag rug and vinyl furniture, and the knockout Tut's Fever by artist Red Grooms, a delightful homage to the neo-Egyptian picture palaces of the 1920s. For more information, go to www.movingimage.us

the Silvercup Studios in neighboring Long Island City. The worthwhile **American Museum of the Moving Image** (35th Avenue at 36th Street, tel: 718-784 0077; closed Mon and Tues; charge) is dedicated to the glory days of New York when it was known as "Hollywood on the Hudson." *(See box opposite.)*

Although traditionally a Greek enclave, Astoria has attracted immigrants from other parts of the world. Along main drags like **Steinway Street** and **Broadway** are Greek delis, Italian bakeries, Asian markets and restaurants. Despite the movie stars working nearby, the side streets remain fairly quiet.

Long Island City ⓮ has much to offer visitors. An aging industrial section, it was discovered in the early 1980s by the artist community. Until recently, MoMA QNS was relocated here while it awaited the completion of its new venue in Manhattan. Other cultural institutions remain – at 43rd Avenue at 36th Street is the **Museum for African Art** (tel: 718-784 7700; closed Tue and Wed; charge), which

moved here from Soho. As with MoMA, MAA's move here is a temporary sojourn while it awaits new premises on Fifth Avenue (which seem to be a long time coming). The **P.S.1 Contemporary Art Center** is at 22–25 Jackson Avenue at 46th Avenue (tel: 718-784 2084; closed Mon and Tues; charge). An exuberant museum space dedicated to showing the work of emerging artists, this is one of the city's most exciting venues.

Sculpture parks

A landmark is the **Isamu Noguchi Garden Museum** (32–37 Vernon Boulevard, tel: 718-721 1932; closed Mon and Tues; weekend shuttle bus from Manhattan; charge). Almost 250 works by the Japanese sculptor are displayed in 13 galleries created from a converted factory building, while others encircle a garden of the artist's design. The overall effect is one of harmony and serenity, a far cry from Manhattan's screaming streets.

Just up Vernon Boulevard at Broadway, more outdoor art can be

Map on page 196

Innovative P.S.1, affiliated with the Museum of Modern Art, has its premises in an old public schoolhouse.

BELOW: AMMI's *Tut's Fever* movie palace by artist Red Grooms.

Staten Island is more than just a ferry. You can admire pretty neighborhoods, stroll through wetlands, or even visit a little corner of Tibet.

BELOW: ceiling of the Main Hall, Snug Harbor Cultural Center.

enjoyed in the 4½-acre (1.8- hectare) **Socrates Sculpture Park** (tel: 718-956 1819). Started by artists, this expanse of grass was proclaimed an official city park. The view of Manhattan from here, through giant sculptures (shows twice a year) is mesmerizing. It's open from 10am until sunset.

A neighborhood well worth exploring is **Forest Hills** ⓯. Best known for the **West Side Tennis Club**, once host to the US Open, this section of Queens was inspired by the English "Garden Suburb" movement. Planning began in 1906 with a low-cost housing endowment, but in 1923, the project only half completed, residents took over the management and began vetting newcomers. The mock-Tudor district turned fashionable and styled itself "lawn tennis capital of the western hemisphere."

For a change of pace, a day at the racetrack can be fun. Events at **Aqueduct** (Rockaway Boulevard and 108th Street in Ozone Park, tel: 718-641 4700), include the Wood Memorial and the Turf Classic.

Staten Island

Once upon a time in New York, there was an island with roads paved by oyster shells, where yachts swayed by resort hotels, European-style finishing schools were founded, and where Americans first played tennis.

Could this be **Staten Island** ⓰, the second-smallest and least known borough? To most New Yorkers, the island is just the place where the famous ferry goes. As the poet Edna St Vincent Millay wrote: "We were very tired, we were very merry – we had gone back and forth all night on the ferry." Yes, come for the ride, but try to spend at least a little time on Staten Island itself.

The ferry lands at **St George** ⓱, where part of the extensive ferry collection is shown at the **St George Ferry Terminal**. Two blocks away is the **Staten Island Institute of Arts & Sciences** (tel: 718-727 1135; closed Mon; small charge), housed in a dignified 1918 building at 75 Stuyvesant Place.

Snug Harbor Cultural Center (1000 Richmond Terrace, tel: 718-448 2500) is a short bus ride from St George. The handsome visitors center first opened in 1831 as a home for retired seamen. Now its 83 acres (34 hectares) of wetlands and woodlands house a school and play host to concerts.

Within the center's grounds is the **Staten Island Botanical Garden**, with a famous orchid collection and the new Chinese Scholar's Garden. Here, too, is the **Staten Island Children's Museum** (tel: 718-273 2060; closed Mon; charge), a great interactive experience for kids.

East of the Staten Island Ferry Landing is the **Rosebank** ⓲ section of the island, home to its earliest Italian-American community. The **Garibaldi Meuci Museum** (480 Tompkins Avenue tel: 718-442 1608; closed Mon; charge), com-

memorates Antonio Meuci, who invented a telephone years before Alexander Graham Bell. Exhibits focus on this and other of his inventions, as well as his friendship with Italian hero Giuseppe Garibaldi, who stayed with Meuci on his 1850 visit to New York. This simple frame house was Meuci's home until his death in 1889.

A bus or taxi ride away, the **Alice Austen House Museum** (2 Hylan Boulevard, tel: 718-816 4506; closed Mon–Wed; charge) is a garden-surrounded cottage that was the home of a pioneering woman photographer from 1866 to 1945.

Because a glacier ridge runs through the middle of the island, its six hills: **Fort**, **Ward**, **Grymes**, **Emerson**, **Todt** and **Lighthouse** are the highest points in New York City. Stately mansions with breathtaking views stand on the ridge of Todt Hill, the highest point along the eastern seaboard south of the state of Maine.

Take a taxi up **Signal Hill**, a narrow hairpin lane. Along the way, alpine homes peek out of the cliff, half hidden by rocks and trees. At the top, beyond the super views from the ridge, is the core of the island. Called the **Greenbelt** (tel: 718-667 2165 for information about walking trails), this enormous expanse of meadows and woodland has been preserved by a civic plan that tightly controls or entirely prohibits development. The heart of it all is **High Rock Park**, a 90-acre (36-hectare) open space.

On **Lighthouse Hill**, around the bend, is an idyllic corner imported from the Himalayas; the **Jacques Marchais Museum of Tibetan Art** (*see page 168*). Less than a mile away on Richmond Road is intriguing **Historic Richmond Town** ⓳, a restored 17th-and 18th-century village showing 300 years of life on Staten Island *(see page 168)*.

Verrazano-Narrows Bridge ⓴ features in many of the island's best easterly views. When the bridge was built in 1964 it was the longest suspension bridge in the world. The Verrazano connects Staten Island to Brooklyn and, long controversial, is known as the bringer of great

Map on page 196

The most historic restaurant in New York City is located on Staten Island, the Old Bermuda Inn. It opened in 1716, and you can have dinner or Sunday brunch in the landmark colonial house at 2512 Arthur Kill Road, Rossville, tel: 718-948 7600. The Wedding Cottage on the same grounds is a high-end B&B.

BELOW: the Verrazano-Narrows Bridge connects Staten Island to Brooklyn.

Edgar Allan Poe lived in the Bronx for three years before his death in 1849.

BELOW: the Bronx Zoo is the largest urban zoo in America.

change to the island. The traffic that poured across its magnificent span brought Staten Island's fastest and least controlled boom in construction. Now, strict laws are in place to ensure that it doesn't happen again.

The Bronx

In 1641, a Scandinavian, Jonas Bronck, bought 500 acres (200 hectares) of the New World from Native Americans. After building his home on virgin land, he and his family found the area remote and lonely, so they threw parties for friends. The Indian land was called Keskeskeck, but the name was changed, the story goes, by Manhattanites asking their neighbors, "Where are you going on Saturday night?" and being answered, "Why, to the Bronck's."

The tale is certainly questionable, but **The Bronx ㉑** *had* been virgin forest, and *did* begin with Jonas' farm. Idyllic woods seem unimaginable here, a far cry from today's Bronx, but a part of the original hemlock forest remains untouched in the virgin 250-acre (100-hectare)

New York Botanical Garden ㉒ (200th St and Southern Boulevard, tel: 718-817 8700; closed Mon; charge). The 1901 **Enid A. Haupt Conservatory** is the grandest structure on the grounds, a veritable crystal palace that includes a central Palm Court and connecting greenhouses. There are plenty of outdoor gardens to explore, including the spectacular **Rose Garden** and the **Everett Children's Adventure Garden**, which features kid-size topiaries and mazes.

The 265-acre (107-hectare) **Bronx Zoo/Wildlife Conservation Park ㉓** (tel: 718-367 1010; charge) is the country's largest urban zoo – and shares **Bronx Park** with the **Bronx Botanical Gardens**. Some of the most popular exhibits include the World of Darkness (nocturnal animals), the Aquatic Bird House and the Butterfly Zone. There's a Children's Zoo, a monorail ride through Wild Asia, and a 40-acre (16-hectare) complex with moats to keep the big cats away from their prey – that would be you. The Congo Gorilla Forest has acres of forest, bamboo thickets and baby lowland gorillas.

The zoo is at the geographic heart of the Bronx, but its nostalgic and architectural heart may well be the **Grand Concourse**. This Champs Elysées-inspired boulevard began as a "speedway" across rural hills. As the borough became more industrialized, the Concourse achieved a classy role as the Park Avenue of the Bronx, stretching as it does for more than 4 miles (6 km).

Museums and poets

North of the Grand Concourse, poet **Edgar Allan Poe's cottage** sits humbly amid high-rise housing on **Kingsbridge Road**. Poe moved here in 1846, hoping the then country air would be good for his consumptive young wife and cousin,

Virginia. But she died at an early age, leaving Poe frayed and destitute; the haunting poem *Annabel Lee* was a reflection of his distress. The cottage has been a museum since 1917, and is run by the Bronx County Historical Society (tel: 718-881 8900; open weekends only; weekdays for organized groups). On the Grand Concourse itself, at 165th Street, is the **Bronx Museum of the Arts** (tel: 718-681 6000; closed Mon and Tues; charge), which hosts contemporary exhibitions.

The Little Italy of the Bronx is the **Belmont** section, just east of the Bronx Zoo. **Arthur Avenue**, near the fork of Crescent Avenue and East 187th Street, teems with people who flock here from all over the city to buy cured meats, pasta and freshly baked bread. It's also a great place for restaurants.

Stop in at the Belmont Library, around the corner at East 186th Street and Hughes Avenue, where the **Enrico Fermi Cultural Center** has books and research materials about the contributions made by Italians to American life. The staff, of course, speak Italian and will help with queries in either language.

Nipple of Knowledge

Lying west of the Grand Concourse is Bronx Community College's most famous landmark, the tile-roofed, bust-lined colonnade, the **Hall of Fame of Great Americans**. It wraps around a building designed by Stanford White. No longer in use as a library, the building's great copper dome was known by scholars as the Great Green Nipple of Knowledge. Above University Heights is **Riverdale ㉔**, in the northwest. It's hard to believe this is the Bronx, as the curvy roads wind through hills lined with mansions.

A drive down Sycamore Avenue to Independence and West 249th Street leads to **Wave Hill** (tel: 718-549 3200; varying hours; charge). This formerly private estate, now a city-owned environmental center, has greenhouses and public gardens overlooking the Hudson. It is one of the most beautiful spots in New York City and, combined with its summer concerts and dance performances, makes a visit here worthwhile and memorable.

East of Riverdale, **Van Cortlandt Park** stretches from West 240th to West 263rd streets, and includes stables, tennis courts and acres of playing fields. The fine **Van Cortlandt House Museum** (tel: 718-543 3344; closed Mon; charge), overlooks the park's lake from a perch at Broadway and 242nd Street. Built in 1748 by Frederick Van Cortlandt, son of a leading Dutch colonial-era merchant, its rooms are filled with some of the family's original furnishings and possessions.

On the park's other side, **Woodlawn Cemetery** is permanent home to about 300,000 New Yorkers. Herman Melville, Duke Ellington and five former mayors are just a handful of the celebrities taking their rest

Map on page 196

So neat, so poor, so unfurnished, and yet so charming a dwelling I never saw.
– A GUEST'S COMMENTS AFTER VISITING POE'S BRONX COTTAGE

BELOW: kids cooling off on hot city streets.

Map on page 196

The graffito on the wall behind this girl playing under a water hose in the Bronx reads "Home of the Yankees."

BELOW:
Yankee Stadium, home of champions.

in the elaborate mausoleums. Over 300 acres (120 hectares) of shady trees, hills and streams have made this a popular place for strolling since it opened in 1863.

Farther east is **Orchard Beach**, a popular summer destination with nature trails, riding stables and a public golf course. Past the turn-off for Orchard Beach, the highway passes Co-op City, the sprawling, brown-towered housing development dating from the 1960s that looms over the horizon like a massive urban beehive. Coop City has its own school, stores and about 50,000 tenants.

The road ends at **City Island ㉕**, the borough's slice of New England quaintness. Accessible by car, city bus, or by boat, this 230-acre (93-hectare) island off the northeast Bronx coast has remained quietly detached from the rest of the city.

The boatyards along **City Island Avenue** eventually yielded masterworks like *Intrepid*, the 1968 winner of the America's Cup race. Today, this main street sports attractions ranging from fishing gear

emporiums and craft shops to galleries and seafood restaurants. Also along the avenue is stately **Grace Church**, a fine example of Gothic Revival architecture. At No. 586, look out for the romantic hideaway **Le Refuge Inn** (tel: 718-885 2478), with both food and rooms to offer.

Yankees at home

The opposite end of the borough – in location and reputation – is the **South Bronx**. Its best-known landmark is **Yankee Stadium ㉖** (161st Street at River Avenue, tel: 718-293 6000). The stadium is known as The House That Ruth Built, though actually, this is the house built for Ruth; its shortened right field was designed for baseball player Babe Ruth's special home-run record.

Other stars of the stadium include Joe DiMaggio, Lou Gehrig, Mickey Mantle, and the team that, in the 1990s, won the World Series three years in a row. In fact, more championship flags and American League pennants have flown over Yankee Stadium than over any other baseball field in the country. ❑

RESTAURANTS, BARS AND CAFÉS

Restaurants

Blue Ribbon
280 5th Ave (between 1st and Garfield Pl), Park Slope, Brooklyn. Tel: 718-840 0404. Open: D only daily. **$$$**
No reservations means a wait for the excellent New American menu.

Bohemian Hall and Beer Garden
29-19 24th Ave, Astoria, Queens. Tel: 718-274 4925. Open: D daily, L Sat–Sun. **$$**
Reasonably priced goulash and *kielbasa*, washed down with plenty of beer is something they've been doing here for 95 years.

The Grocery
288 Smith St (between Sackett and Union sts), Carroll Gds, Brooklyn. Tel: 718-596 3335. Open: D only Mon–Sat. **$$$**
Local four-star, one room phenom serving New American cuisine.

Karyatis
35-03 Broadway (between 35th and 36th sts), Astoria, Queens. Tel: 718-204 0666. Open: D daily. **$$**
Popular, upscale Greek.

Peter Luger Steakhouse
178 Broadway (at Driggs Ave) Wmsburg, Brooklyn. Tel: 718-387 7400. Open: L & D daily. **$$$$**
Brooklyn's oldest restaurant still holds the title of "King of all Steak Places." No credit cards.

Oznot's Dish
79 Berry St (at N. 9th),Wmsburg. Brooklyn. Tel: 718-599 6596. Open: L & D daily. **$$**
Oznot's has an off-beat Mediterranean/Middle-Eastern menu and serves a great weekend brunch: Cardamom French toast, the Eggs of Gibraltar, Green Eggs and Sam, etc.

Planet Thailand
133 N. 7th St (at Berry), Wmsburg, Brooklyn. Tel: 718-599 5758. Open: L & D daily. **$**
Warehouse-sized, screamingly popular (read "noisy"), trendy, tasty Thai.

Thomas Beisl
25 Lafayette Ave (at Ashland Pl), Ft. Greene. Tel: 718-222 5800. Open: L Tues–Fri, D daily, Br Sat–Sun. **$$**
Viennese bistro, best food in the Brooklyn Academy of Music district. The chef is formerly of the venerable Café des Artistes.

River Café
1 Water St (at Fulton Ferry). Tel: 718-522 5200. Open: L & D daily. **$$$$**
Unsurpassed location and views of Manhattan from under the Brooklyn Bridge combined with genuine haute cuisine make this a magical spot. Bookings difficult.

Water's Edge
44th Drive and East River (at Vernon Blvd), Queens. Tel:

718-482 0033. Open: L & D Mon–Fri, D only Sat. **$$$$**
From the Long Island City location, this romantic spot serves delicious food with an emphasis on fresh fish. A free ferry service is available from Manhattan.

Bars and Cafés

Almondine, 85 Water St, in trendy DUMBO, is a great place to dip into coffee and pastries or sandwiches while touring the galleries.

Athens Café, 32-07 30th Avenue (at 31st St) in Astoria, Queens, is a lively sidewalk café for pastry and coffee and people-watching.

Bliss Vegetarian Café, 191 Bedford Ave, in

Williamsburg serves breakfast 'til 4pm

Also in Williamsburg is **Hurricane Hopeful (Chowder Bar)**, 218 N. 7th St (between Bedford and Berry), a funky surfer bar with day trips to Rockaway Beach in the summer.

Juniors, 386 Flatbush Ave, Ext. at De Kalb Ave, Brooklyn, is a dessert spot where the cheese-cake is a NYC tradition.

PRICE CATEGORIES

Prices for a three-course dinner per person with half a bottle of wine:
$ – under $20
$$ = $20–$45
$$$ = $45–$60
$$$$ = over $60

RIGHT: grab a dog and take me out to the ballgame.

TRANSPORTATION

GETTING THERE AND GETTING AROUND

GETTING THERE

By Air

East of Manhattan on Long Island, New York's two major airports, **John F. Kennedy International** and **LaGuardia**, are respectively 15 and 8 miles (24 km and 13 km) from the city, with driving time to/from Kennedy estimated at just under one hour. In practice, heavy traffic can sometimes double this, so leave lots of time if you're catching a flight. Most charters and domestic flights, and some international flights use LaGuardia, although more are now flying from JFK.

New York's third airport, **Newark**, is actually in New Jersey and, although further away from Manhattan than JFK and LaGuardia, it can often be easier to reach.

By Sea

Stretching along the Hudson River from 48th to 52nd streets in Manhattan, the efficient and well-organized **Passenger Ship Terminal**, tel: 212- 246 5450, at Piers 88, 90 and 92, has customs facilities, baggage handling, rooftop parking and good bus connections to Midtown.

By Rail

Trains arrive and depart from Manhattan's two railroad terminals: **Grand Central Terminal** at Park Ave and 42nd St, and **Pennsylvania Station** at Seventh Ave and 33rd St. City buses stop outside each terminal and each sits atop a subway station. **Amtrak information**, tel: 212-582 6875, or (toll-free) 1-800-872 7245.

By Road

From the south, the **New Jersey Turnpike** leads into lower Manhattan via the Holland Tunnel or Lincoln Tunnel (Midtown) and offers access farther north via the George Washington Bridge. From the northwest, the **New York State Thruway** connects with the Henry Hudson Parkway leading into northern Manhattan. Driving in from the Long Island airports, access is via the Midtown Tunnel or across the Triborough Bridge and down Manhattan's East River Drive.

The city's main bus terminal, the **Port Authority** (Eighth Ave between 40th and 42nd St), sits atop two subway lines and is serviced by long-distance bus companies (including **Greyhound**, tel: 1-800-231 2222) as well as local commuter lines. City buses stop outside. A modern, air-condi-tioned terminal with several shops and facilities, it tends to attract its share of riff-raff; although well-policed, it's not the sort of place to trust strangers or to leave bags unguarded.

GETTING AROUND

On Arrival

Orientation

Generally, avenues in Manhattan run north to south; streets run east to west. Even-numbered streets tend to have one-way eastbound traffic; odd-numbered streets, westbound traffic. There are very few exceptions. Most avenues are one-way, either north or south, the major exception being Park Avenue which is wide enough for two-way traffic north of 44th St.

Buses do not run on Park Avenue but do run on most other avenues, as well as on major cross-streets (also two-way): Houston, 14th, 23rd, 34th, 42nd, 57th, 66th, 86th, 116th, 125th and a few others. Subway trains cross town at 14th and 42nd St but there is no north–south line east of Lexington Ave or west of Eighth Ave and Broadway above 59th St.

TRANSPORTATION

Airport/City Transportation

AirTrain is an airport rail system that the Port Authority of New York and New Jersey has built connecting **JFK** and **Newark** airports with the region's existing rail transportation network. At all AirTrain rail-link terminals, travelers are able to check their flight times and board AirTrain for a short ride to their airline terminals. AirTrain arrives every few minutes and is approximately 10 minutes from each terminal.
AirTrain JFK information:
tel: 1-718-244 4444 or go to www.airtrainjfk.com
AirTrain Newark information:
tel: 1-888-EWR INFO or www.airtrain-newark.com
The New York Airport Service (tel: 212-875 8200) operates **buses** to and from both **JFK** ($15) and **LaGuardia** ($12) airports to Manhattan. Pick up and drop-off points include: Port Authority Bus Terminal, Penn Station and Grand Central Terminal. New Jersey Transit (tel: 973-762 5100) and Olympia Airport Express (tel: 212-964 6233) operate regular express buses between **Newark** airport and Manhattan, the former to the Port Authority Bus Terminal at Eighth Ave and 41st St, the latter to Penn Station and Grand Central and Lower Manhattan.

A **minibus** service from all three airports to many major Manhattan hotels is provided by **Super Shuttle Blue Vans** (tel: 1-800-451 0455 or 1-800-258 3826) offering a door-to-door transportation service at fares averaging $20. Hotel pick-up and drop-off can be priced lower. These can be booked at airport ground transportation centers or from courtesy phones.

The **cheapest routes** from JFK to the city are AIR TRAIN, transferring to the A subway line at the Howard Beach subway station or via Green Bus Lines to the Lefferts Boulevard subway station (from which A trains run to Brooklyn, Lower Manhattan and the West Side), or to the Kew Gardens-Union Turnpike station (E and F trains to Queens and mid-Manhattan). From LaGuardia, the Triboro Coach Corporation operates the Q-33 bus to the 74th St subway station in Jackson Heights, Queens, from which various trains run to Manhattan. For information about this and other routes to and from airports, call 1-800-AIR RIDE.

Note that 12 airlines maintain a joint ticket office at the Satellite Airlines Terminal (125 Park Ave, tel: 212-986 0888) opposite Grand Central, which is also a drop-off and pick-up spot for buses to JFK and LaGuardia.

There is also a cellular phone rental office located here.

Public Transportation

Subways and Buses

Subways and buses run 24 hours, less frequently after midnight, with the fare payable by exact change as well as by MetroCard pass (available at subway ticket booths), which allows free transfers within two hours of use. Unlimited-ride passes good for seven or 30 days are also available, as is a day pass sold at newsstands, hotels and electronic kiosks in some subway stations. For general **bus and subway information** call: 718-330 1234; for details about the **MetroCard pass**, call 212-METROCARD (1-800-METRO-CARD from outside the city).

PATH (Port Authority Trans Hudson) trains run under the Hudson River from six stations in Manhattan to New Jersey, including Hoboken and Newark. The flat fare is reasonable; for more information call 1-800-234 PATH.

Taxis

Taxis, all metered, cruise the streets and must be hailed, although there are official taxi stands at places like Grand Central Terminal and Penn Station. Be sure to flag down an official yellow cab, not an unlicensed gypsy cab. In 2004, base rates on taxi fare increased to $2.50. The flat rate for a taxi to or from JFK is now $45 (up from $35).

One fare covers all passengers up to four (five in a few of the larger cabs). Between the hours of 4 and 8pm, there is a $1 surcharge on all taxi rides.

Car Services

Delancy   212-228 6666
Good for Downtown.
Princess   212-684 6227
Limos and town cars.
Tel Aviv   212-777 7777
Reliable, especially to airports.

Private Transportation

By Car

Driving around Manhattan is not fun, but there is a range of firms at all airports from which cars can be rented. In order to rent a car, you must be at least 21, have a valid driver's license and at least one major credit card. Be sure you are properly insured.

CAR RENTAL

Alamo:
US   1-800-327 9633
International 1-800-522 9696
Avis:
US   1-800-331 1212
International 1-800-331 1084
Budget:
US   1-800-527 0700
International 1-800-527 0700
Dollar:
US   1-800-800 4000
International 1-800-800 6000
Enterprise:
US   1-800-325 8007
International 1-800-325 8007
Hertz:
US   1-800-654 3131
International 1-800-654 3001
National:
US   1-800-227 7368
International 1-800-227 3876
Thrifty:
US   1-800-331 4200
International +1-918-669 2499

ACCOMMODATIONS

ACTIVITIES

A – Z

A CCOMMODATIONS

LOOK OUT FOR A WIDE VARIETY OF DISCOUNTS AND PROMOTIONS

Choosing a Hotel

The old adage that New York has more of everything than virtually anywhere else is only a slight exaggeration when it comes to hotel accommodations. The following list is hardly exhaustive, but instead represents a sampling of the best hotels in Manhattan in the budget-to-luxury price range, plus a few inexpensive places of distinction, and some alternative accomodations.

Be mindful that with the exception of "Luxury," these categories are not hard and fast. When mak-

ing reservations, ask specifically about special weekend or corporate rates and package deals. American telephone reservations staff are notorious for quoting only expensive rates, but many hotels offer an ever-changing variety of discounts and promotions.

It's a good idea to book a room by credit card and secure a guaranteed late arrival, in the foreseeable circumstance that your flight is interminably stacked up over the airport or your 40-minute limo ride from the airport turns into a two-hour nightmare of traffic jams. New York City is the last place on

earth anyone wants to find themselves stranded late at night without a hotel room.

In addition to regular hotels, we have included a few "suite hotels" and bed and breakfast accommodation services.

The former are basically apartments, available from a few nights, up to a room for a month. The latter are modeled on those in the UK and Europe. As with small B&Bs everywhere, reservations should be made as far in advance as possible. *Be sure to specify if you want a room where smoking is allowed.*

ACCOMMODATIONS LISTINGS

MIDTOWN

HOTELS

Luxury

The Algonquin
59 West 44th St
Tel: 212-840 6800,
1-800-548 0345
Fax: 212-944 1618
www.algonquinhotel.com
Once a haven for New

York's literary Round Table set, and still an all-time favorite *(see photo opposite)*, the Algonquin retains an atmosphere of low-key, oak-paneled charm. Clubby and Victorian in demeanor, civilized in its treatment of guests, it's near theaters and is not as expensive as its competitors. A recent

renovation managed to upgrade everything and change very little.

Drake SwissHotel
440 Park Ave (at 56th St)
Tel: 212-421 0900,
1-800-372 5369
Fax: 212-371 4190
www.swissotel-newyork.com
A Swiss-owned model of decorum and efficiency, much favored by corporate executives for its

clean, hushed, board-room atmosphere. Very large and very comfortable rooms.

Hotel Inter-Continental
111 East 48th St
Tel: 212-755 5900
Fax: 212-644 0079
www.new-york.interconti.com
Opened in the 1920s as The Barclay, this hotel blends executive-class efficiency with majestic spaces and a full range of pampering services. Public rooms include two fine restaurants, a clothier, and a luxury gift shop.

New York Palace
455 Madison Ave (at 50th St)
Tel: 212-888 7000,
1-800-NY-PALACE
Fax: 212-303 6000
www.newyorkpalace.com
A grandiose monument to lavish, American-style pomp and excess. Appointed in a style that can only be called post-modern rococo, the Palace has a regime of flawlessly detailed service that can make the average guest feel like an imperial Pasha. In its brashly high-style way, it's a *very* New York experience.

Omni Berkshire Place
21 East 52nd St
Tel: 212753 5800,
1-800-THE-OMNI
Fax: 212-754 5018
www.omnihotels.com
Although it's been acquired by the Omni chain, the Berkshire retains its old-fashioned grace and attention to personal service. Known by some guests as "a junior Plaza," it's comfortable and comforting, a tastefully appointed oasis of calm in the heart of the Midtown shopping and business bustle.

Le Parker Meridien
118 West 57th St
Tel: 212-245 5000,
1-800-543 4300
Fax: 212-307 1776
www.parkermeridien.com
Part of the internationally known French chain: modern, airy, with an excellent restaurant, and health facilities that include a swimming pool.

Peninsula New York
700 Fifth Ave (at 55th St)
Tel: 212-247 2200,
1-800-262 9467
Fax: 212-903 3943
www.peninsula.com
One of the city's most lavish hotels, where richly appointed rooms go for about $500 (slightly less with corporate rates). The hotel's health club and spa is truly luxurious. It's also in a prime location on Fifth Avenue.

Renaissance New York
714 Seventh Avenue
Tel: 212-765 7676,
1-800-682 5222
Fax: 212-765 1962
www.renaissncehotels.com
A star of the recently improved and cleaned up Times Square, with 300-plus rooms, most of them featuring large-screen televisions, over-sized bathtubs and other ample comforts. Very convenient for theaters, restaurants, Midtown businesses.

The Royalton
44 West 44th St
Tel: 212-869 4400,
1-800-635 9013
Fax: 212-869 8965
www.morganshotelgroup.com
Another chic and ultra-modern creation from Ian Schrager of Studio 54 fame. Every line and appointment – from the lobby to the lavatories – is as boldly, coldly futur-

istic as the set of a sci-fi film, complete with state-of-the-art video and stereo gadgetry. Still, the Royalton bends over backwards to provide the scurrying, "can-do" pampering expected by its clientele. Convenient to the theater district.

St Regis
2 East 55th St
Tel: 212-753 4500,
1-800-759 7550
Fax: 212-350 6900
www.starwood.com
A grand Edwardian wedding cake of a building, filigreed and charmingly muraled (by the likes of Maxfield Parrish). The St Regis is a magnet for somewhat older, moneyed guests who appreciate the ambiance of a more regal age than our current times. The convenient location doesn't hurt, either.

The Sherry-Netherland
781 Fifth Ave (at 59th St)
Tel: 212-355 2800
Fax: 212-319 4306
www.sherrynetherland.com
An old-fashioned luxury hotel redolent of a bygone era, with such a faithful club of visitors that reservations must be made well in advance. Grandly expansive spaces, both public and in the 40 rooms and suites (the rest of the building is private apartments), with royal treatment to match.

The Westin New York
270 West 43rd St
Tel: 212-921 9575
Fax: 212-921 9576
www.westinny.com
Architecturally dazzling with its multicolored-mirrored exterior, this 45-story hotel has become a visual attraction in the Times

Square area and is one of the new luxury hotels in the neighborhood.

Expensive

Hudson Hotel
356 West 58th St
Tel: 212-554 6000
Fax: 212-554 6001
www.morganshotelgroup.com
Another Ian Schrager invention, but a little less expensive than the Royalton since rooms are smaller. Trendy and stylish, it's a favorite due to location (by the Time Warner Center) and its restaurant, Cafeteria, is a magnet for the nightlife scene.

Hotel Iriquois
49 West 44th St
Tel: 212-840 3080,
1-800-332 7220
Fax: 212-398 1754
www.iriquoisny.com
Built in the early 1900s,

PRICE CATEGORIES

Price categories are for a double room for one night, usually with a Continental breakfast:
Luxury: over $300
Expensive: $250–$300
Inexpensive: ranging from $200–$250
Budget: under $200

this once-shabby hotel has received a facelift and now offers upscale single, double and suite accommodations on the same block as more expensive hotels.

New York Hilton and Towers
1335 Avenue of the Americas
Tel: 212-586 7000,
1-800-HILTONS
Fax: 212-315 1374
www.newyorktowers.hilton.com
A typical Hilton: huge, modern, impersonal but consistent.

The Paramount
235 West 46th St (between Broadway and Eighth Ave)
Tel: 212-764 5500,
1-800-225 7474
Fax: 212-354 5237
www.solmelia.com
A fashion statement in the heart of Times Square (and one of Ian Schrager's ever-growing roster of hotels). The rooms and public spaces, designed by Philippe Starck, dazzle and amaze: amenities include beds with headboards made of reproductions of famous paintings, a fitness club, a supervised kids' playroom, and The Whiskey, a trend-setting small bar. Rooms are small, but well-equipped. Good value for what it achieves.

The Plaza
Fifth Ave (at 59th St)
Tel: 212-759 3000,
1-800-759 3000
Fax: 212-759 3167
www.fairmont.com
One of New York's grand hotels *(see photo, p218)*, the Plaza underwent a renovation that restored its Edwardian-style splendor. Rooms have antiques; the high ceilings deco-

rated with charming murals; and the service close to Old World elegance. The Oak Bar and the Edwardian Room are Old Money's favorite pre- and post-theater spots.

Millennium UN Plaza One
United Nations Plaza (44th St and First Ave)
Tel: 212-758 1234,
1-800-222 8888
Fax: 212-702 5051
www.millennium-hotels.com
The clientele is obvious, although its location can be inconvenient. Others appreciate the busy atmosphere as United Nations' representatives bustle through the heroically proportioned lobby. Benefits to non-ambassadorial guests include rooms with views of the East River, a fitness center, tennis court and pool.

W New York
541 Lexington Ave
Tel: 212-755 1200
Fax: 212-319 8344
www.whotels.com
The flagship of a chain of sybaritic hotels-as-spas, W's interior was designed by entertainment architect David Rockwell and features Zen-like rooms where grass grows on the windowsills and quilts are inscribed with New Agey aphorisms. There's a juice bar, a spa with good fitness facilities, and a trend-setting restaurant called Heartbeat. Can be pricey for this category.

The Waldorf-Astoria
50th St and Park Ave
Tel: 212-355 3000,
1-800-925 3673
Fax: 212-872 7272
www.waldorf.com
The most famous hotel

in the city during its heyday in the 1930s and 1940s, with a pre-war panache that's been restored to something like its early glory. The look of the lobby and public spaces combines H.G. Wells's heroic concept of the future with Hollywood's Cecil B. DeMille's view of Cleopatra's Egypt; the combination never fails to lift the spirits. Most rooms have an old-world charm, and the location is convenient, not only to Midtown shopping, but to the theater and business districts.

CAT NAPS

Sleep for the weary is available at MetroNaps on the 24th floor of the Empire State Building. "Pods" are single occupancy only and cost $14 for 20 minutes. 10am-6pm Mon-Fri; lunch optional. Tel: 212-239-3344 or www.metronaps.com

---

Inexpensive

Hotel Pennsylvania
401 Seventh Ave (at 33rd St)
Tel: 212-736 5000,
1-800-223 8585
Fax: 212-790 8712
www.hotelpenn.com
With 1,700 rooms, this large hotel is centrally located across from Madison Square Garden and Penn Station. Its range of packages makes it good value and few can compete with its history. Built in 1919 by the Pennsylvania Railroad, the building was designed by the renowned firm of McKim, Mead & White. The hotel's Café Rouge

Ballroom played host to many of the Big Band Era's greats including Count Basie, Duke Ellington and the Glenn Miller Orchestra – who immortalized the hotel and its phone number in the 1938 hit *Pennsylvania 6-5000*. It has kept the same phone number ever since.

The Wyndham Hotel
42 West 58th St
Tel: 212-753 3500,
1-800-257 1111
Fax: 212-754 5638
www.hotelwyndham.com
A charming 1920s hotel liked by Carnegie Hall musicians and known for its spacious rooms and very reasonable rates. It's near Fifth Avenue shopping and Midtown restaurants, and only a short walk from leafy Central Park.

Milford Plaza Hotel
270 West 45th St (at 8th Ave)
Tel: 212-869 3600,
1-800-221 2690
Fax: 212-642 4694
www.milfordplaza.com
Located in the very hectic Broadway theater district and not far from Times Square, this hotel is large and gets a lot of traffic from tour groups. If you're taking in a Broadway show, the Milford Plaza is a smart way to save on overnight accomodations.

Wellington Hotel
871 Seventh Ave (at 55th St)
Tel: 212-247 3900,
1-800-652 1212
Fax: 212-581 1719
www.wellingtonhotel.com
The sidestreet entrance in a congested neighborhood is useful and the location is great for Central Park, Lincoln Center, and Carnegie Hall. A reliable standby for reasonable rates.

Budget

Comfort Inns are at several locations:
Comfort Inn Javits Center
442 West 36th St
Tel: 212-714 6699
Fax: 212-714 6681
www.comfortinn.com
Very far west, but good access to public transportation. Perfect for conventioneers.
Comfort Inn Manhattan
42 West 35th St
Tel: 212-947 0200,
1-800-221 5150
Fax: 212-594 3047
www.comfortinnmanhattan.com
Near Macy's and other shopping.
Comfort Inn Midtown
129 West 46th St
Tel: 212-221 2600,
1-800-517 8364
Fax: 212-764 7481
www.applecorehotels.com
In the heart of the theater district, and NYC's only smoke-free hotel. The formula is much the same at this extremely reasonably priced hotel group. Rooms are fairly small, but well situated locations make up for it.
Habitat Hotel
130 East 57th St
Tel: 212-753 8841,
1-800-497 6028
Fax: 212-838 4767
www.stayinny.com
New to the budget category, this excellently located hotel can't be beaten for the price. Recently renovated rooms are compact, and baths are shared.
La Quinta Manhattan
17 West 32nd St
Tel: 212-736 1600,
1-800-551 2303
Fax: 212-563 4007
www.applecorehotels.com
Like others in the Apple Core Hotels group, rates at this 182-room hotel, a short walk from Macy's and Madison Square Garden, are extremely reasonable, especially considering that the comfortable rooms come with such conveniences as data ports and voice mail. There's also a lobby café with entertainment, a restaurant with room service, and – rare in this price category – an open-air rooftop bar where music and snacks can be enjoyed in summer, along with views of the Empire State Building.
Pickwick Arms Hotel
230 East 51st St
Tel: 212-355 0300,
1-800-PICKWIK
Fax: 212-755 5029
www.pickwickarms.com
The recently redecorated rooms are about the size of a postage stamp at this popular budget hotel, which is on a pleasant tree-lined street across from a city "pocket park". The least expensive rooms have shared baths. It's a short walk from the United Nations and other Midtown attractions, and also close to Second Avenue's strip of restaurants and good-time Irish bars.
Super-8 Hotel Times Square
59 West 46th St

Tel: 212-719 2300,
1-800-567 7720
Fax: 212-768 3477
www.applecorehotels.com.
More reasonably priced lodging from the Apple Core Hotel group, especially considering this is geared for the business traveler. Located between 5th and 6th avenues, there's the usual on-demand movies and free local phone calls, plus a business center with computers and a fax machine, a conference room that seats 30 people and an 80-seat meeting room. Budget to inexpensive rooms are available.

PRICE CATEGORIES

UPPER EAST AND WEST SIDES

HOTELS

Luxury

The Carlyle
35 East 76th St
Tel: 212-744 1600,
1-800-227 5737
Fax: 212-717 4682
www.thecarlyle.com
Posh, reserved and serene in its elegance, The Carlyle remains one of the city's most highly acclaimed luxury hotels. The appointments are exquisite, the furnishings antique and the service tends to be on the formal side. Home of Café Carlyle (Woody Allen plays here) and Bemelmans Bar, two of the city's most enduring and upscale evening spots. The Carlyle is a favorite with royalty.
Mandarin Oriental
80 Columbus Circle
Tel: 212-247 2000,
1-800-492 8122
Fax: 212-805 8882
www.mandarinoriental.com/newyork
One of the city's newest luxury hotels, tucked into the aerie of the Time Warner Center at Columbus Circle. Spectacular views, hushed surroundings and the latest of everything make this a sought-after spot for high-end visitors to the city.
The Pierre
2 East 61st St
Tel: 212-838 8000,
1-800-743 7734
Fax: 212-758 1615
www.fourseasons.com
Justly renowned as one of New York's finest hotels, with a fabulous pedigree of guests that goes back to its open-

ing in the early 1930s. (It's now run by the Four Seasons luxury chain.) The location on Fifth

Avenue is perfect for those intent on business or Midtown shopping, and there is a lovely view of Central Park. Rooms are large and elegant; service is top flight; and dining in the Café Pierre or having afternoon tea in the beautiful Rotunda are among the city's most civilized experiences.

Trump International Hotel & Tower
1 Central Park West
Tel: 212-299 1000,
1-800-44-TRUMP
Fax: 212-299 1150
www.trumpintl.com

Overlooking Central Park with sweeping views provided by floor-to-ceiling windows, the hotel comes complete with a spa, fitness center and indoor pool. As flashy as its namesake, the hotel houses a celebrated restaurant, Vong, and has an enormous silver globe sculpture marking its spot at Columbus Circle.

Expensive

The Lucerne Hotel
201 West 79th St
Tel: 212-875 1000,
1-800-492 8122
Fax: 212-579 2708
www.newyorkhotel.com

Great location to experience the trendy Upper West Side in a landmark building where bars and restaurants exist side-by-side with families in brownstones conducting their daily life. The Nice Matin on the corner has become one of the area's better and popular restaurants.

The Melrose New York Hotel
140 East 63rd St (at Lexington Avenue)

Tel: 212-838 5700,
1-800-223 1020
Fax: 212-888 4271
www.melrosehotel.com

Seasoned New Yorkers will remember this as the once posh Barbizon Hotel for Women. The Melrose is now a perfect haven for the shopaholic with its proximity to Madison Avenue designer shops, and Bloomingdale's is just a few blocks south. Spacious fitness facilities keep the stylish shoppers in shape for just about anything.

The Franklin
164 East 87th St
Tel: 212-369 1000,
877-847 4444
Fax: 212-369 8000.
www.franklinhotel.com

Once a bargain for the Upper East Side, this boutique hotel has upgraded and is slightly more expensive, but be on the lookout for special rates. The atmosphere is charming, the breakfast delicious, the beds heavenly and the sheets are linen. Plasma TV screens, WiFi access, and in-room movies from a library of classic films.

Hotel Excelsior
45 West 81st St
Tel: 212-362 9200,
1-800-368 4575
Fax: 212-721 2994
www.excelsiorhotelny.com

An old-fashioned hotel dating from the 1920s, recently renovated, and located on a pleasant block between Central Park West and Columbus Avenue shopping. It's convenient for museums, shopping and Central Park. Can be expensive, but given the location, worth it.

Hotel Wales
1295 Madison (at 92nd St)
Tel: 212-876 6000,
1-800-428 5252
Fax: 212-860 7000
www.waleshotel.com

The Wales was once known for its low rates and splendid views of Central Park. Today it costs more, but still offers a great location in the upmarket Carnegie Hill neighborhood, close to Museum Mile and Central Park. You can feast on the best breakfast in NY next door at Sarabeth's Kitchen, or enjoy the light breakfast offered in the hotel's tea salon, also the setting for afternoon teas and chamber music.

Inexpensive

Beacon Hotel
2130 Broadway (at 75th St)
Tel: 212-787 1100,
1-800-572 4969
Fax: 212-724 0839
www.beaconhotel.com

This busy and friendly Upper West Side favorite is adjacent to the Beacon Theater, where popular music groups play. Deals are to be had for families

who book rooms with fold-away couches. The location is a great launch pad thanks to the West 72nd St and Broadway public transportation hub with subway and bus connections that lead just about anywhere.

Gracie Inn
502 East 81 St
Tel: 212-628 1700,
1-800-404 2252
Fax: 212-697 3772
www.gracieinn.com

Located on an easternmost sidestreet in a very quiet part of town near Gracie Mansion (the mayor of New York's official residence), this is really more like a cross between a city townhouse and a country inn. From small, single-room "studios" to larger "penthouse" accommodations, rates are subject to reduction depending on the length of stay.

Comfort Inn – Central Park West
31 West 71 St
Tel: 212-721 4770,
1-877-727 5236
Fax: 212-579 8544
www.comfortinn.com/ires/hotel/ny209

A boutique hotel at bargain prices in an excellent location on the Upper West Side. It's less than a block from Central Park.

Budget

Malibu Hotel
2688 Broadway
Tel: 212-663 0275
Fax: 212-678 6842

At 103rd St on the Upper West Side, this budget hotel's a little bit of a trek, but compact and renovated rooms have cable TV, CD players, etc. The cheapest rooms have shared bathrooms. As an added bonus, guests (mostly students and younger travelers) receive free passes to popular nightclubs.

The Milburn
242 West 76th St
Tel: 212-362 1006,
1-800-833 9622
Fax: 212-721 5476
www.milburnhotel.com
A bargain 16-floor hotel with refurbished rooms that have TVs and kitch-enettes; it also has a fitness facility. Situated on a quiet side street within walking distance of Lincoln Center.

Quality Hotel on Broadway
215 West 94th St
Tel: 212-866 6400,
1-800-834 2972
Fax: 212-866 1357
www.affinia.com
Good location and near transportation hub at 96th St and Broadway. Events at nearby Symphony Space are usually interesting.

MURRAY HILL/GRAMERCY PARK/CHELSEA

HOTELS

Luxury

Inn at Irving Place
56 Irving Place
Tel: 212-533 4600,
1-800-685 1447
Fax: 212-533 4611
www.innatirving.com
A pair of graceful townhouses transformed into a facsimile of a country inn, with a cozy fireplace-lit tea salon, and 12 elegant rooms and suites featuring four-poster beds. A two-block walk from Gramercy Park and a short distance from Union Square. There's a nice little restaurant on the Inn's lower level that provides guests with room service.

Morgans
237 Madison Ave (at 37th St)
Tel: 212-686 0300,
1-800-334 3408
Fax: 212-779 8352
www.morganshotelgroups.com
The original brainchild of Ian Schrager and the late Steve Rubell, and, surprising for ultra trend-conscious New York, still one of the most fashionable temporary addresses in Manhattan; an ultra-modern enclave for hip young movie stars and

other millionaires. The decor's original stark grays have been replaced by warmer tones, but there's still a minimalist ambiance at work. Service is extraordinarily pampering; it is said there is *nothing* the staff won't do for its privileged guests.

W New York Union Square
201 Park Ave South (at 17th St)
Tel: 212-253 9119,
1-877-W-HOTELS
Fax: 212-253 9229
www.whotels.com
Bordering the fashionable Flatiron District, this stylish hotel has one foot in Gramercy Park and the other in a Downtown "attitude". Everything here is top-of-the-line, including trendy bar and restaurant "Olives".

Expensive

Hampton Inn Chelsea
108 West 24th St
Tel: 212-414 1000
Fax: 212-647 1511
www.hershahotels.com.
hamptoninnchelsea.htm
Hi-tech modern decor sets the tone at this Chelsea spot situated at the doorstep of the gallery scene stretching West Shopping opportunities abound on nearby Avenue of the Americas.

The Roger Williams Hotel
131 Madison Ave (at 31st St)
Tel: 212-448 7000,
877-847 4444
Fax: 212-448 7007
www.rogerwilliamshotel.com
The Roger Williams has exchanged its sleek, stark style for a warmer approach, using bold colors and natural wood. The lobby has a soaring atrium, while the bedrooms are home-from-home cozy, with lots of space, thick bathrobes, down comforters to curl up under, CD players and VCRs in each room. Penthouses have lovely little balconies with great views of the Empire State Building.

Inexpensive

The Chelsea Hotel
222 West 23rd St
Tel: 212-243 3700
Fax: 212-675 5531
www.hotelchelsea.com
A red-brick, Victorian landmark of bohemian decadence, home to beatnik poets, then Warhol drag queens, then Sid Vicious, and now... some of all of the above, plus "ordinary" guests. For some, a stay at the Chelsea can be part of a ritual pilgrimage to all that is hip Down-

town, as redolent with arty history as West Village streets and Lower East Side clubs. Accommodations vary from a few inexpensive "student rooms" to suites, with the price mirroring the standard of the amenity. Long-stay discounts may be available; enquire.

Gershwin Hotel
7 East 27th St
Tel: 212-545 8000
Fax: 212-684 5546
www.gershwinhotel.com
Artsy with intimate feel, this medium-sized hotel

PRICE CATEGORIES

Price categories are for a double room for one night, usually with a Continental breakfast:
Luxury: over $300
Expensive: $250–$300
Inexpensive: ranging from $200–$250
Budget: under $200

just north of Madison Square Park has very attractive package rates for families and for weekend stays.

Jolly Madison Towers Hotel
22 East 38th St
Tel: 212-802 0600
Fax: 212-204 9334
www.jollymadison.com
Right around the corner from some much more expensive places to stay is a Murray Hill affordable "find" where

excellent room rates can be discovered for the asking.

Marriott ExecuStay Aurora
554 Third Ave (bet. 36th and 37th Sts)
Tel: 212-953 5707,
1-800-877 2800
Fax: 212-953 5755
www.stayatexecustay.com/nyc
Fully equipped apartments for long- and

short-term stays; the surrounding area is a little bit busy, but it's a great bargain for New York nevertheless.

Murray Hill East Suites
149 East 39th St
Tel: 212-661 2100,
1-800-248 9999
Fax: 212-818 0724
These are excellent value, situated in the heart of Murray Hill between Lexington and Third aves. Each suite has a kitchen.

Ramada Inn Eastside
161 Lexington Ave at 30th St
Tel: 212-545 1800,
1-800-625 5980
Fax: 212-679 9146
www.applecorehotels.com
A cozily refurbished early-1900s hotel, with a friendly staff and 100 reasonably priced rooms, some with views of the Empire State Building. The location, within walking distance of Midtown and Downtown, is convenient.

GREENWICH VILLAGE/SOHO/ LITTLE ITALY/LOWER MANHATTAN

HOTELS

Luxury

Hotel Gansevoort
18 Ninth Ave at 13th St
Tel: 212-206 6700,
1-877-426 7386
Fax: 212-255 5858
www.hotelgansevoort.com
The Meatpacking District's first luxury hotel *(see photo opposite)*, has a huge rooftop bar and swimming pool, as well as breathtaking views of the Downtown skyline and sunsets. Bedrooms are fashionably appointed (think neutral colors and a single orchid). If it faces west, the Hudson River will be on the horizon and the Meatpacking action will be taking place directly below, non-stop. You need never leave the room.

The Mercer Hotel
147 Mercer St
Tel: 212-966 6060,
888-918 6060
Fax: 212-965 3838
www.mercerhotel.com

In the heart of Soho, a converted 1890s landmark building with 75 rooms that feature high loft ceilings, arched windows and (for New York City) spacious bath facilities. Andre Balazs, the owner, also owns Chateau Marmont in LA, and the clientele here is similarly stylish. Hotel facilities include a second-floor roof garden, a library bar with 24-hour food and drink service, and the highly regarded, ever popular Mercer Kitchen restaurant.

The Millenium Hilton Hotel
55 Church St
Tel: 212-693 2001,
1-800-445 8667
Fax: 212-571 2317
www.newyorkmillenium.hilton.com
Adjacent to Wall St and its "canyons"of financial movers and shakers, this Hilton hotel affords the opportunity to be near Hudson River breezes across the way at Battery Park City – after being pampered by the large selection of in-house services.

The Soho Grand
310 West Broadway
Tel: 212-965 3000,
1-877-965 3236
Fax: 212-965 3200
www.sohograd.com
A sophisticated yet totally comfortable 15-story addition to downtown Manhattan, with industrial-chic decor throughout, and stunning upper-floor views. The service at the Grand is excellent, and the lobby and bar is the rendezvous of choice for cool media types, music stars and others in town to see and be seen. As befits a place owned by the heir to the Hartz Mountain pet empire, pets are welcome (in rooms far from other guests who might be allergic). Exercise, grooming and feeding services are available – and if you arrive without an animal companion, the management will provide a complimentary bowl of friendly goldfish, just one of the tasks the pleasant staff will be happy to provide.

Expensive

Holiday Inn Wall Street
15 Gold St
Tel: 212-232 7700,
1-800-HOLIDAY
Fax: 212-425 0330
www.holidayinnwsd.com
After all that profit taking on the right New York Stock Exchange investments, make a stop at Century 21 shopping emporium around the corner and spend, spend, spend!

The Maritime Hotel
363 West 16th St(at Ninth Ave)
Tel: 212-242 4300
Fax: 212-242 1188
www.themaritimehotel.com
On the north, less fren-

tic end of the Meatpacking District, the lobby bar is more famous than the hotel itself as a place to be seen. With its distinctive architecture and funky port-hole windows, you'll never lose sight of where you're staying.

Inexpensive

Best Western Seaport Inn
33 Peck Slip
Tel: 212-766 6600,
1-800-HOTEL-NY
Fax: 212-766 6615
www.bestwestern.com/seaportinn
A block from South Street Seaport, this converted 19th-century warehouse has 72 rooms featuring Federalist-era antiques and modern amenities like VCRs and mini-fridges. Some rooms on the sixth floor have Jacuzzis and/or terraces with good views of the Brooklyn Bridge.
Holiday Inn Downtown
138 Lafayette St
Tel: 212-966 8898,
1-800-HOLIDAY
Fax: 212-966 3933
www.holidayinn-nyc.com
In a renovated historic building, this hotel right on the edge of Chinatown is much nicer than you might expect from an international chain hotel group.

Budget

Abingdon Guest House
13 Eighth Avenue (between West 12th and Jane sts)
Tel: 212-243 5384
Fax: 212-807 74731
www.abingdonhouse.com
It's romance on ashoe-string at this nine-room hostelry between the West Village and the

Meatpacking District. Accommodation is spread between two townhouses, and each of the tiny rooms is individually decorated: some have four-posters, some fireplaces. The rooms facing Eighth Avenue can be a little noisy, so ask for the Garden Room in the back. Preferably a two-night minimum stay; no smoking allowed.
Riverview Hotel
113 Jane Street at West St
Tel: 212-929 0060
Fax: 212-675 8581
www.hotelriverview.com
Aptly named, this popular Greenwich Village spot faces the Hudson River and all the waterfront activity that rolls on by. It's a little bit of a walk to public transportation, but it's along some of the city's most picturesque blocks.
Washington Square Hotel
103 Waverly Place
Tel: 212-777 9515,
1-800-222 0418
Fax: 212-979 8373
www.washingtonsquarehotel.com
An almost century-old hotel that offers the per-

fect Village locale. The rooms are small but nicely appointed. In a former incarnation, this was the seedy Hotel Earle, where Papa John wrote the 1960s rock classic, *California Dreaming*.

ALTERNATIVES

Anco Studios
Tel: 212-717 7500,
1-888-701 7500
www.ancostudios.com
B&B as well as vacation studio accommodations for short term on the Upper East Side. From budget to expensive.
City Lights Bed & Breakfast, Ltd
Tel: 212-737 7049
www.citylightsny.com
Offers a full range of B&B listings.
Marmara-Manhattan
301 East 94th St
Tel: 212-427-3100
www.marmara-manhattan.com
Suite stays of 30 days or more are required, but prices are extremely reasonable for an Upper East Side historic district room.

PRICE CATEGORIES
Price categories are for a double room for one night, usually with a Continental breakfast:
Luxury: over $300
Expensive: $250–$300
Inexpensive: ranging from $200–$250
Budget: under $200

New York also has reliable **hostel-style** accommodations, like the **New York International Youth Hostel** at 891 Amsterdam Ave, tel: 212-932 2300, www.hinewyork.org. The **YMCA-Vanderbilt** at 224 West 47th St, tel: 212-756 9600, www.hostelnewyork.com, is the best of four Ys in Manhattan, while the **92nd St Y de Hirsch Residence** at 1395 Lexington Ave, tel: 212-415 5650, has a 30 day minimum for furnished rooms. Details on: www.92y.org/content/de_hirsch_residence. The **Brandon Residence for Women**, 340 West 85th St, tel: 212-496 6901, www.thebrandon.org, is located on abeautiful Upper West Side block; dormitory-style rooms for single women.

A CTIVITIES

THE ARTS, NIGHTLIFE, EVENTS, SHOPPING, SPORTS AND TOURS

It's just possible that there may be somebody somewhere who comes to New York for a rest. But it's certainly the least likely place to choose, because in The Big Apple there's something happening 24 hours, every day of the year. A comprehensive calendar of events is included in the *Official NYC Guide* published by the NYC & Company & Visitors Information Center, 810 Seventh Ave, New York, NY, 10019, tel: 212-397 8222; 1-800-NYCVISIT. Information is also available online at www.nycvisit.com, or tel: 212-484 1222 when you arrive.

THE ARTS

Theater

Few Broadway theaters are actually on Broadway. The alternative to Broadway is off-Broadway, where performances scarcely differ in quality from the former category, although they are performed in smaller theaters. The vast majority of off-Broadway theaters, and indeed, the more experimental off-off-Broadway theaters, are Downtown – particularly in the East Village area. Here you'll find the influential **Joseph Papp Public Theater**, a complex of several theaters in

one building at 425 Lafayette St, tel: 212-260 2400. The **Theater for the New City** at 155 First Ave, tel: 212-254 1109 and **LaMama E.T.C.**, 74A East 4th St, tel: 212-475 7710, are both nearby and show new work by experimental theater artists.

Interesting off-Broadway productions can also be found around Union Square at the **Union Square Theatre**, 100 East 17th St, tel: 212-307 4100; in Soho at the **Soho Playhouse**, 15 Vandam St, tel: 212-615 6432; and in the West Village, at the **Lucille Lortel Theater**, 121 Christopher St, tel: 212-239 6200 and the **Cherry Lane Theater**, 38 Commerce St, tel: 212-727 3673. Near Times Square, the group of off-Broadway theaters on West 42nd St between Ninth and Tenth avenues are known as **Theater Row**, of which the best-known is **Playwrights Horizons**, tel: 212- 279 4200. One block north, **The Westside Theatre**, 407 West 43rd St, tel: 212-239-6200 is home to new dramatic comedy. On the Upper West Side the **Promenade Theater**, 2162 Broadway at 76th St, tel: 580 1313, is a fine venue.

The *New York Times* offers good listings (as do *The New Yorker, Time Out New York* and *New York* magazines; these are worth checking regularly). A use-

ful telephone number for ticket prices, availability and/or information about current shows is NYC/On Stage, tel: 212-768 1818, www.TDF.org.

Dance

Numerous renowned dance troupes are based in the city, including the Martha Graham Dance Company, Paul Taylor Dance Company, Alvin Ailey American Dance Theater and the Dance Theater of Harlem.

Performance venues:
Aaron Davis Hall, City College, 138 Convent Ave. Tel: 212-650 7148.
Brooklyn Academy of Music (BAM), 30 Lafayette Ave, Brooklyn. Tel: 718-636 4100.
City Center, 131 West 55th St. Tel: 212-581 1212.
Cunningham Studio, 55 Bethune St. Tel: 212-691 9751.
Danspace Project, St Mark's Church, Second Ave at East 10th St. Tel: 212-674 8194.
Dance Theater Workshop, 219 West 19th St. Tel: 212-924 0077.
The Joyce Theater, 175 Eighth Ave. Tel: 212-242 0800.
Wave Hill, 249th St and Independence Ave, Riverdale, the Bronx. Tel: 718-549 3200. Beautiful spot with outdoor, site-specific performances (summer only).

Magazines with listings, such as *The New Yorker*, *Time Out New York* and *New York* publish dance performances, as does NYC/On Stage, tel: 212-768 1818.

Concert Halls

Lincoln Center for the Performing Arts, on Broadway between 62nd and 66th St, is the city's pre-eminent cultural center. It's home to America's oldest orchestra, the New York Philharmonic, which gives 200 concerts annually in **Avery Fisher Hall**, while nearby **Alice Tully Hall** houses the Center's Chamber Music Society. The New York City Opera and New York City Ballet perform at different times in the **New York State Theater**.

Also in this complex are the **Metropolitan Opera House**, home of the Metropolitan Opera Company and, in spring, the American Ballet Theater; the excellent **Vivian Beaumont Theater**, the **Mitzi E. Newhouse Theater**, and the **Walter Reade Theater** (where the New York Film Festival is held); the **Julliard School of Music**, and **The New York Public Library for the Performing Arts** (tel: 212-870-1630), an excellent reference source for music and the arts. Tours of Lincoln Center are offered daily between 10am and 5pm; for details, call 212-875 5350. For information about current performances, call 212-LINCOLN (546-2656).

New York's oldest joke concerns the tourist who asks how to get to **Carnegie Hall** and is told "practice, practice." It's far quicker to take the N or R subway to 57th St and walk to Seventh Ave or catch a crosstown 57th St bus to this century-old hall, where the world's greatest performers have appeared. For information, call 212- 247 7800.

Venues for classical (and other) music also include **Town Hall**, 123 West 43rd St, tel: 212-840 2824; **Merkin Concert Hall**, 129 West 67th St, tel: 212-501 3330; the **Kaye Playhouse**, 695 Park Ave at 68th St, tel: 212-772 4448; **Brooklyn Center for the Performing Arts**, Brooklyn College, tel: 718-951 4500; and the **Brooklyn Academy of Music (BAM)**, 30 Lafayette Ave, Brooklyn, tel: 718-636 4100.

Opera

In addition to the performances of the New York City Opera and the Metropolitan Opera at Lincoln Center, opera can be enjoyed at cozier venues, including:
Amato Opera Company Theatre, 319 Bowery. Tel: 212-228 8200.
DiCapo Opera Theater, 184 East 76th St. Tel: 212-288 9438.

Contemporary Music

Apollo Theater, 253 West 125th St. Tel: 212-531 5300.
Beacon Theater, Broadway at 74th St. Tel: 212-496 7070.
Madison Square Garden, Seventh Ave, between 31st and 33rd Streets. Tel: 465-MSG1 (6741).
Radio City Music Hall, Sixth Ave and 50th St. Tel: 212-247 4777.
Symphony Space, 2537 Broadway. Tel: 212-864 5400.
Town Hall, 123 West 43rd St. Tel: 212-840 2824.

And just out of town at:

Continental Airlines Arena, The Meadowlands, East Rutherford, New Jersey. Tel: 201-935 3900.
Nassau Coliseum, Uniondale, Long Island. Tel: 516-794 9300.

Art Galleries

Note: most galleries are closed on Mondays. There are well over 400 art galleries in the Naked City, in various neighborhoods – in **Midtown** along 57th St between Sixth Ave and Park Ave; on the **Upper East Side** along upper Madison Ave; in **Chelsea** (particularly around West 22nd and West 24th streets near Tenth Ave); in the **Meatpacking District** around 13th and 14th streets between Tenth Avenue and the West Side Highway ,and a few remain in **Soho** (Bonino; Swiss Institute; DeitchProjects; Phyllis Kind; Lennon, Weinberg).

From the mid-1990s onward, most of Soho's best-known galleries either closed or moved to **Chelsea,** where the big gallery scene is happening these days. Some others re-located to the more traditional 57th St or Fifth Ave/Madison Avenue area (Gagosian, Leo Castelli), while still others fled to Brooklyn's DUMBO or Queens.

As with restaurants, boutiques and clubs, galleries spring up overnight and disappear just as quickly. True art fans should consult the listings in weekly magazines like *New York* or *Time Out New York*, as well as the art section of The *New York Times* on Friday and Sunday. A free monthly, *Gallery Guide*, can be picked up at various arty locations.

It's also worth checking out the following places, most of which have some sort of artist participation:
AIR Galleries, 511 West 25th St. A women's art collective.
Artists Space, 38 Greene St. New trends, new artists, also visual screenings and performance art.
New Museum of Contemporary Art, 556 West 22nd St (temporary new location). Video installations, sculpture and other works.
Printed Matter, 535 West 22nd St. Books on, by and for artists.
P.S. 1 Contemporary Art Center, 22–25 Jackson Ave, at 46th Ave,

Long Island City, Queens. Tel: 718-784 2084. Up-and-coming artists, multi-media installations, and much more. Affiliated with the Museum of Modern Art and always worth checking out.
White Columns, 320 West 13th St (entrance on Horatio St), in the West Village.

Multi-Media

Performance art, multi-media presentations and various uncategorizable events are held at spots around the city, including:
Dia Center for the Arts, 548 West 22nd St. Tel: 212-989 5566 (reopens 2006).
The Kitchen, 512 West 19th St. Tel: 212-255 5793.
La Mama, 74A East 4th St. Tel: 212-475 7710.
P.S. 122, 150 First Ave. Tel: 212-477 5288.
Symphony Space, 2537 Broadway (at 95th St). Tel: 212-864 5400.

NIGHTLIFE

Clubs appear and disappear in New York even more abruptly than do restaurants. While flagship music venues like the Village Vanguard seem eternal, others, especially the ultra-chic dance clubs, are more ephemeral, seeming to rise and fall (or fail) literally overnight. With these clubs, it's even more important to consult up-to-date listings in publications like the *New Yorker*, *New York* magazine, *Time Out New York* and the *Village Voice*.

The following represent a range of clubs offering various types of live and recorded music, as well as comedy, cabaret acts and even poetry readings. Because cover charges, reservation policies and show times vary from club to club and act to act, it's best if you call and ask for specific details geared to a specific night.

Jazz

Midtown

Birdland, 315 West 44th St. Tel: 212-581 3080. Elegant jazz club and restaurant. Big-name big bands and jazz greats are the norm, along with smaller well-known or up-and-coming groups holding sway from around 9pm, with a second set at 11pm.
Iridium, 1650 Broadway (at 51st St.) Tel: 212-582 2121. Relocated from the Upper West Side when it opened in early 1994, this club and restaurant has also presented some of the jazz world's most gifted denizens. Definitely worth checking out, especially Monday night when guitar legend Les Paul is often holding court to admirers.

Uptown

Smoke, 2751 Broadway (between 105th and 106th St). Tel: 212-864 6662. Latin jazz, jazz, blues and soul vocalists at this Uptown haunt; no cover charge most nights.

Downtown

Blue Note, 131 West 3rd St. Tel: 212-475 8592. The West Village is home to the most famous jazz clubs in the world, and first and foremost there's the Blue Note; it's been packed virtually every night for years. The reason is simple: the club presents the very best of mainstream jazz and blues, from time-honored greats to more contemporary acts. The line-up here has featured such luminaries as the Modern Jazz Quartet, Etta James, Joe Williams, Betty Carter, the Count Basie Orchestra... the list goes on and on. For die-hard fans, there's a late-night session that jams until 4am, after the last set.
Cajun, 129 Eighth Ave at 16th St. Tel: 212-691 6174. Jazz and blues bands predominate here, although the occasional 1930s Bix Biederbecke-style bands slip in, as do authentic Cajun bands, washboards and all.

The Jazz Standard, 116 East 27th St. Tel: 576 2232. Everything from duos to nine-piece bands and beyond in this basement club. There's a popular restaurant, "Blue Smoke" upstairs, but food downstairs, too. Closed Mondays.
S.O.B.'s, 204 Varick St. (at Houston St.) Tel: 212-243-4940. Funky, global jazz, lots of Brazilian beat, but runs the gamut of international dance music.
Village Vanguard, 178 Seventh Ave South. Tel: 212-255 4037. Born over half a century ago in a Greenwich Village basement, this flagship club cut its teeth helping to launch fabulous talents like Miles Davis and John Coltrane. In its adulthood, it hardly keeps up with the "vanguard" anymore, but presents the greats and near-greats of what is now the mainstream. It's also a chance to catch acts that rarely tour. The VV is a terrific evening out, but an extremely popular one – call the club well in advance for reservations to avoid disappointment.

Rock, Dance, Blues

Midtown

B.B. King's Blues Club & Grill 237 West 42nd St. Tel: 212-997 4144. In the heart of Times Square, the legendary bluesman's New York venture (there are others around the country, including Memphis) packs them in for the best of the biggest names in R & B. This often includes the King himself, stroking the only woman who's never let him down – his trusty guitar, Lucille.
Crobar, 530 West 28th St. Tel: 212-629 9000. Very far west, upper Chelsea nightspot. Popular with the large dance-club, late-night crowd.
Rodeo Bar, 375 Third Ave at East 27th St. Tel: 212-683 6500. A kitschy Wild West theme; a loose and lanky atmosphere, and (sometimes) live performances by "cowboy rock" bands.

Roseland, 239 West 52nd St. Tel: 212-247 0200. Historically, a venue for traditional ballroom dancing; lately, also for private parties, special events and performances by alternative rock bands or DJ-driven dancing to classic R&B. Check the website, www.roselandballroom.com for schedules.

Swing 46, 349 West 46th St. Tel: 212-262 9554. An all-swing jazz and supper club with dance lessons every night and live bands. George Gee and his 15-piece Make Believe Ballroom Orchestra get the joint jumping whenever they appear. There is a cover charge.

Downtown

Arlene Grocery, 95 Stanton St, between Ludlow and Orchard. Tel: 212-358 1633. A low-key, dress-down Lower East Side venue for rock, folk, funk and everything in between. No admission fee.

The Bitter End, 147 Bleecker St. Tel: 212-673 7030. A Greenwich Village landmark, the Bitter End books an eclectic mishmash of folk, folk rock, soft rock, blues, some comedy and cabaret... whatever. A classic example of eternal bohemianism, it's popular with young adult tourists and can be mobbed on weekends.

CBGB & OMFUG, 315 Bowery at Bleecker St. Tel: 212-982 4052. The club where punk started in America, still the quintessential grubby rock venue; in effect, a museum to the spirit of '77. In the midst of the Bowery, CBGB has a beaten-down anti-glamour that's quite charming if you can appreciate it. You may not have heard of any of the young bands, because CBGB continues to encourage up-and-coming groups with bad haircuts, although occasional name bands do show up.

Irving Plaza, 17 Irving Pl. Tel: 212-777 6800. A ramshackle hall near Union Square that's gone through more than one incarnation, currently featuring everything from top rock bands to Sunday swing dancing.

Joe's Pub at The Public Theater, 425 Lafayette St. Tel: 212-239-6200. Singers, performance artists, musicians: quite the eclectic mix, adjacent to Joseph Papp's legendary theatre.

Knitting Factory, 24 Leonard St. Tel: 212-219 3055. Tribeca eclectic music mecca which also features the next wave in other performance arts. Totally unpredictable, casual and cool.

Mercury Lounge, 217 East Houston St. Tel: 212-260 4700. Intimate Lower East Side club with excellent acoustics, catering to a more sophisticated alternative music crowd than usual.

The Village Underground, 130 West 3rd St. Tel: 212-777 7745. For those who miss the eclectic mix that was Tramps in Chelsea, its former booker picks the groups that appear here.

Webster Hall 125 East 11th St. Tel: 212-353 1600; www.websterhall.com. Discount passes available online for this large, crowded East Village club that attracts a young crowd. Open Wednesdays to Saturdays from 10pm, it offers all-night dancing to everything from rock, reggae and R&B to house, techno and who knows; theme nights range from "runway parties" to 1960s psychedelia.

Comedy and Cabaret

Midtown

Caroline's Comedy Club, 1626 Broadway (between 49th and 50th St.) Tel: 212-757 4100. A plush restaurant and club with a continuous roster of young comic hopefuls along with some of the biggest names in the "biz," since so many of them live in New York and it's a chance not to have to tour. An evening here can also be your big opportunity to laugh your way onto American television; some of the shows from Caroline's are videotaped for national cable TV consumption.

Gotham Comedy Club, 34 West 22nd St. Tel: 212-367 9000. A Chelsea club that runs the stand-up comedy gamut from unknown first-timers to the irrepressible and unmissable all-star acerbic wit, Jackie Mason.

Danny's Skylight Room at the Grand Sea Palace, 346 West 46th St. Tel: 212-265 8133. A lively Theater District piano bar and cabaret room, located in a popular Thai restaurant. Shows starts around 9pm during the week, but tend to be earlier on weekends.

Don't Tell Mama, 343 West 46th St. Tel: 212-757 0788. Very jolly spot, long favored by a theatrical crowd. In the front there's often a sing-along at the piano bar. The back room is a non-stop cabaret featuring comedians and torch singers. Leave inhibitions behind, and bring cash (no credit cards accepted).

The Oak Room, Algonquin Hotel, 59 West 44th St. Tel: 212-840 6800. A dark, intimate piano bar with great singers (Harry Connick, Jr played here before he made it big. It's also an opportunity to dress up in cocktail finery. Dinner is served here, too.

Le Jazz Au Bar, 41 East 58th St. Tel: 212-308 9455. Specializes in legendary female jazz vocalists and has a clubby atmosphere for dinner, but like the location, it's expensive.

Uptown

Café Carlyle, 35 East 76th St. Tel: 570 7184. In the elegant Carlyle Hotel, an upper-crusty institution of sorts for the social set. Depending on who's singing, playing or both, there's a hefty cover charge and always a two-drink minimum. On Mondays, Woody Allen sits in with the New Orleans Jazz Band headed by Eddy Davis.

Comic Strip, 1568 Second Ave at 82nd St. Tel: 861 9386. A casual, popular proving ground for young stand-up kamikazes, both known and unknown. Open seven days a week, with three shows on popular Friday and Saturday nights.

Stand-Up NY, 236 West 78th St, at Broadway. Tel: 212-595 0850. Small Upper West Side club that often takes the inventive approach of searches for "funniest doctor", "funniest banker" (really?) with hilarious results.

Feinstein's at the Regency, 540 Park Avenue at 61st St. Tel: 307 4100. Singer Michael Feinstein is so devoted to cabaret that he opened his own high-end club in the luxurious Regency Hotel.

Downtown

The Comedy Cellar, 117 MacDougal St. Tel: 212-254 3480. A cramped basement room where the tables are packed so close together that, even if you don't get the jokes, you may make some new friends. The show starts at 9pm.

The Duplex, 61 Christopher St. Tel: 212-255 5438. A landmark of the gay West Village, attracting a friendly and mixed audience.

Boston Comedy Club, 82 West 3rd St. Tel: 212-477 1000. Remember the film *Animal House*? That's basically the atmosphere at this rowdy Downtown joint.

Nuyorican Poet's Café, 236 East 3rd St. (between Aves B and C). Tel: 212-505-8183. Everything from the spoken word to comedy and music at this cutting-edge East Village outpost.

Movies

Movie theaters are scattered all over town, with first-run films often shown at cinemas in Midtown; in the East and West 60s in multiplex film houses; on East 34th St near Third Ave; and in Greenwich Village. The city's daily newspapers, weekly papers and color magazines carry complete listings, as well as, usually, the performance times.

There are at least a score of venues that are devoted to showing revival, cult, experimental and genre films which never make the mainstream circuit. The theaters are often small and intimate, with a neighborhood feel, and the films are usually subtitled.

Theaters include the **French Institute/Alliance Française**, 22 East 60th St, tel: 212-355 6100 and the **Japan Society**, 333 East 47th St, tel: 212-832 1155, which specialize in foreign-language showings. Places such as **Anthology Film Archives**, 32 Second Ave, tel: 212-505 5181; **Cinema Village**, 22 East 12th St, tel: 212-924 3363; and **Angelika Film Center**, 18 West Houston (at Mercer St), tel: 212-777 FILM), and the **Film Forum**, 209 West Houston St, tel: 212-727 8110, all show films of a special nature.

Independent and foreign films are a specialty at the **BAM Rose Cinemas** at the Brooklyn Academy of Music, 30 Lafayette Ave, Brooklyn, tel: 718-636 4100, and at the **Walter Reade Theater** at Lincoln Center, tel: 212-875 5600, where the annual New York Film Festival takes place every fall.

Rarely seen movies or obscure directors are featured at the **American Museum of the Moving Image** in Queens, tel: 718-784 0077, as well as at the **Museum of Modern Art**, tel: 212-708 9400.

During the summer **Bryant Park**, behind the Public Library at 42nd St, shows free outdoor movies; call 212-512 5700 for a current schedule.

EVENTS

January

Martin Luther King Day Parade.
National Boat Show, Javits Convention Center.
Outsider Art Fair, Puck Building, Lafayette St.
Winter Antiques Show, 7th Regiment Armory, Park Avenue.

February

The Art Show, 7th Regiment Armory, Park Avenue.
Black History Month.
Chinese New Year, celebrations in Chinatown (sometimes Jan).
Empire State Building Run-Up race.
Westminster Kennel Club Dog Show, Madison Square Garden.

March

Artexpo New York, Javits Convention Center.
Circus Animal Walk, Ringling Brothers, Barnum & Bailey Circus, Queens Midtown Tunnel.
Greek Independence Day Parade.
International Cat Show, Madison Square Garden (sometimes Feb).
New York City Opera (through April), Lincoln Center.
St Patrick's Day Parade Fifth Avenue.
Whitney Biennial exhibition, Whitney Museum.

April

American Ballet Theater (to June) at Lincoln Center.
Earth Day Celebrations.
Easter Parade on Fifth Avenue.
Cherry Blossom Festival at Brooklyn Botanic Garden (sometimes May).
Greater New York International Auto Show, Javits Convention Center.
Macy's Spring Flower Show.
New York Yankees baseball season begins.

May

Belmont Racetrack opens.
Fleet Week, Intrepid Sea-Air-Space Museum.
Great Five Borough Bike Tour Race & Festival, Staten Island.
New York beaches open.
New York City Ballet (to June) at Lincoln Center.
Ninth Avenue International Food Festival.
Salute to Israel Parade, Fifth Avenue.
Tribeca Film Festival.
Ukrainian Festival, 7th St and Second Avenue.
Washington Square Art Show.

June

Buskers Fare Festival, Lower Manhattan.
Central Park Summer Stage shows (through Aug), Rumsey Playfield, Central Park.
Downtown River to River Festival.
Feast of St Anthony, Little Italy.
Free Metropolitan Opera performances in parks of all five boroughs (through Aug).
Gay and Lesbian Pride Day Parade, Fifth Avenue.
JVC Jazz Festival throughout the city.
Mermaid Parade, Coney Island, Brooklyn.
Midsummer Night Swing dancing at Lincoln Center (through July).
Museum Mile Festival.
Puerto Rican Day Parade, Fifth Avenue.

July

Free New York Philharmonic concerts in major parks. Free concerts at South Street Seaport.
Macy's Fourth of July Fireworks, East River.
Mostly Mozart Festival (to Aug) at Lincoln Center.
Museum of Modern Art Summergarden concerts.
Thunderbird American Indian Midsummer Pow Wow, Queens County Farm Museum.
Washington Sq. Music Festival.

August

Harlem Week celebrations, including the Harlem Jazz and Music Festival.
The New York International Fringe Festival.
New York Giants football season begins.
Tugboat Challenge in Hudson River, sometimes early Sept.
US Open Tennis Championships, USTA National Tennis Center, Queens (through mid-Sept).
Wigstock/HOWLFestival

September

Annual Mayor's Cup Race, South Street Seaport.
Broadway on Broadway, Times Square.
Feast of San Gennaro Festival, Little Italy.
German-American Steuben Day Parade.
Metropolitan Opera (to April), Lincoln Center.
"New York is Book Country" Fair, Fifth Avenue (sometimes early Oct).
New York Philharmonic (to March), Lincoln Center.
Richmond County Fair (Labor Day weekend), Staten Island.
UN General Assembly opens.
Washington Square Art Show.
West Indian American Day Carnival (Labor Day), Eastern Parkway, Brooklyn.

October

American Ballet Theater (to mid-Nov), City Center.
Aqueduct Race Track opens, Queens.
Big Apple Circus (to Jan), Lincoln Center.
Columbus Day Parade, Fifth Avenue.
Halloween Parade, Greenwich Village.
Hispanic Day Parade, Fifth Avenue.
New York Film Festival (to Nov), Lincoln Center.
New York Rangers hockey and **New York Knicks** basketball starts, Madison Square Garden.

Next Wave Festival (through Dec), Brooklyn Academy of Music (BAM).
Pulaski Day Parade, Fifth Avenue.

November

Christmas Holiday Spectacular (to Jan), Radio City Music Hall.
Macy's Thanksgiving Day Parade.
The Nutcracker (to Jan), New York City Ballet at Lincoln Center.
National Horse Show, Madison Square Garden.
New York City Ballet (through Feb), Lincoln Center.
New York City Marathon, Staten Island to Central Park.
Veterans' Day Parade, Fifth Avenue.

December

Lighting of Christmas Tree, Rockefeller Center.
Lighting of Giant Chanukah Menorah, Fifth Avenue.
New Year's Eve Celebration in Times Square.
New Year's Eve Midnight Run, Central Park.

SHOPPING

What to Buy

Shopping is a major pastime in New York: there isn't much to be found anywhere that can't be found here, and usually more of it. **Art**, of course, is a good bet to buy. Apart from the major auctioneers, **Sotheby's** and **Christies** – where record prices are set for world-famous works – there are hundreds of art galleries in which to choose something appropriate.

Antiques can be found in Greenwich Village along Bleecker and West 4th Sts, and on side streets off University Place; along upper Madison Ave, on 60th St near Third Ave; and on Lafayette St below Houston St, as well as at a few indoor art "malls" around the city, including the **Manhattan Art & Antiques Center**, 1050 Second Ave, tel: 212-355 4400; the **Metropolitan Art & Antiques Pavilion**, 110 West 19th St, tel: 212-463 0200; and the **Chelsea Antiques Building**, 110 West 25th St, tel: 212-929 0909.

The city's famous **department stores** offer something for almost everyone but differ somewhat in their clientele: the most famous are **Bloomingdale's** (1000 Third Ave at 59th St) with its new Soho location and **Macy's** (151 West 34th St), which sell everything from housewares to furniture and clothing. **Lord & Taylor** (424 Fifth Ave at 39th St); and **Saks Fifth Avenue** (611 Fifth Ave) tend to concentrate on clothes.

Soho and the Upper East Side are generally where the highest proportion of classy clothing boutiques can be found, with Madison Avenue Uptown thick with expensive possibilities. There's another stretch of elegance along Fifth Avenue from Rockefeller Center to the Plaza Hotel, with **Takashimaya** (693 Fifth Ave), **Ferragamo** 661 Fifth Ave), **Henri Bendel** (712 Fifth Ave), **Prada** (724 Fifth Ave) and **Bergdorf Goodman** (754 Fifth Ave). The Swedish import **H & M** has been a huge success at 640 Fifth Avenue just across from St Patrick's Cathedral.

Electronic and photographic suppliers can be found almost everywhere, including Times Square and on Lexington Avenue near Grand Central Terminal. A few outlets are less than scrupulous, so it's best to do some comparison shopping before actually buying. *(See p229 for some recommendations).*

The real bargains are often Downtown: along Orchard St on the Lower East Side; in Chinatown; on Canal St between Sixth and Third avenues, and in the East Village, particularly the cross streets between First and

Second avenues. Savvy New York shoppers also flock to Manhattan's **flea markets**, including the eclectic weekend **Chelsea antiques market** on Sixth Ave between 25th and 27th streets and the **Sunday flea market** at Columbus Ave and 77th St on the Upper West Side.

There are some excellent antiquarian and second-hand bookstores around town, especially the **Strand Book Store**, 828 Broadway at 12th St, tel: 212-473 1452, which claims to have two million volumes in stock and is a wonderful place to browse. (There's also a Strand in the South Street Seaport, at 95 Fulton St, tel: 212-732 6070.)

The transformation of Soho from an urban art colony to a major shopping mecca has brought names like **Pottery Barn** and **Eddie Bauer**; **Bloomingdale's** now has a downtown store at 504 Broadway, joined by other "uptown" names such as **Ralph Lauren,Zara and Prada**. East of Soho, interesting small boutiques can be found on Elizabeth and Mott streets, in Nolita ("North of Little Italy").

In Chelsea, meanwhile, **Old Navy**, **Filene's Basement** and other suburban franchises are doing a booming business in the old "Ladies Mile" emporiums lining Sixth Avenue between 18th and 23rd streets.

The Upper West Side is home to the stylish shops of Columbus

Avenue **(Betsey Johnson, Eileen Fisher, Banana Republic, April Cornell, Putamayo)** as well as to Manhattan's best-known gourmet delicatessen, the wonderful **Zabar's**, at 2245 Broadway, tel: 212-787 2000.

Other food meccas around town include **Citarella**, at 2135 Broadway; **Dean & DeLuca**, at 560 Broadway in Soho (with many branches around town); **Chelsea Market**, 75 Ninth Ave (between 15th and 16th Sts); **Eli's Vinegar Factory** at 431 E. 91st St, and **Grace's Marketplace**, at 1237 Third Ave on the Upper East Side and **Whole Foods** with locations in Chelsea (250 7th Ave at 24th St), and in the Time Warner complex at Columbus Circle.

Major crosstown arteries (8th, 14th, 23rd, 34th, 42nd, 57th, 86th, 125th) are usually good for shopping, but the best discovery may be made on a sidestreet.

Clothes Stores

Women's Clothes

Agnès b, 1063 Madison Ave,tel: 212-570 9333; 103 Greene St. Tel: 212-431 0552.
Betsey Johnson, 138 Wooster St (and several other locations). Tel: 212- 995 5048.

WOODBURY COMMON

Woodbury Common outlet mall features 220 stores where savings are 25 to 65 percent off the original retail price. Designers include Donna Karan, Armani, Gucci, Max Mara, Burberry, Betsey Johnson, Nike, Polo Ralph Lauren, Brooks Brothers and Versace. Buses make the one-hour journey several times a day from the Port Authority Terminal, and overnight packages are also available. For details, go to www.chelseapremiumoutlets.com

D&G, Dolce & Gabbana, 434 West Broadway. Tel: 212-965 8000.
DKNY (Donna Karan) Madison, 655 Madison Ave. at 60th St. Tel: 212-233-DKNY.
Eileen Fisher, 1039 Madison Ave. Tel: 212-879 7799; 341 Columbus Ave. Tel: 212-362 3000; 103 Fifth Ave. Tel: 212-924 4777.
OMO-Norma Kamali, 11 West 56th St. Tel: 212-957 9797.
April Cornell, 487 Columbus Ave. Tel: 212-799 4342.
Nicole Miller, 780 Madison Ave. Tel: 212-288 9779; 134 Prince St. Tel: 212-343 1362.

Men's Clothes

Alfred Dunhill, 711 Fifth Ave. (between 55th and 56th sts). Tel: 212-753 9292.
Brooks Brothers, 346 Madison Ave at 44th St). Tel: 212-682 8800.
J. Press, 7 East 44th St. Tel: 212-687 7642.
Paul Stuart, Madison Ave at 45th St. Tel: 212- 682 0320.
Sean, 224 Columbus Ave. Tel: 212-769 1489; 132 Thompson St. Tel: 212- 598 5980.

Men's and Women's Clothes

A/X Armani Exchange, 645 Fifth Ave. Tel: 212-980 3037; Time Warner Ctr at Columbus Circle. Tel: 212-823 9321; 568 Broadway. Tel: 212- 431 6000.
Barneys New York, 660 Madison Ave. Tel: 212-826 8900.
Brooks Brothers, 346 Madison Ave. Tel: 212-682 8800.
Burberry's, 9 East 57th St. Tel: 212-371 5010; 131 Spring St. Tel: 212-925 9300
Calvin Klein, 654 Madison Ave. Tel: 212- 292 9000.
Comme des Garçons, 520 West 22nd St. Tel: 212-604 9200.(closed Mondays)
Emporio Armani, 601 Madison Ave. Tel:212-317 0800; 410 West Broadway. Tel: 646-613 8099.
J. Crew, 91 Fifth Ave. Tel: 212-255 4848.

Polo-Ralph Lauren, 867 Madison Ave. Tel: 212- 606 2100; 379 West Broadway. Tel: 212-625 1660.
Urban Outfitters, 628 Broadway. Tel: 212-475 0009 *(see below)*.

For Kids and Teens

Urban Outfitters, (several locations): 2081 Broadway at 72nd St. Tel: 212-579 3912; 360 Ave. of the Americas at Washington Place. Tel: 212-677 9350.
Space Kiddets, 46 East 21 St. Tel: 212-420 9878
Old Navy (several locations):150 West 34th St. Tel: 212-594 0049; 610 Ave of the Americas. Tel: 212-645 0663; 503 Broadway at Broome St. Tel: 212-226 0838.

Designer Discounts

Century 21, 122 Cortlandt St. Tel: 212-227 9092 (located Downtown by the site of the former World Trade Center, but loved by Uptown ladies).
Daffy's, 111 Fifth Ave. Tel: 212-529 4477 and Uptown branches.
Filene's Basement, 620 Avenue of the Americas. Tel: 212-620 3100 (Chelsea), and at 2222 Broadway (79th St). Tel: 212-873 8000.
Loehmann's, 101 Seventh Ave (Chelsea). Tel: 212-352 0856.

Cameras, Computers and Electronics

B & H Photo-Video, 420 Ninth Ave. Tel: 212-444 6600 (closed Saturdays).
Circuit City, 52-64 East 14th St. Tel: 212-387 0730 (and other Uptown locations).
Harvey Electronics, 2 West 45th St. Tel: 212-575 5000.
J&R Computer World, 15 Park Row. Tel: 212-238 9000, 1-800-221 8180.
Sony Style, 550 Madison Ave. Tel: 212-833 8800.
Willoughby's, 298 Fifth Ave at 33rd St (closed Saturday). Tel: 212-564 1600 (established in 1898 and still selling cameras as well as other electronics.)

CLOTHES CHART

The chart listed below gives a comparison of United States, European and United Kingdom clothing sizes. It is always a good idea, however, to try on any article before buying it, as sizes between manufacturers can vary enormously.

● **Women's Dresses/Suits**

US	Continental	UK
6	38/34N	8/30
8	40/36N	10/32
10	42/38N	12/34
12	44/40N	14/36
14	46/42N	16/38
16	48/44N	18/40

● **Women's Shoes**

US	Continental	UK
4½	36	3
5½	37	4
6½	38	5
7½	39	6
8½	40	7
9½	41	8
10½	42	9

● **Men's Suits**

US	Continental	UK
34	44	34
—	46	36
38	48	38
—	50	40
42	52	42
—	54	44
46	56	46

● **Men's Shirts**

US	Continental	UK
14	36	14
14½	37	14½
15	38	15
15½	39	15½
16	40	16
16½	41	16½
17	42	17

● **Men's Shoes**

US	Continental	UK
6½	—	6
7½	40	7
8½	41	8
9½	42	9
10½	43	10
11½	44	11

Music Stores

West 48th Street is particularly good for music instrument stores. You may want to check out more than one along here, but be sure to go to **Manny's Music** at 156 West 48th St. Tel: 212-819 0576.

Other music stops include:
Bleecker Bob's, 118 West 3rd St. Tel: 212- 475 9677. Good for rare recordings.
Colony Records, 1619 Broadway. Tel: 212-265 2050. In business for almost 60 years.
House of Oldies, 35 Carmine St. Tel: 212- 243 0500.Vintage vinyl in Greenwich Village.
J&R Music World, 23 Park Row. Tel: 212-732 8600. Downtown near City Hall; great jazz and classical recordings.
Jazz Record Center, 236 West 26th St (8th Floor). Tel: 212-675 4480. Chelsea's best for jazz.
Sam Ash, 160 West 48th St. Tel: 212-719 2299. Good for seeking out musical instruments.
Tower Records, 692 Broadway. Tel: 212-505 1500; 1961 Broadway at 66th St. Tel: 212-799 2500.
Virgin Megastore, Times Square (45th St). Tel: 212-921 1020; 52 East 14th St. Tel: 212-598 4666.

Sports Equipment and Clothes

Niketown, 6 East 57th St. Tel: 212-891-NIKE (6453.)
Paragon Sporting Goods, 867 Broadway. Tel: 212-989 8686.
Patagonia, 101 Wooster St. Tel: 212-343 17764. 26 Columbus Ave. Tel: 917-441 0011.
Scandinavian Ski & Sports, 16 East 55th St. Tel: 757 8524.
Modell's (several locations), 51 East 42nd St. Tel: 212-661 4242; 1535 Third Ave at 86th St. Tel: 212-996 3800.
NBA Store, (National Basketball Assocation), Fifth Ave at 52nd St. Tel: 212-515-NBA1
Super Runners Shop, (several locations), Grand Central Terminal. Tel: 646-487 1120.

Toys

Children's General Store, Grand Central Terminal. Tel: 212-284 0004.
FAO Schwarz, 767 Fifth Ave at 58th Street. Tel: 212- 644 9400. Venerable kids' store with polished floors and sparkling ceilings selling toys you won't find in other shops.
Penny Whistle, 448 Columbus Ave. Tel: 212- 873 9090; 1283 Madison Ave. Tel: 212-369 3868.
Toys R Us, Broadway at 44th St,. Times Square. Tel: 1-800-869 7787. Megastore complete with working indoor Ferris wheel.
West Side Kids, 498 Amsterdam Ave at 84th St. Tel: 212-496 7282.

SPORTS

Participant Sports

New York offers a wide array of recreational facilities. Many are found in the city's **parks** – including Central Park, where roads are closed to traffic on summer weekends for the benefit of bicyclists and in-line skaters. For general information call the Department of Parks and Recreations at 1-800 201 PARK.

Tennis can be played in Central Park and various other parks; it's also available at private facilities such as the Midtown Tennis Club, 341 Eighth Ave, tel: 212-989 8572; the Manhattan Plaza Racquet Club, 450 West 43rd St, tel: 212-594 0554; and the HRC Tennis Club, Piers 13 and 14 near Wall St, tel: 422 9300. The largest public tennis facility is the USTA National Tennis Center in Queens, home of the US Open, tel: 718-760 6200.

Horses can be hired at the Claremont Riding Academy, 175 West 89th St, tel: 212-724 5100, for riding along Central Park's miles of bridle trails; at Kensington Stables in Brooklyn,

tel: 718-972 4588, for riding in Prospect Park, and other places around the city.

Ice skating is available at both Wollman (tel:212-439 6900) and Lasker Rinks in Central Park in winter; also at Rockefeller Center, tel: 212-332 7654; and year-round at Sky Rink, Pier 61 at the Hudson River, tel: 212-336 6100, part of Chelsea Piers.

Baseball and **softball** diamonds are located in city parks, as are miles of **jogging** tracks and trails. (The New York Road Runners Club maintains a running center, tel: 212-860 4455.)

And **rowboats** can be hired at the Central Park Lake boathouse (and at Prospect Park in Brooklyn, Kissena Park in Queens and Van Cortlandt Park in the Bronx), as can **bicycles**.

You'll find public **golf courses** at Pelham Bay Park, Van Cortlandt Park (both in the Bronx) and at Latourette Park in Staten Island, among other Outer Borough parks.

There are several public indoor and outdoor **swimming pools** including 348 East 54th St, and the Asser Levy Pool at 23rd St and FDR Drive. Call 718-699 4219 for information. In addition, day rates are available at the YMCAs at 224 East 47th St, tel: 756 9600 and 5 West 63rd St, tel: 212-787 4400, both of which have swimming pools and exercise facilities. Manhattan hotels with pools include the Parker Meridien, Regal UN Plaza,and the Sheraton Manhattan.

For numerous sports in one place, try the **Chelsea Piers Sports and Entertainment Complex** (tel: 212- 336 6666; www.chelseapiers.com), which stretches along the Hudson River between 17th and 23rd streets. Facilities include a multi-tiered **golf driving range**, **boating**, **bowling**, **horseback riding** and **in-line skating**; day passes are available at the sports/fitness center, which has an Olympic-size swimming pool, a sundeck, running track and **rock climbing** wall.

Spectator Sports

New York is understandably proud of its top-rated teams, the Mets and Yankees, who play **baseball** from April to October at Shea Stadium in Flushing, tel: 718-507 8499 and Yankee Stadium in the Bronx, tel: 718-293 6000. The New York Knicks (tel: 212-465 6741) play **basketball** between October and May at Madison Square Garden, where the New York Liberty (tel: 212-564-WNBA) professional women's team can be seen in summer. College team schedules are listed in the sports sections of daily papers.

Ice hockey season runs from October to April, with the the New York Rangers at Madison Square Garden (tel: 212-465 7561) and the Islanders playing at Nassau Coliseum on Long Island (tel: 516-794 4100). Madison Square Garden is also the main site for important events in **boxing** and **tennis**, although the US Open is at the **National Tennis Center** in Flushing Meadows-Corona Park, Queens (tel: 718-760 6200) from late August to September.

The **football** season starts in late August and lasts through December or January, with both the New York Giants (tel: 201-935 8222) and New York Jets (tel: 516-560 8100) playing at Giants Stadium in the Meadowlands, East Rutherford, NJ.

Soccer takes place between March and September, when the MetroStars play matches at the Meadowlands (tel: 201-583 7000). **Cricket** matches are held on summer Sundays in Van Cortlandt Park in the Bronx, as well as on Randall's Island in the East River and various parks in Brooklyn and Staten Island.

The closest thoroughbred **horse-racing** is at Aqueduct Racetrack in Queens (subway from Eighth Ave and 42nd St), tel: 718-641 4700, and Belmont Park in Elmont, Long Island (Long Island Railroad from Pennsylvania Station), tel: 516-488 6000.

TOURS

Sightseeing Tours

Among the dozens of tour operators offering sightseeing trips around the city, the most popular include: **Gray Line New York**, tel: 212-445 0848,1800-669 0051, which features double-decker buses with hop-on, hop-off itineraries; **Circle Line**, tel: 212-563 3200, which operates boat trips around Manhattan, as well as harbor cruises from South Street Seaport; and **NY Waterway**, tel: 1-800-533 3779, featuring harbor cruises, entertainment cruises and boat trips to Yankee Stadium during baseball season. **Shearwater Sailing**, tel: 212-619 0885 cruises near the Statue of Liberty in a beautiful, 1929 double-masted schooner.

Spirit Cruises, tel: 1-866-211 3805 offers dinner,entertainment, sightseeing afloat.

Other interesting touring options include:
Art Horizons International, tel: 212-969 9410. Visits to galleries, museums and artists in their studio lofts.
Big Onion Walking Tours, tel: 212-439 1090. Historic, ethnic neighborhoods with zing.
Central Park Bicycle Tours, tel: 212-541 8759. Guided bike tours, including rentals, through the wilds of Central Park.
Central Park Conservancy, tel: 212-360 2726. Free walking tours. Also **Urban Park Rangers Tours**, tel: 1888-NY PARKS.
Elegant Tightwad Shopping Tours, tel: 1-800-808 4614. Designer showroom tours, sample sales.
Harlem Heritage Tours, tel: 212-280 7888. Walk around the streets with a local resident and hear the history and stories.
Harlem Spirituals/New York Visions, tel: 212-391 0900, Uptown Sunday Gospel tours.
Hush Tours, tel: 212-714 3527. Hip-hop culture tours.
Municipal Art Society, tel: 212-935 3960. Architectural walks.
92nd St Y, tel: 212-415 5599. An in-depth look at neighborhood attractions.
New York MovieTours, tel: 212-304-9022,1-800-MOVIE-TOUR, tours of famous locations.
Radio City Music Hall, tel: 212-247 4777. Go behind the big gold curtain and find out who plays the gigantic Wurlitzers.
The **Lower East Side Tenement Museum** at 90 Orchard St, tel: 212-431 0233, offers walking tours through a neighborhood rich with 19th-century immigrant history, led by local historians. Call for a current schedule.

Another view of the immigrant experience is provided by the **Museum of Chinese in the Americas**, 70 Mulberry St, tel: 212-619 4785, which sponsors walks around one of the city's most fascinating ethnic enclaves.

TRANSPORTATION

ACCOMMODATIONS

ACTIVITIES

A – Z

A-Z

A SUMMARY OF PRACTICAL INFORMATION, ARRANGED ALPHABETICALLY

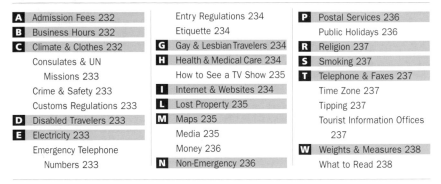

A dmission Fees

Fees to attractions range from about $6 to $15. A few, like the Museum of Modern Art, cost extra; we've indicated this with the words "large charge," while a few cost under $2 ("small charge"). On Thursdays or Fridays after 4pm, certain museums are free, or post a suggested donation.

B usiness Hours

New Yorkers work long and hard in a city where this is generally seen to be an advantage. Normal business hours are 9am–5/6pm but stores, particularly, tend to

stay open much later. They can get crowded at lunchtime. Some shops also open on Sundays. Banking hours are nominally 9am–3 or 4pm but increasingly, banks are opening as early as 8am and staying open until late afternoon or early evening. ATM machines are everywhere.

The Port Authority Bus Terminal (Eighth Ave at 42nd St) stays open 24 hrs: Tel: 212-564 8484 Penn Station (Seventh Ave at 32rd St) is open 24 hr. Long Island Railroad Information: Tel: 718-217 5477; New Jersey Transit Info: Tel: 973-762 5100. Grand Central Terminal closes at 1:30 AM. MetroNorth Information: Tel: 212-532 4900.

C limate & Clothes

New York has four distinct seasons, and is at its best during the spring and fall months. Summer temperatures hover in the mid-70s to mid-80s°F (24–29°C), although heatwaves where the mercury rises to 100°F (37.8°C) may occur, and uncomfortable humidity is often the rule, especially in July and August.

September and October sometimes usher in a balmy, dry "Indian summer" that fills parks and office plazas with sun worshipers. Winter temperatures can drop below 10 or 15°F (–12 or –9°C), with the average temperature for January closer to 32°F

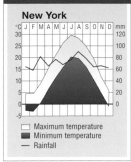

CLIMATE CHART

New York

- ☐ Maximum temperature
- ■ Minimum temperature
- — Rainfall

(0°C). The average annual rainfall is 44 ins (112 cm) and the average snowfall is 29 ins (74 cm). Raincoats are a good idea all year-round.

Except for casual wandering, dress tends to be a little bit more formal compared to other US cities. It's always advisable to ask about proper dress codes for restaurants, clubs, etc.

Crime & Safety

Despite its recent reputation as a "caring, sharing New York," parts of the city are still reasonably dangerous and visitors should not be lulled into any false sense of security. Miscreants whose lives are devoted to exploiting the unwary will be quick to seize advantage of your bewilderment, so adopt the typical New Yorker's guise of looking street-smart and aware at all times.

Ostentatious displays of jewelry or wealth invite muggers;

foolhardy excursions into deserted regions at night (such as Central Park or Battery Park) are equally unwise. Lock your hotel door even when you are inside, and travel to places like Harlem in a group. And even though Times Square has thrown off its seedy mantle, the streets around it attract pickpockets.

Although the subways are much safer than they were, women traveling alone late at night should stay on alert. Once through the turnstile, stay within sight – or at least within shouting range – of the ticket booth. When boarding, try to get on a carriage where there are other women. In emergencies, **dial 911 for police, fire or ambulance**.

Police Precincts

Call for non-emergencies only:

Downtown
1st, 16 Ericsson Place (West Canal St). Tel: 212-334 0611.
5th, 19 Elizabeth St (Chinatown). Tel: 212-334 0711.
6th, 233 W. 10th St (Greenwich Village). Tel: 212-741 4811.
7th, 19 Pitt St (Lower East Side). Tel: 212-477 7311.
9th, 321 E. 5th St. Tel: 212-477 7811.
10th, 230 W. 20th St. Tel: 212-741 8211.
13th, 230 E. 21st St. Tel: 212-477 7411.
17th, 167 E. 51st St. Tel: 212-826 3211.
Midtown South, 375 W. 35th St. Tel: 212-239 9811.
Midtown North, 524 W. 42nd St. Tel: 212-767 8400.

Uptown
19th, 153 E. 67th St. Tel: 212-452 0600.
20th, 120 W. 82nd St. Tel: 212-580 6411.
Central Park, Transverse Road at 86th St. Tel: 212-570 4820.
23rd, 162 E. 102nd St. Tel: 212-860 6411.
24th, 151 W. 100th St. Tel: 212-678 1811.
25th, 120 East 119th St. Tel: 212-860 6511.
26th, 520 West 126th St. Tel: 212-678 1311.
28th, 2271 Eighth Ave (near 123rd St). Tel: 212-678 1611.
30th, 451 W. 151st St. Tel: 212-690 8811.
32nd, 250 W. 135th St. Tel: 212-690 6311.
33rd, 2120 Amsterdam Ave. Tel: 212-927 3200.
34th, 4295 Broadway. Tel: 212-927 9711.

Customs Regulations

For a breakdown of up-to-date US Customs regulations, visit www.customs.ustreas.gov. Tel: 202-354 1000.

Disabled Travelers

Disabled travelers can obtain information about rights and special facilities from the **Mayor's Office for People with Disabilities**, 52 Chambers St, Room 206, New York, NY 10007. Tel: 212-788 2830.

Electricity

The United States uses 110 volts. Electrical adaptors are easy to purchase from stores.

Emergency Telephone Numbers

For all emergencies: police, fire ambulance, dial **911**.
Dental Emergency: Tel: 212-573 9502.
24-hr Pharmacy: CVS at Second Ave and 72nd St: Tel: 212-249 5699 (and many others.)

CONSULATES & UN MISSIONS

Australia Mission to the UN
150 East 42nd Street
Tel: 212-351 6600
British Consulate-General
845 Third Avenue
Tel: 212-745 0200
Canadian Consulate-General
1251 Avenue of the Americas
Tel: 212-596 1783

Consulate General of Ireland
345 Park Avenue
Tel: 212-319 2555
New Zealand Mission to the UN
1 UN Plaza
Tel: 212-826 1960
Consulate of South Africa
333 East 38th Street
Tel: 212-213 4880

Sex Crimes Report Line: Tel: 212-267 7273.

Suicide Prevention Hotline: Tel: 212-532 2400.

For all non-emergency services, *see page 236.*

Entry Regulations

For a breakdown of up-to-date US entry regulations, visit http://travel.state.gov/visa/index.html. The Visa Office's emailbox for enquiries and quick general information is usvisa@state.gov. Tel: 202-663 1225.

Etiquette

New York is a fast-paced town, whose residents are possessed of a restless energy that legend says is necessary for survival. Few people seem to have time for anything not on their mental schedule, and even asking for directions in the street is best done with an awareness of this, ideally while moving at the same pace and in the same direction as the informant.

New Yorkers have persuaded themselves that living at breakneck speed, always under pressure, is what gives them their edge and makes Manhattan the center of the universe (which all New Yorkers believe implicitly). It may also explain why few people live out their latter years in the city, if, indeed, they survive long enough to make that choice.

The city is undeniably stimulating and exciting, not only for the wealth of its social and cultural pleasures but also because of its almost 24-hour street life. Its neighborhoods offer boundless diversions to the eye and ear.

A casual stroll in almost any direction rewards the explorer with guaranteed serendipity. Rockefeller Plaza at lunchtime, Soho's West Broadway on Saturday, Central Park on Sunday, or Washington Square on any summer weekend will provide a visitor with as much entertainment as the best Broadway show.

G ay & Lesbian Travelers

The Gay and Lesbian Hotline, tel: 212- 989 0999 (closed mornings), provides information to gay men and women about all aspects of gay life in New York including recommendations of bars, restaurants, accommodations, legal counseling, etc. The **Lesbian, Gay, Bisexual and Transgender Community Center,** 208 West 13th St, tel: 212- 620 7310, is another large and helpful organization. Bookshops such as the **Oscar Wilde Memorial Bookshop** at 15 Christopher St, tel: 212-255 8097, stock various useful publications, and can often offer advice.

H ealth & Medical Care

Medical services are extremely expensive. Always travel with comprehensive travel insurance to cover any emergencies. **Physicians Home Care,** tel: 718-238 2100, make house calls on a non-emergency basis.

Hospitals with Emergency Rooms

Midtown/Downtown

Bellevue Hospital, First Ave and East 27th St. Tel: 212-562 4141.

Beth Israel Medical Center, First Ave at East 16th St. Tel: 212-420 2840.

NYU Medical Center, 550 First Ave at 33rd St. Tel: 212-263 7300.

St Luke's-Roosevelt Hospital, 59th St between Ninth and Tenth avenues. Tel: 212-523 6800.

St Vincent's Hospital, Seventh Avenue at 11th Street. Tel: 212-604 7000.

Uptown

Columbia Presbyterian Medical Center, 622 West 168th St. Tel: 212-305 2500.

Lenox Hill Hospital, 77th St and Park Ave. Tel: 212-434 2000.

Mount Sinai Hospital, Fifth Ave and East 100th St. Tel: 212-241 6500.

New York Hospital, 525 East 68th St. Tel: 212-746 5454.

I nternet & Websites

WiFi (wireless internet facility) is available in Union Square and seven areas in Lower Manhattan. More and more hotels are gearing up to provide WiFi in their bedrooms, too. E-mail can be sent from most branches of FedEx/Kinko's copy shops or from computers at many libraries.

Branches of the New York Public Library including the **Science, Industry and Business Library,** 188 Madison Ave at 34th St, tel: 212-592 7000; one-hour limit per day, by appointment. There are also many commercial internet "café" sites. Just to name a few: **EasyEverything, Inc.,** 234 West 42nd St.

Café 101, 101 Park Avenue at 41st St.

Cybercafe, 250 West 49th St.

CITY WEBSITES

Several boroughs have their own websites, listed here under "Tourist Information." Other websites that provide helpful information include: **www.newyork.citysearch.com** for listings and reviews of current arts and entertainment events, as well as restaurants and shopping. It's excellent for links to every conceivable aspect of New York City. **www.nyc.gov,** the official site of the City of New York, contains news items, mayoral updates, city agency information and parking regulations. **www.nycvisit.com,** is the NYC & Co website, which includes links to Central Park. **www.nypl.org** is for everything you ever wanted to know about the New York Public Library. There's also an online information service.

TRANSPORTATION
ACCOMMODATIONS
ACTIVITIES
A – Z

Lost Property

The chances of retrieving lost property are not high, but the occasional public-spirited individual may turn items in to the nearest police precinct.

To inquire about items left on public transportation (**subway and bus**), tel: 212-712 4500, open Mon, Wed, Fri 8am–12pm, Thur 11am–6.45pm. Or call 311. (see Non-Emergency Services, page 236).

Lost or Stolen Credit Cards

All 1-800 calls are free of charge: **American Express**, tel: 1-800-528 4800. **Visa**, tel: 1-800-847 2911. **Diners Club**, tel: 1-800-234 6377. **MasterCard**, tel: 1-800-826 2181.

Maps

NYC & Co has good maps at their visitors center and online through their website: www.nycvisit.com. Subway and bus maps are available at subway station booths, or from the New York City Transit Authority booth in Grand Central and the Long Island Rail Road information booth in Penn Station, as well as the MTA booth at the Times Square Visitors Center. Maps may also be obtained online through the Metropolitan Transit Authority website: www.mta.info

The best detailed street map (Manhattan only) is actually a book called Manhattan Block by Block: A Street Atlas, published by Tauranac Maps, 3rd Edition, 2004, sold in bookstores.

Media

Print

The internationally known New York Times is the paper of choice for most well-informed readers, with its bulky Sunday edition listing virtually everything of consequence. On a daily basis, two tabloids compete for the rest of the audience: the New York Post, famed for its garish headlines and downmarket appeal; and the Daily News, which until outsold (by the Los Angeles Times and The New York Times), boasted of having the largest daily circulation of any newspaper in America. There are two "commuter" dailies distributed free in the mornings: AM New York and Metro. The free weekly Village Voice has comprehensive listings and classified ads, as does the free New York Press. Respected local magazines include New York, the New Yorker and Time Out New York.

Television

The three major networks – all with New York headquarters – are **ABC**, 77 West 66th St, tel: 212-456 7777; **CBS**, 51 West 52nd St, tel: 212- 975 4321; and **NBC**, 30 Rockefeller Plaza, tel: 212-664 4444. **Fox News Service,** has national offices at 1211 Ave of the Americas, tel: 212-556 2500 and **CNN** has new offices at the Time Warner Center at Columbus Circle.The **Public Broadcasting System** (PBS) can be found on channels 13 and 21 on the VHF band (for those without cable).

HOW TO SEE A TELEVISION SHOW

With advance planning, it's possible to join the audience of a New York-based TV show, many of them shown overseas. For more details, go to the NYC & Company Information Center or check www.nycvisit.com. Here's just a selection:
● **Late Show with David Letterman**
Tapings of this popular, wacky talk show are Mon–Fri at 5.30pm. Audience members must be 16 or older; proper ID required. Tickets can be applied for online, or by visiting the show's theater and making an in-person request. Standby tickets may be available by calling the theater at 9.30am on the day of broadcasting.
Late Night Tickets, Ed Sullivan Theatre, 1697 Broadway, New York, NY 10019. Tel: 212-975 1003 or 975 2476.
www.lateshowaudience.com
● **NBC Today Show Through the Window**
Tapings of this early-morning show are Mon–Fri from 7–9am. An audience is encouraged to watch from the streets outside – and perhaps be televised – but be prepared to get there by dawn.The best spot to stand is at the southeastern corner. Go to the kiosks at 30 Rockefeller Plaza for information.
● **Saturday Night Live**
Tapings of this venerable comedy show are on Saturday from 11.30pm–1am. Audience members must be 16 or older. A ticket lottery is held each August. Only one email per person sent in August will be accepted, for two tickets each. Standby tickets are given out for the dress rehearsal and the live show at 7am on the 49th St entrance, but do not guarantee admission. Send email to: www.snltickets@nbc.com. NBC Tickets, tel: 212-664 4537; www.nbc.com.
● **NBC Studio Tour**
To ensure that you will at least see the studios of Saturday Night Live and other programs (as long as they're not taping), you could go on the NBC Studio Tour. Attractions include blue-screens to let you "join" presenters on the sets. Tours start at the NBC Experience Store at 30 Rockefeller Plaza, every 15 minutes, 7 days a week (www.nbcsuper-store.com, tel: 664 7174, charge).

The other three local stations are affiliated with the **Fox** (5), **UPN** (9) and the **WB** (11) networks. These channels broadcast nationally aired shows as well as local programming. In addition, there are half a dozen UHF stations which broadcast in Spanish and other languages.

Various **cable companies** offer 50 or more basic cable and movie channels, although the exact number differs from borough to borough and whether or not there is a satellite connection which provides hundreds of channels. Most hotels offer cable in guest rooms as well as – for a fee – up-to-the-minute Hollywood movies. A few Manhattan public access TV programs (particularly late at night) are pretty sexually explicit, so you may want to make sure the kids are in bed before tuning in.

Money

The dollar bill comes in denominations from $1 through $5, $10, $20, $50, $100 and up. It is always green, although bearing the head of different presidents. There is a $2 bill, although this is considered unlucky and is rarely seen. Coins begin with the penny (1¢) and ascend through the nickel (5¢), dime (10¢), quarter (25¢), half-dollar (50¢) and the infrequent $1 coin, which is also unpopular as it closely resembles a quarter.

Cash advances on major credit and debit cards can be obtained from bank tellers and bank ATMs (automatic teller machines) which are marked with the corresponding stickers (i.e. Cirrus, Plus, Visa, MasterCard, American Express, etc.) Most of these charge a fee for withdrawing cash. Credit cards are accepted almost everywhere int the city, although not all cards at all places.

There are numerous outlets for exchanging currency in New York, and a few banks still charge a fee to cash traveler's checks. Traveler's checks (as long as they are in dollar amounts) are accepted in most hotels and good restaurants, so long as they are accompanied by proper identification. Be sure to keep your passport handy.

Thomas Cook Currency Services, tel: 1-800-287 7362; 1590 Broadway at 48th St, tel: 212-265 6063; 1271 Broadway at 32nd St, tel: 212-679 4877; and 511 Madison Ave at 53rd St, tel: 212-753 0117.

Thomas Cook's offices also sell and cash traveler's checks, as do the numerous **American Express** offices around town, including 374 Park Ave, tel: 212-421 8240.

There is also an automated self-change kiosk at the **Times Square Visitors Center** at 1560 Broadway (between 46th and 47th streets).

Citibank offers exchange facilities at most of its 200 or so branches around the five boroughs. Tel: 1-800-285 3000.

N on-Emergency Services

New York has a new three digit number to be dialed for information and non-emergency services whether the caller is a resident or a visitor. Calls to **311** are answered by a live operator, 24 hours a day, seven days a week, and services are provided in over 170 languages. The purpose of a call can be as wide-ranging as tourist destination inquiries, making a complaint about noise or a taxi; finding out about tax-free shopping weeks which are held several times a year, or locating lost and found items on public transportation.

P ostal Services

Manhattan's main post office on Eighth Ave between 31st and 33rd streets is open 24 hours a

PUBLIC HOLIDAYS

As with many other countries in the world, the United States has gradually shifted most of its public holidays to the Monday closest to the actual dates, thereby creating a number of three-day weekends. Holidays that are celebrated no matter what day on which they fall are:
New Year's Day (January 1).
Independence Day (July 4).
Veterans' Day (November 11).
Christmas Day (December 25).

Other holidays are:
Martin Luther King Jr Day (third Mon in Jan).
President's Day commemorating Lincoln and Washington (third Mon in Feb).
Memorial Day (last Mon in May).
Labor Day (first Mon in Sept).
Columbus Day (second Mon in Oct).
Election Day (first Tues in Nov, every four years).
Thanksgiving (fourth Thurs in Nov).

day for stamps, express mail and certified mail. To find out where post office branches are located throughout the five boroughs, and to enquire about mailing rates and methods, call the Postal Service Consumer Hotline: 1-800-275 8777.

R eligion

New York is approximately 70 percent Christian, 11 percent Jewish, 1.5 percent Muslim, 7.4 percent agnostic, with Buddhists, Hindus and others also represented. Some 6,000 churches, temples and mosques are scattered throughout the city's five boroughs. Consult the *Yellow Pages* or ask at the desk of your hotel for the nearest.

S moking

There is currently a no-smoking law in effect in virtually all New York City bars, restaurants and offices. Be sure to request a smoking room when booking a place to stay.

T elephone & Faxes

Most Manhattan attractions have the established **212** telephone code, which has been in existence for decades; newer places might use the **646** or **917** prefix. Brooklyn, Queens, Staten Island and Bronx numbers are prefixed by **718** (or the newer **347** or **917**). Regardless of the number you are calling *from,* the area code of the number being called must now be used: e.g., in a 212 area, calling another 212 number, the 212 prefix must still be used, preceded by 1.

Toll-free calls are prefixed by **800, 888** or **877**; remember to dial **1** first when calling these numbers. **Telephones** accepting credit cards can be found in various centers, including Grand Central and Penn stations. Hotels also usually add on a hefty charge. **Telephone dialling cards,** available from Korean shops and

TIPPING

Most New Yorkers in the service industries (restaurants, hotels, transportation) regard tips as a God-given right, not just a pleasant gratuity. The fact is, many people rely on tips to make up for what are often poor hourly salaries. Therefore, unless service is truly horrendous, you can figure on tipping everyone from bellmen and porters (usually 50¢ a bag; or $1 if only one bag); to hotel doormen ($1 if they hail you a cab); hotel maids ($1 a day, left in your room when you check out), rest room attendants (at least 25¢) and room-service waiters (approximately 15 percent of the bill unless already added on). In restaurants, the best way to figure out the tip is to double the tax (which adds up to a little more than 16 percent; add or subtract a dollar or two depending on how the service was). In taxis, tip as much as 15 percent of the total fare, with a 50¢ minimum.

other places, are an inexpensive way to make calls.

Cell phone usage is widespread. There is a cellular phone rental office at the Satellite Airlines Terminal (125 Park Ave, tel: 212-986 0888) opposite Grand Central Terminal, which is also a drop-off and pick-up spot for buses to JFK and LaGuardia.However, anyone staying for more than a few days, or who makes repeated trips to NY, might consider buying one: prices are cheap compared to many cities.

Most major hotels offer **fax services**; faxes can also be sent from many of the copy and printing shops, as well as from the numerous branches of FedEx-Kinko's (see *Yellow Pages* for locations), which offer computer access and **e-mail** for a fee.

Useful Numbers

- **International calls**, dial: 011 (the international access code), then the country code, city code and local number.
- **Directory help**, including toll-free numbers, dial: 555-1212 preceded by the area code you are calling from.
- **Wrong number refunds**, dial: 211.
- **Current time**, dial: 976 1616.
- **Emergencies**, *see page 223.*

Time Zone

New York is in the Eastern Standard Time zone (EST). This is five hours behind London; one hour ahead of Chicago and three hours ahead of California.

Tourist Information Offices

NYC & Company Visitors Information Center, 810 Seventh Ave, New York, NY 10019, tel: 212-397 8222, 1-800-NYCVISIT; www.nycvisit.com, has brochures, maps and information about special hotel packages and discount admission programs to various attractions.

They also publish the *Official NYC Guide*, a listing of activities, hotels, tours and restaurants. Visitors are welcome in person at NYC & Co.'s **Visitor Information Center,** tel: 212-484 1222 (the same address as above), located between 52nd and 53rd streets, open Mon–Fri 8:30 am–6pm, weekends 9am–5pm. There's also an information kiosk by Downtown's **City Hall Park** at Broadway and Park Row. **www.nyc.gov** is another useful website for nformation about NYC, events and regulations. **The Times Square Visitors Center** is at the Embassy Theater, 1560 Broadway between 46th and 47th streets. A source of citywide info, there's a ticket counter for shows, and e-mail and currency facilities. Open daily 8am–8pm; it organizes free walking tours of Times Square.

The Greater Harlem Chamber of Commerce, 200 West 136th St., New York, NY 10030. Tel: 212-862 7200. An essential source of information about tours, events and landmarks in Harlem. There's also an information kiosk at **163 West 125th St**, dispensing brochures and maps.

The Bronx Tourism Council, 198 East 161st St. Bronx NY 10032. Tel: 718-590-BRONX. Offers information about art, music and other events.

The Brooklyn Tourism and Visitors Center, Tel: 718-802 4994. Provides information on culture, shopping, history, local parks, events and historic sites.

The Queens Tourism Council, Tel: 718-263 0546; www.discoverqueens.info provides museum and cultural attraction information and well as tours.

The Council on Arts & Humanities for Staten Island, Tel: 1-866-474 3862; www.statenislandarts.org Lists cultural events and places of interest.

W eights & Measures

The United States uses the Imperial system of weights and measures. Metric weights and measures are rarely used.

What to Read

A New Deal for New York by Mike Wallace, Bell & Weiland, Gotham Center Books, 2002.

At The Theatre: An Informal History of New York's Legitimate Theatres. Dodd Mead & Company, 1984.

The Encyclopedia of New York City, edited by Kenneth T. Jackson. Yale University Press, 1995.

History Preserved: A Guide to New York City Landmarks and Historic Districts by Harmon H. Goldstone and Martha Dalrymple. Schocken Books, 1976.

Literary Neighborhoods of New York by Marcia Leisner. Starhill Press, 1989.

Lower East Side Memories: A Jewish Place in America by

Hasia R. Diner. Princeton University Press, 2002.

Lucia, Lucia by Adriana Trigiani. Random House, 2004.

Manhattan '45 by Jan Morris. Oxford University Press, 1987.

More Than Petticoats: Remarkable New York Women by Antonia Petrash, The Globe Pequot Press, 2002.

The Movie Lover's Guide to New York by Richard Alleman. Perennial Library/Harper & Row, 1988.

New York: An Illustrated History by Ric Burns, Knopf, 1999.

On Broadway: A Journey Uptown Over Time by David W. Dunlop. Rizzoli International Publications, 1990.

Uptown & Downtown: A Trip Through Time on New York Subways by Stan Fischler. E.P. Dutton, 1976.

You Must Remember This. An Oral History of Manhattan from the 1890s to World War II by Jeff Kisseloff. Harcourt Brace Jovanovich, 1988.

Waterfront, A Journey Around New York by Phillip Lopate, Crown, 2004.

The WPA Guide to New York City, Federal Writers Project Guide to 1930s NY. The New Press, 1995.

Other Insight Guides

With more than 500 titles in five different formats, Insight Guides cover the world. There are 40 titles devoted to the United States, ranging from Alaska to Florida, from Seattle to Orlando.

Museums and Galleries of New York City is a large-format, fully illustrated guide to 79 renowned institutions. **Shopping in New York** and **Eating in New York** each contain hundreds of detailed listings. **Insight Pocket Guide: New York** includes the author's personal recommendations and a pull-out map. **Insight Compact Guide: New York** is a highly portable companion. Three laminated **Insight Fleximaps** – one covering the city in general, museums and galleries, and children's attractions – are easily foldable and immensely durable.

LIFE IN THE CITY: GOOD BACKGROUND READING

Fifth Avenue: The Best Address by Jerry E. Patterson. Rizzoli International Publications, 1998. Describes the gradual development of the city's most famous boulevard, from rocky dirt path, to shanty row to elegant thoroughfare.

Flatbush Odyssey: A Journey Through the Heart of Brooklyn by Alan Abel. McClelland & Stewart, 1997. A fond reminiscence by an expat writer (now a Canadian) who grew up in one of Brooklyn's most picturesque neighborhoods.

Gotham: A History of New York to 1898 by Mike Wallace and Edwin G. Burrows. Oxford University Press, 1998. Pulitzer prize-winning narrative about the city's early years; in-depth, with an emphasis on some of its characters.

Low Life by Luc Sante. Vintage Books, 1992. Everything you

always wanted to know about the gangs, gangsters and general riff-raff who thrived at the edge of New York's society in the 19th century.

New York Characters by Gillian Zoe Segal. W.W. Norton Co., 2001. An exuberant and sympathetic account of 66 New Yorkers, photographed in their distinctive environments.

Still Life in Harlem by Eddy L. Harris. Henry Holt and Company, Inc., 1996. A well-written autobiographical take on this famed Uptown neighborhood, with poignant details.

Writing New York: A Literary Anthology edited by Philip Lopate. The Library of America, 1998. Observations about life in New York by such literary folk as Henry David Thoreau, Walt Whitman, Maxim Gorky and F. Scott Fitzgerald. A must for city-philes.

NEW YORK STREET ATLAS

The key map shows the area of New York covered by the atlas section. An index of street names and places of interest shown on the maps can be found on the following pages. For each entry there is a page number and grid reference.

Map Legend

═══	Freeway with Exit
─ ─ ─	Freeway (under construction)
═══	Divided Highway
───	Main Road
───	Secondary Road
───	Minor road
───	Track
─ ·· ─	International Boundary
─ ─ ─	State/County Boundary
─ • ─	National Park/Reserve
✈	Airport
†	Church (ruins)
†	Monastery
🏰	Castle (ruins)
∴	Archaeological Site
∩	Cave
★	Place of Interest
🏠	Mansion/Stately Home
☀	Viewpoint
▼	Beach
	Freeway
	Divided Highway
	Main Roads
	Minor Roads
	Footpath
─·─·─	Railroad
	Pedestrian Area
	Important Building
	Park
Ⓜ	Subway
🚌	Bus Station
❶	Tourist Information
✉	Post Office
✝	Cathedral/Church
☪	Mosque
✡	Synagogue
𝟙	Statue/Monument
▯	Tower

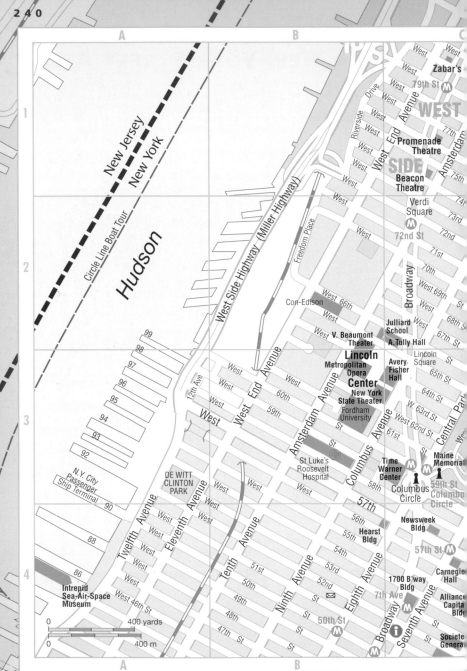

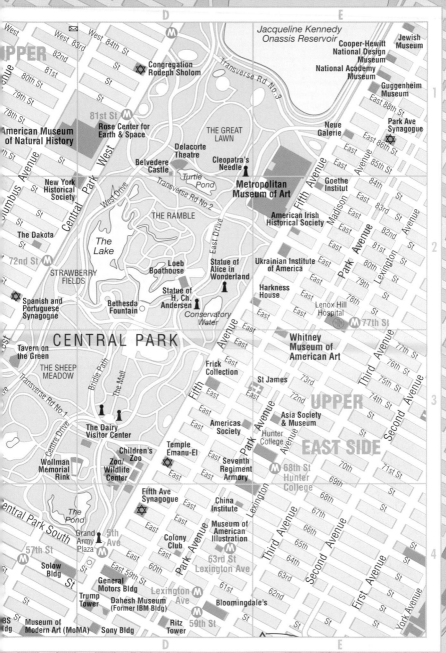

West 82nd St

West 83rd St

West 84th St

UPPER

81st

80th St

79th St

78th St

American Museum of Natural History

th St

Columbus Avenue

New York Historical Society

The Dakota

72nd St

STRAWBERRY FIELDS

Spanish and Portuguese Synagogue

Tavern on the Green

THE SHEEP MEADOW

Transverse Rd No 1

Central Park West

West Drive

Central Park Drive

Congregation Rodeph Sholom

81st St

Rose Center for Earth & Space

Delacorte Theatre

Belvedere Castle

Turtle Pond

Transverse Rd No.2

THE RAMBLE

The Lake

Loeb Boathouse

Bethesda Fountain

Statue of H. Ch. Andersen

Statue of Alice in Wonderland

Conservatory Water

East Drive

THE GREAT LAWN

Cleopatra's Needle

Metropolitan Museum of Art

American Irish Historical Society

Ukrainian Institute of America

Harkness House

Jacqueline Kennedy Onassis Reservoir

Transverse Rd No.3

Neue Galerie

Goethe Institut

Lenox Hill Hospital

Cooper-Hewitt National Design Museum

National Academy Museum

Jewish Museum

Guggenheim Museum

East 88th St

Park Ave Synagogue

East 86th St

East 85th Avenue

East 84th

East 83rd St

East 82nd

East 81st St

East 80th St

East 79th St

East 78th

Madison Avenue

Fifth Avenue

Park Avenue

Lexington Avenue

CENTRAL PARK

Bridle Path

The Mall

Centre Drive

The Dairy Visitor Center

Wollman Memorial Rink

Children's Zoo/ Wildlife Center

Temple Emanu-El

Fifth Ave Synagogue

Frick Collection

St James

Americas Society

Whitney Museum of American Art

Asia Society & Museum

Hunter College

77th St

East 77th St

East 76th St

East 75th St

East 74th St

73rd

72nd

UPPER

EAST SIDE

Third Avenue

Second Avenue

57th St

Solow Bldg

Central Park South

The Pond

Grand Army Plaza

5th Ave

General Motors Bldg

Trump Tower

Dahesh Museum (Former IBM Bldg)

Colony Club

China Institute

Museum of American Illustration

Seventh Regiment Armory

68th St Hunter College

71st St

70th

69th

68th

67th

66th

65th

64th

63rd

62nd

Museum of Modern Art (MoMA)

Sony Bldg

East 59th St

Lexington Ave

Ritz Tower

Bloomingdale's

59th St

60th

61st

Lexington Ave

Lexington Ave

63rd

First Avenue

York Avenue

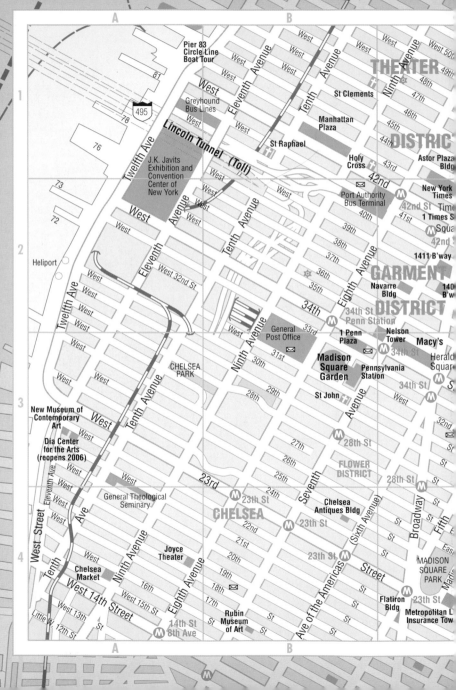

Pier 83
Circle Line
Boat Tour

West

West

West

West

West

West

West

West 50t

West

West 48th

THEATER

St Clements

47th

46th

Greyhound
Bus Lines

West

West

Manhattan
Plaza

45th

44th

DISTRIC

West

St Raphael

43rd

Holy
Cross

Astor Plaza
Bldg

Lincoln Tunnel (Toll)

West

West

West

42nd

New York
Times

J.K. Javits
Exhibition and
Convention
Center of
New York

West

Port Authority
Bus Terminal

42nd St

Time

1 Times S

West

West

40th

41st

Squa

73

West

39th

42nd

72

West

38th

Heliport

Eleventh

37th

1411 B'way

West

West 32nd St

36th

GARMENT

West

35th

Navarre
Bldg

140
B'w

34th

West

34th St

DISTRICT

Penn Station

West

General
Post Office

33rd

1 Penn
Plaza

Nelson
Tower

Macy's

West

31st

Madison
Square
Garden

34th St

Herald
Squar

CHELSEA
PARK

30th

Pennsylvania
Station

West

28th

29th

34th St

S

West

St John

32nd

New Museum of
Contemporary
Art

West

27th

28th St

St

Dia Center
for the Arts
(reopens 2006)

West

26th

FLOWER
DISTRICT

28th St

West

25th

23rd

General Theological
Seminary

24th

23rd St

Chelsea
Antiques Bldg

St

CHELSEA

22nd

23rd St

West Street

West
Ave

21st

Seventh

23rd St

St

Joyce
Theater

20th

23rd St

MADISON
SQUARE
PARK

Chelsea
Market

19th

Street

West 14th Street

16th

18th

Flatiron
Bldg

23rd St

West 15th St

17th

Rubin
Museum
of Art

St

Metropolitan L
Insurance Tow

West 13th
St

14th St
8th Ave

Little W. 12th St

7th Ave Bldg
7th Ave Bldg
West 7th Ave
Seventh Avenue
Broadway
Societe Generale
Alliance Capital Bldg
West 54th St
West 56th St
Sixth Avenue
52nd
CBS Bldg
American Folk Art Museum
Museum of Modern Art (MoMA)
St Thomas
Solow Bldg
Trump Tower
General Motors Bldg
Dahesh Museum of Art (Former IBM Bldg)
Sony Bldg
Lexington Ave
East 61st
East 60th St
Bloomingdale's
59th St
Third Ave
East 59th St
58th St
East 57th Street
Second Avenue

Rockefeller Center
Radio City Music Hall
Museum of Arts & Design
Central Synagogue
56th
919 Third Ave
55th
Chase Bldg
49th St
50th St
Rocket. Center
GE Bldg
Olympic Tower
Lever House
Park Ave Plaza
McGraw-Hill Bldg
Rockefeller Plaza
St Patrick's Cathedral
Seagram Bldg
Citigroup Center
909 Third Ave
Murdoch's Fox News Bldg
Times Square Visitors Center
MID-TOWN
DIAMOND DISTRICT
Mutual of America Bldg
345 Park Ave
Lexington Ave
54th
East 53rd St
Manhattan Arts & Antiques Center

Conde Nast Bldg
International Center of Photography
51st St
52nd
Verizon Bldg
Grace Bldg
St Gotham Book Mart
JP Morgan Chase
UBS #299
51st
East 50th
800 Third Ave Bldg
Third Avenue
Second Avenue
First Avenue
Beekman Pl

42nd St Bryant Park
N.Y. Public Library
St
Lincoln Bldg
Helmsley Bldg
MetLife Bldg
Grand Central Terminal
Graybar Bldg
49th
48th
47th
46th
45th
1 Dag Hammarskjöld Plaza
Hammarskjöld Plaza
American Standard (Radiator) Bldg
Lord & Taylor
Fifth Avenue
East
Vanderbilt Ave
Depew Pl
Pershing
Chrysler Bldg
44th
43rd
42nd
2 UN Plaza
1 UN Plaza
Statue of Peace
United Nations Headquarters
United Nations Plaza

Whitney Museum of American Art (Midtown)
42nd St Grand Central
Chanin Bldg
101 Park Ave
Former Mobil Bldg
41st
40th
Former Daily News Bldg
Ford Foundation Bldg
Secretariat Bldg
Hammarskjöld Library

MURRAY HILL
Empire State Bldg
Lutheran Church in America
Morgan Library
39th
38th
37th
36th
35th
Exit Plaza
Tudor City Pl
U Thant Island
Queens Midtown Tunnel (Toll)

33rd St
34th Street
33rd
32nd
31st
30th
29th
28th
St GABRIEL'S PARK
TUDOR
E 34th St Heliport
East

New York Life
28th St
27th
26th
25th
24th St
Lexington Avenue
Third Avenue
Second Avenue
First St
Franklin D. Roosevelt Drive
N.Y.U. Medical Center
East

0 400 yards
0 400 m

D   E

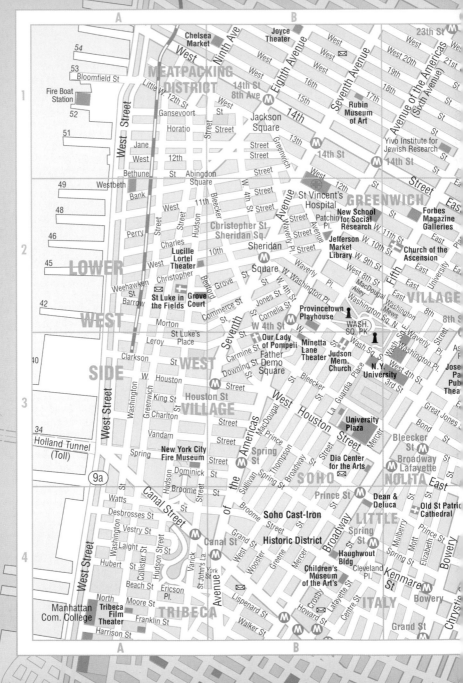

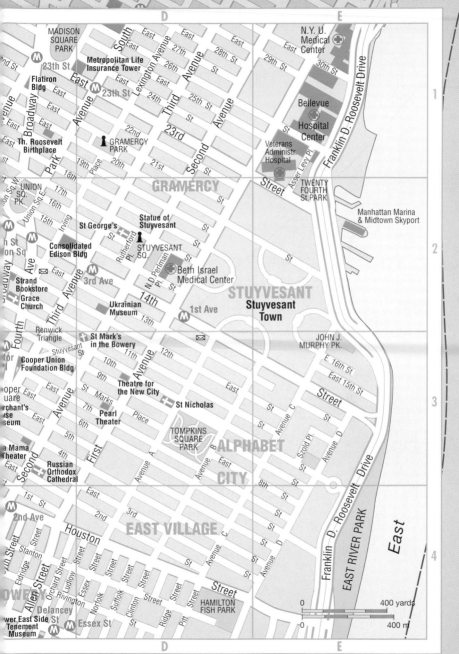

MADISON
SQUARE
PARK

Metropolitan Life
Insurance Tower

South

East 27th St

East 28th St

East 26th

East 25th St

Lexington Avenue

24th St

N.Y.U.
Medical
Center

East 29th St

30th St

Bellevue

Hospital
Center

Veterans
Administr.
Hospital

Franklin D. Roosevelt Drive

Asser Levy Pl.

Broadway

Flatiron
Bldg

East

23th St

23th St

East

Third Avenue

23rd

22nd
St

21st

Second Avenue

GRAMERCY
PARK

20th

Th. Roosevelt
Birthplace

19th St

18th

Park

TWENTY
FOURTH
St PARK

Street

UNION
SQ.
PK.

17th

16th

15th

Irving

Union Sq.

GRAMERCY

St

St

Manhattan Marina
& Midtown Skyport

St George's

Consolidated
Edison Bldg

3rd Ave

Statue of
Stuyvesant

STUYVESANT
SQ.

Beth Israel
Medical Center

Rutherford Pl.

N.D. Perlman Pl.

St

St

St

St

STUYVESANT

Stuyvesant
Town

Strand
Bookstore

Grace
Church

Third Avenue

Fourth

14th

Ukrainian
Museum

13th

1st Ave

JOHN J.
MURPHY PK.

Ave

Renwick
Triangle

Stuyvesant St

St Mark's
in the Bowery

11th

12th

Avenue

E. 16th St

East 15th St

Street

Cooper Union
Foundation Bldg

10th

9th

St Marks

Theatre for
the New City

East

St

Avenue C

Avenue D

Szold Pl.

Cooper
Square

Merchant's
House
Museum

East

7th

6th

Pearl
Theater

Place

St Nicholas

TOMPKINS
SQUARE
PARK

ALPHABET

St

St

St

St

5th

First

4th

Russian
Orthodox
Cathedral

Avenue A

CITY

East

8th

St

La Mama
Theater

Second

East

1st St

2nd Ave

2nd

3rd

Houston

EAST VILLAGE

C

Avenue C

Avenue D

Franklin D. Roosevelt Drive

EAST RIVER PARK

East

Stanton

Eldridge Street

Allen Street

Orchard Street

Ludlow Street

Essex Street

Norfolk Street

Suffolk Street

Clinton Street

Ridge Street

Pitt

Street

Street

HAMILTON
FISH PARK

Delancey St

Lower East Side
Tenement
Museum

Essex St

0   400 yards

0   400 m

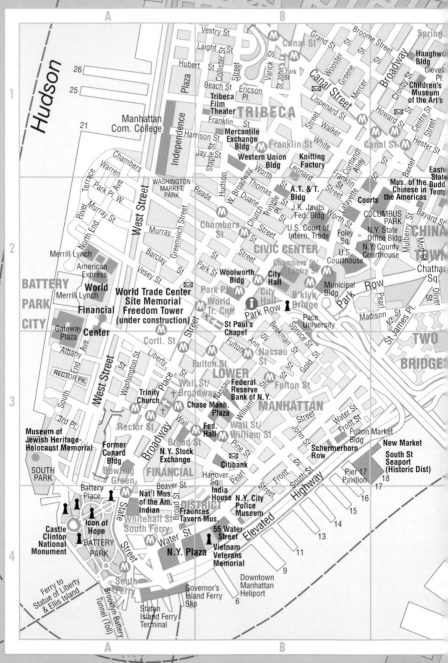

EAST VILLAGE

East 5th St
East 6th St

East Houston Street

Prince St
Mott St
Elizabeth St
Spring St

Bowery Street

nmare

Bowery

BOWERY

Stanton Street

Rivington Street

Orchard Street

Ludlow Street

Essex Street

Suffolk Street

Street

East 2nd St
East 3rd St
East 4th St

Avenue C
Avenue D

Street

HAMILTON FISH PARK

Roosevelt Drive
Franklin D.

Delancey

Delancey Street

Essex St

Lower East Side
Tenement Museum

St
Clinton St
Attorney St
Ridge St
Pitt St

Columbia Street

Baruch Pl.
Nangin St

Baruch Dr.

LITTLE ITALY

Grand St

Street

LOWER EAST

Grand St

Norfolk St

Broome Street

Delancey

Willett St
Pitt St

A.A. Kazan

Lewis St

Street

PARK

EAST RIVER

Williamsburg Bridge

Chrystie St
Forsyth

Allen St
Eldridge St
Orchard St
Ludlow St
Essex Street
Hester St

Canal St

SEWARD PARK

Dickstein Place

Confucius Plaza
vision

Broadway

Forsyth St

E Broadway

Straus Sq.

Street

East Broadway

Broadway

Henry Street

Madison Street

Grand St

SIDE

enry St

Pike Street

Rutgers St

Clinton St

Montgomery St

Gouverneur St

Jackson Street

Cherry St.

Monroe St

Cherry St

Water St

Cherry St
Water St
South St

evated Highway

South St

Franklin D. Roosevelt Drive

Corlears Hook

Manhattan Bridge

35
Circle Line Boat Tour
43

East

klyn Bridge

Wallabout Bay

Marshall St

John Street

Plymouth Street

Pearl St

Water Street

Little St

Evans St

Water St
Main St
Washington St

Front St

Jay St

Front Street

Bridge St

Hudson St

Brooklyn

Furman Street
Columbia Heights
Everit St
Elizabeth Pl.
Doughty St

Queens

York Street

Gold Street

Poplar St
Middagh St
Cranberry St
Orange St
Henry St
Fulton St

Prospect St

Expressway

Borough Hall

0   400 yards
0   400 m

D   E

STREET INDEX

ART & PHOTO CREDITS

Jenny Acheson/Axiom 125, 149
Alamy 7R, 24
Jim Anderson/Woodfin Camp 215
Bartel 187T
Nathan Benn/Corbis 195
Bettmann/Corbis 6TR, 17, 21, 31, 36
Bernard Boutrit/Woodfin Camp 77, 120, 127T, 129, 139, 146L
Bodo Bondzio 96T, 128, 155
Brooklyn Museum of Art/Central Photo Archives 201T, 201
Children's Museum of Manhattan/Ann Chwatsy 68
Doug Corrance 66/67, 86, 89, 107, 117, 128T, 162T, 203T, 206T, 208
Grace Davies Photography 200
Jerry Dennis 197
Nigel Francis/Robert Harding Picture Library 82
Wolfgang Fritz 111T
Blaine Harrington 210T
Dallas & John Heaton 191
Lewis W. Hine/George Eastman House/Getty Images 25
Hans Höfer 202
Hotel Gansevoort 221
Scott Houston/Corbis 43
Hulton Archive/Getty Images 27
Illustrated London News 16
Image Bank/Getty Images 58
Britta Jaschinski/Apa 78, 79, 90, 91, 112, 113, 122, 123, 137L, 141, 142, 149T, 151, 166, 167, 173, 177, 178T, 199t, 199, 211
Catherine Karnow 2/3, 12/13, 42, 47, 50, 51, 56, 57, 59, 87, 88, 92, 97, 107T, 109T, 111, 119T, 134, 138T, 138, 140, 159, 162, 163, 164, 165, 175, 176, 178, 185, 188, 192T, 203, 204, 205, 206, 207, 209
Katz/Laif 49, 108, 199
Library of Congress 208T
Bob Krist 37, 40, 41, 44, 45, 64/65, 104, 133, 160, 161
Anna Mockford & Nick Bonetti/Apa 4B, 63, 73, 85T, 88T, 98T, 119, 127, 135, 137R, 145T, 155T, 183T, 184, 185T, 186, 189, 190, 193, 194, 218, 223, 231, 236

Gail Mooney/Corbis 76
Peter Morgan/Reuters/Corbis 10/11
Courtesy of Mount Vernon Hotel Museum and Garden 110
Museum of Jewish Heritage 181
New York Public Library 19
Richard Nowitz 72, 153
PA/EPA 34
Panther/Powerstock 187
Tony Perrottet/Apa 1, 4/5, 5BR, 7L, 8CT, 8BL, 38/39, 52, 75T, 85, 87T. 94T, 94, 98, 116, 121, 130, 143, 156T, 156, 157, 158, 160T, 172, 174, 177T, 188T, 190T, 225
Photolibrary.com/Index Stock 83, 124
Private Collection, Paris, France/Lauros-Giraudon/Bridgeman 48
PS1 Contemporary Arts Center/Eileen Costa 205
Carl Purcell 192
Radio City Music Hall/Kozlowski 96
Rubin Museum of Art 139T
Mark Read/Apa 3B, 5BL, 6BL, 46, 77T, 93, 95, 105. 109, 120T, 137T, 146R, 148T, 148, 152, 165T, 170, 171, 172T, 174T, 180, 228
Mike Segar/Reuters 35
Michael Setboun/Corbis 60
Shannon Stapleton/Reuters/Corbis 9TR, 210
Time Life Pictures/Getty Images 28
Topham Picturepoint 30, 32, 183
Bill Wassman 14, 33, 63, 75, 145, 147T, 147L, 159T
David Whelan 61, 118, 131T, 150
Marcus Wilson-Smith 53
Mike Yamashita/Woodfin Camp 147R

Pages 54/55: All pictures by the Ronald Grant Archive
Pages 80/81: Top row left to right: Tony Perrottet, Britta Jaschinski
Bottom row: Anna Mockford &

Nick Bonetti, Battman, Doug Corrance, Bill Wassman
Pages 100/101: all pictures Museum of Modern Art
Pages 102/103: Top row left to right: Katz/Laif, Marcus Wilson Smith
Center row: Anna Mockford & Nick Bonetti, Tony Perrottet
Bottom row: Topham Picturepoint, Catherine Karnow, Topham Picturepoint
Pages 114/115: Top row left to right: Bob Krist, Museum of the City of New York, Bascove, detail of Pershing Square Bridge, 1993 ©Bascove Museum Purchase, Topham Picturepoint
Center row: Courtesy of The Metropolitan Museum of Art, Museum of the City of New York Paulo Cornino, First Night Game, Yankee Stadium, 1945, Gift of the Artist, Jewish Museum/John Parnell
Bottom row: Mike Yamashita/Woodfin Camp
Pages 168/169: Top row left to right: Tony Perrottet, Bill Wassman, Skyscaper Museum
Center row: Bernard Boutrit/Woodfin Camp
Bottom row: Tony Perrottet, Grace Davies Photography, Bernard Boutrit/Woodfin Camp

Works of art have been reproduced with the permission of the following copyright holders:
False Mirror, 1928, Rene Magritte ©ADAGP, Paris and DACS, London 2005
Marilyn Monroe 20 Times, 1962 Andy Warhol ©The Andy Warhol Foundation for the Visual Arts, Inc/ARS, NY and DACS, London 2005

Map Production: James Macdonald, Maria Randell, Laura Morris and Stephen Ramsay

©2005 Apa Publications GmbH & Co. Verlag KG, Singapore Branch

GENERAL INDEX